Bread Cook Book

By the Editors of

Better Homes and Gardens

Meredith Press, Des Moines

Printed in the United States of America

Bread

The aroma of home-baked bread says welcome to a busy family, creates a friendly and homey atmosphere that invites good will, relaxed conversations. Breads take many forms. You can produce crusty, golden loaves of a yeast bread, make a quick coffeecake, or count on muffins, biscuits, waffles, pancakes, or tempting sandwiches to turn any meal into an occasion. Hot breads are special, but this does not mean they should be saved only for the special events. Treat your family as well as your guests. Even a speedy short-cut bread will lift a meal from the ordinary. Serving your own bread will be a rewarding experience.

Contents

Take your pick from an array of recipes

← Here's a preview of the good baking in store for you. On top are Perfect White Bread, Ham Salad on Rye, and "Oh Boy" Waffles. Date Muffins and pretty Raisin-Nut Braid adorn the middle shelf. Take-two Sandwich, Peaches 'n Crepes in the chafing dish, Orange Lattice Coffeecake, and Italian Bread Sticks complete the picture. Now, on with the baking!

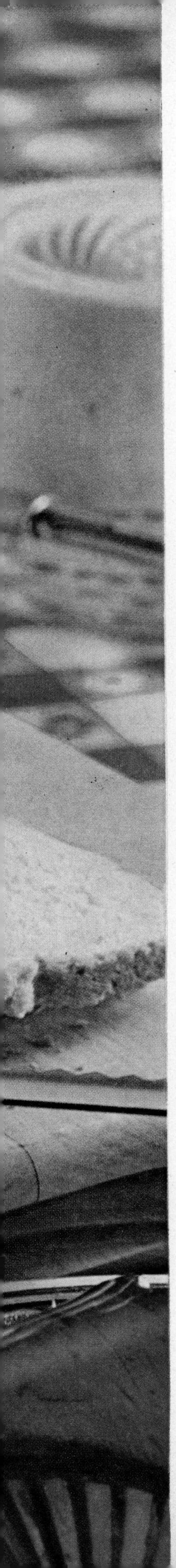

Yeast Breads

Feel the springy aliveness of yeast dough as you work with it. Create distinctive flavors with spices and herbs. Shape fancy rolls and braids; then add gaiety with swirls of icing

Slice your way through crusty goodness

← The ability to bake fine yeast bread has always been the mark of a good cook. The matchless aroma and flavor of bread fresh from the oven are the best reputation-builders we know. Make our Perfect White Bread and you'll rate tops.

This seal tells you that every recipe in your Bread Book is *endorsed* by the Better Homes & Gardens Test Kitchen. Each recipe has been tested over and over till it rates superior—in family appeal, practicality, and in deliciousness.

Better Homes and Gardens TEST KITCHEN

Tasty Yeast Loaves

Yeast Bread Basics

There's a wonderful personal satisfaction in baking bread. You feel magic in your hands as you knead the simple ingredients to a bouncy round of dough. And you know the real thrill of creative cooking when you take the beautiful, fragrant loaves from the oven.

A perfect loaf of yeast bread is pretty and plump. It has a tender, golden-brown crust which may be crisp; or it may be shiny and soft from a swish of butter over the top while the loaf is still hot.

Look for an even "shred" or "break" along the sides, just below the crust. The texture should be fine grained. A slice feels soft and springy, and just a bit moist.

Most breads are made by the straight-dough process, in which all ingredients are combined at one time. Bread may also be made by the sponge process, in which the yeast is allowed to work in a thin, batter-like mixture before being combined with the other ingredients in the recipe.

• Flours most used for bread baking are all-purpose flours made from a combination of hard wheat and soft wheat.

Always buy enriched flour. This is wheat flour to which iron and some of the B-vitamins have been added. Therefore, enriched flour has the essential iron and vitamin value of whole-wheat flour.

• When you use all-purpose flour for baking you will get a more accurate measure (and a better product) if you sift the flour *before* measuring. If you do measure by simply spooning unsifted flour, remove 2 level tablespoons of flour from each measured cup. Then the weight of the cup of unsifted flour will be more equal to the weight of a cup of sifted flour.

Whether you sift or don't sift *before* measuring, you should sift all the dry ingredients together after measuring (as directed in each recipe). By doing this, you get a more uniform blending of the dry ingredients.

Note: Instantized all-purpose flour is a granulated flour and can't be sifted. Don't adjust the recipe when you use this flour.

• Choose active dry yeast, or compressed yeast. Either may be used successfully.

Yeasts is a living plant. The growth of yeast in the bread dough produces a gas which forms bubbles. These bubbles expand and cause the dough to "rise." Yeast grows best at a temperature between 80° and 85°. A high temperature will kill yeast; a low temperature retards growth.

Soften active dry yeast in warm water (110°) and compressed yeast in lukewarm water (85°). Both take 5 to 10 minutes.

Active dry yeast should always be softened in water. To soften compressed yeast, use water, milk, diluted evaporated milk, potato water, or a mixture of these. (Scald milk and cool to lukewarm before adding yeast.) On a chilly day the liquid may be slightly warmer; or cooler on a warm summer day.

• Sugar is the raw material from which yeast manufactures the leavening gas; it also adds flavor and aids in browning.

• You add the salt to give flavor, but it also helps control the fermentation.

• All the flour necessary to keep dough from sticking to your hands should be added at time of mixing or kneading. If you add it after it has risen, it may make dark streaks in the bread and coarsen its texture.

• To knead, turn dough out on lightly floured surface. Curve your fingers over dough and push down with heel of palm. Give dough a quarter turn; fold over and push down again. Knead till smooth.

• Place dough in lightly greased bowl; turn once to grease surface. Cover to prevent crust from forming. Let rise in a warm, not hot, place till double.

• Punch down by plunging hand into dough, folding edges toward center, and turning dough over. Let rise again (or shape according to recipe) till double and dough retains a dent when pressed lightly.

Perfect White Bread

This is an easy-to-handle, 2-loaf recipe—

1 package active dry yeast *or*
  1 cake compressed yeast
¼ cup water

• • •

2 cups milk, scalded
2 tablespoons sugar
2 teaspoons salt
1 tablespoon shortening

• • •

6 to 6¼ cups sifted all-purpose flour

Soften active dry yeast in *warm* water (110°) or compressed yeast in *lukewarm* water (85°). Combine hot milk, the sugar, salt, and shortening. Cool to lukewarm. Stir in 2 *cups* of the flour; beat well. Add the softened yeast; mix. Add enough of the remaining flour to make a moderately stiff dough.

Turn out on a lightly floured surface; knead till smooth and satiny (about 8 to 10 minutes). Shape dough in a ball; place in a lightly greased bowl, turning once to grease surface. Cover and let rise in a warm place till double (about 1½ hours).

Punch down. Let rise again till double (45 minutes). Cut in 2 portions. Shape each in a smooth ball. Cover; let rest 10 minutes. Shape in loaves as shown in the pictures. Place in 2 greased 8½x4½x2½-inch loaf pans. Let rise till double (about 1 hour). Bake in hot oven (400°) 35 minutes or till done. Peek in oven after 15 minutes; if tops are browning too fast, cover loaves with foil.

Brush the tops of your loaves with butter for soft shiny crusts.

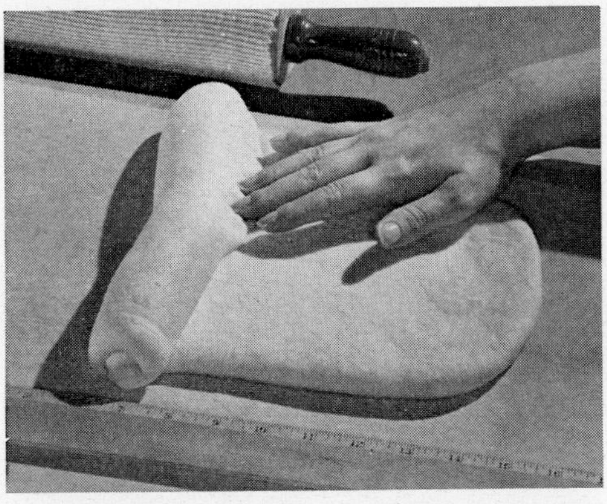

1 To shape loaf, flatten dough with rolling pin in 15x7-inch rectangle. Roll up like jellyroll (start at narrow side), sealing at each turn with fingertips or edge of the hand.

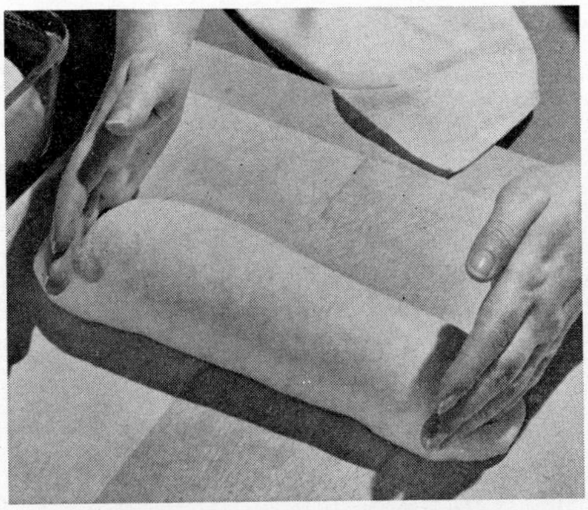

2 Press down on ends of loaf with sides of hands to make 2 thin sealed strips. Fold strips under loaf as you put it in the pan so bread will have smooth crusts at both ends.

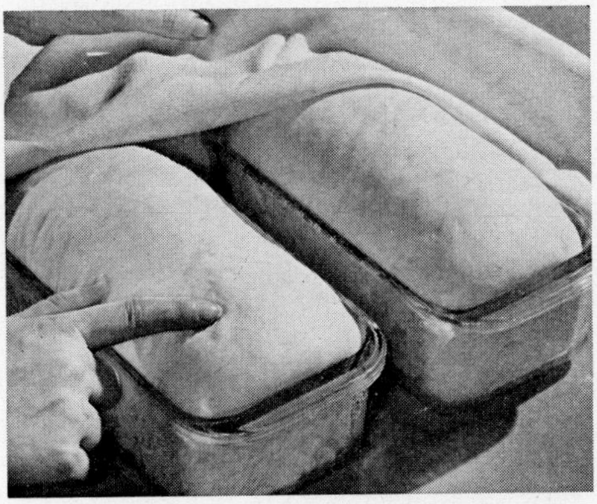

3 Cover loaves and let rise in warm place until double—dough will be puffy and light. To test, press top gently with fingertip —if dent remains, bread is ready to bake.

4 Place loaves on oven rack, leaving space between pans for heat to circulate. When baked, remove from pans; cool loaves on a rack or across top of pans, away from drafts.

Whole-wheat Bread

1 package active dry yeast *or*
  1 cake compressed yeast
¼ cup water
• • •
2½ cups hot water
½ cup brown sugar
3 teaspoons salt
¼ cup shortening
3 cups stirred whole-wheat flour
5 cups sifted all-purpose
  white flour

Soften active dry yeast in ¼ cup *warm* water (110°) or compressed yeast in ¼ cup *lukewarm* water (85°). Combine hot water, sugar, salt, and shortening; cool to lukewarm.

Stir in whole-wheat flour and *1 cup* of the white flour; beat well. Stir in softened yeast. Add enough of remaining flour to make a moderately stiff dough. Turn out on a lightly floured surface; knead till smooth and satiny (10 to 12 minutes).

Shape dough in a ball; place in lightly greased bowl, turning once to grease surface. Cover; let rise in warm place till double (about 1½ hours). Punch down. Cut in 2 portions; shape each in smooth ball. Cover and let rest 10 minutes.

Shape in loaves; place in greased 8½x 4½x2½-inch loaf dishes. Let rise till double (about 1¼ hours). Bake in moderate oven (375°) about 45 minutes. Cover with foil last 20 minutes, if necessary. Makes 2 loaves.

Light Rye Mixer Bread

Your electric mixer does the biggest part of the work for you—

1 package active dry yeast *or*
  1 cake compressed yeast
¼ cup water
1 cup water
2 tablespoons honey
2 tablespoons shortening
2 teaspoons salt
2 to 3 teaspoons caraway seed
1½ cups stirred rye flour
2¼ cups sifted all-purpose
  white flour

Soften active dry yeast in ¼ cup *warm* water or compressed yeast in *lukewarm* water. Combine 1 cup water, honey, shortening, salt, caraway seed, rye flour, ½ *cup* white flour and the softened yeast. Blend on low speed of electric mixer. Beat 2 minutes at medium speed, scraping sides and bottom of bowl constantly. Add remaining flour and stir till smooth. Place in a greased bowl, turning once to grease surface. Cover and let rise in a warm place till double, about 1 hour.

Punch batter down. Spread evenly in a greased 9½x5x3-inch loaf pan. Cover and let rise in a warm place till double, (about 35 minutes). Bake in a moderate oven (375°) for 45 to 50 minutes. If top browns too rapidly, cover the top of loaf loosely with foil after 20 minutes of baking.

You've a treat in store! It will be a favorite with all

Light Rye Mixer Bread is homemade bread at its best. It's sweetened with honey and full of rye flavor. You'll find it makes tasty sandwiches.

Swedish Rye Bread

The flavor is deliciously sweet, with overtones of caraway, or orange if you prefer. It slices nicely; grand for sandwiches and for buffet suppers—

1 package active dry yeast *or*
1 cake compressed yeast
¼ cup water

• • •

¼ cup medium-brown sugar
¼ cup light molasses
1 tablespoon salt
2 tablespoons shortening
1½ cups hot water

• • •

2½ cups stirred medium rye flour
3 tablespoons caraway seed *or*
2 tablespoons grated orange peel

• • •

3½ to 4 cups sifted all-purpose white flour

Soften active dry yeast in ¼ cup *warm* water (110°) or compressed yeast in ¼ cup *lukewarm* water (85°). In a big bowl, combine the brown sugar, molasses, salt and shortening; add the hot water and stir till the sugar dissolves. Cool to lukewarm.

Stir in the rye flour; beat well. Add the softened yeast and caraway seed; mix well. Reserving some of the all-purpose flour for kneading, add enough of the remainder to make a soft dough. Cover; let rest 10 minutes. Turn out on a lightly floured surface and knead till smooth and satiny, about 10 minutes. Place dough in a lightly greased bowl, turning dough once to grease the surface. Cover; let rise in a warm place till double (about 1½ to 2 hours).

Punch down. Turn out on a lightly floured surface and divide into 2 portions. Round each piece of dough in a ball. Cover and let rest for 10 minutes. Pat balls of dough into 2 round loaves and place on opposite corners of a greased baking sheet. (Or shape in 2 oblong loaves and place in two greased 8½x4½x2½-inch loaf pans.)

Cover and let rise in a warm place till almost double (about 1½ to 2 hours). Bake in a moderate oven (375°) for 25 to 30 minutes. Place foil over tops last 10 minutes, if necessary. For soft crust, brush tops with melted butter or margarine while loaves are still hot. Cool on rack. Makes 2 loaves.

To match the picture, first cut the round loaf in quarters, then slice each quarter perpendicular to flat side of next quarter.

Win praises with this plump round of Swedish Rye Bread. Flavor it with caraway seed or with orange peel. It's delicious either way.

Pumpernickel Bread

3 packages active dry yeast *or*
3 cakes compressed yeast
1½ cups water

• • •

½ cup dark molasses
1 to 2 tablespoons caraway seed
1 tablespoon salt
2 tablespoons soft shortening
2¾ cups stirred rye flour
2¼ to 2¾ cups sifted all-purpose white flour

Soften active dry yeast in *warm* water *or* compressed yeast in *lukewarm* water. Combine molasses, caraway seed, salt, shortening, the rye flour, about 1 *cup* of the white flour and the softened yeast. Beat until smooth. Add enough more flour to make a stiff dough. Turn out on a lightly floured surface and knead till smooth and elastic (8 to 10 minutes). Place dough in a greased bowl, turning once to grease surface. Cover and let rise in a warm place until double (about 1½ hours).

Punch down and divide dough into 2 parts. Cover and let rest 10 minutes. Round each part into a smooth ball. Place on opposite corners of a corn meal sprinkled baking sheet. Cover and let rise until double, (about 30 minutes). Bake loaves in a moderate oven (375°) for about 30 to 35 minutes or until well browned. For a chewy crust, brush tops of the loaves with warm water several times during the baking, after the first 20 minutes. Makes 2 round loaves.

Grandma's Oatmeal Bread

Soften 2 packages active dry yeast in ½ cup *warm* water. Combine 1¼ cups boiling water, 1 cup quick-cooking rolled oats, ½ cup light molasses, ⅓ cup shortening, and 1 tablespoon salt; cool to lukewarm. Sift 6 to 6¼ cups all-purpose flour. Stir in 2 *cups* sifted flour; beat well. Add 2 beaten eggs and the yeast; beat well. Add enough remaining flour to make a soft dough. Turn out on lightly floured surface; cover and let rest 10 minutes. Knead till smooth. Place in a lightly greased bowl, turning dough once. Cover; let rise till double (about 1½ hours).

Punch down. Coat 2 well-greased 8½x4½x2½-inch loaf pans with 2 tablespoons rolled oats each. Divide dough in half. Shape in loaves; place in pans. Cover, let double (45 to 60 minutes). Brush with mixture of 1 egg white and 1 tablespoon water; sprinkle lightly with rolled oats. Bake at 375° for 40 minutes. Cover with foil after baking 15 minutes if tops are getting too brown.

Onion Bread

Soften 1 package active dry yeast in ¼ cup *warm* water. Combine 1 envelope onion-soup mix and 2 cups water; simmer covered 10 minutes; add 2 tablespoons sugar, 1 teaspoon salt, 2 tablespoons grated Parmesan cheese, and 2 tablespoons shortening; stir. Cool to lukewarm. Sift 6 to 6½ cups all-purpose flour.

Stir in 2 *cups* of the sifted flour; beat well. Stir in yeast. Add enough remaining flour to make a moderately stiff dough. Turn out on floured surface. Knead till smooth. Place in a lightly greased bowl turning dough once. Cover; let double (1½ hours).

Punch down; divide in half. Cover; let rest 10 minutes. Shape in 2 long loaves, tapering ends. Place on greased baking sheet sprinkled with corn meal. Gash tops diagonally, ⅛ to ¼ inch deep. Cover; let double (1 hour). Bake at 375° for 20 minutes. Brush with mixture of 1 egg white and 1 tablespoon water. Bake 10 to 15 minutes longer.

Hot bread from the oven

← Nothing beats the flavor or the aroma of fresh-baked bread. Treat your family to this one—it's Grandma's Oatmeal Bread.

Herb Bread

1 package active dry yeast
¼ cup warm water
2 tablespoons sugar
2 tablespoons shortening
1½ teaspoons salt
¾ cup milk, scalded
3 to 3½ cups sifted all-purpose flour
½ teaspoon nutmeg
1 teaspoon ground sage
2 teaspoons celery seed
1 slightly-beaten egg

Soften yeast in water. Combine next 4 ingredients; cool to lukewarm. Add about *half* of the flour and mix well. Add nutmeg, sage, celery seed, softened yeast, and egg; beat smooth. Add remaining flour or enough to make a moderately soft dough. Knead on lightly floured surface until smooth (8 minutes). Place in lightly greased bowl, turning dough once. Cover; let double (1½ hours).

Punch down; cover and let rest 10 to 15 minutes. Shape in round loaf; place in greased 8- or 9-inch pie plate. Cover; let rise till almost double (45 to 60 minutes). Bake at 400° for 35 minutes or till done.

Corn-meal Loaves

2 packages active dry yeast
½ cup warm water
1¾ cups milk, scalded
⅓ cup sugar
⅓ cup shortening
1 tablespoon salt
6½ to 7 cups sifted all-purpose flour
2 slightly-beaten eggs
1 cup yellow corn meal

Soften yeast in water. Combine next 4 ingredients. Stir till shortening melts. Cool to lukewarm. Add 2½ *cups* of the flour; beat well. Add softened yeast and eggs; beat till smooth. Add corn meal and remaining flour to make a soft dough. Place on lightly floured surface; knead until smooth (8 to 10 minutes). Place in a greased bowl, turning once. Cover; let double (1½ to 2 hours).

Punch down. Divide in half. Let rest 10 minutes. Shape 2 loaves. Place in 2 greased 9½x5x3-inch loaf pans.* Cover; let double. Carefully brush top with milk; sprinkle with corn meal. Bake at 375° for 45 minutes.

*Or divide dough in eighths and form in 8 small loaves. Bake in 8 greased 4½x2½x2-inch loaf pans in 350° oven for 25 minutes.

Glazed Raisin Loaf

Rich and slightly sweet, it's delicious plain or toasted. And you'll be pleased at how professional the loaves look—

1 package active dry yeast *or*
  1 cake compressed yeast
¼ cup water

• • •

1 cup seedless raisins
¼ cup soft butter or margarine
¼ cup sugar
1½ teaspoons salt
½ cup buttermilk or milk, scalded

• • •

3¾ cups sifted all-purpose flour
2 beaten eggs

Soften active dry yeast in *warm* water or compressed yeast in *lukewarm* water. Combine raisins, soft butter, sugar, salt, and buttermilk; cool to lukewarm. Add 1½ *cups* of the flour; beat well. Add softened yeast and eggs; beat well. Stir in remaining flour or enough to make a soft dough.

Turn out on a lightly floured surface and knead till smooth and elastic (10 to 12 minutes). Place dough in a lightly greased bowl, turning once to grease the surface. Cover and let rise in a warm place till double (about 1½ to 2 hours).

Punch down. Round in ball, cover and let rest 10 minutes. Shape in loaf (see photographs) and place in a greased 9½x5x3-inch loaf pan. Cover and let rise in a warm place till almost double (about 45 to 60 minutes). Bake in a moderate oven (375°) about 30 minutes or till done.

(If browning too fast, place foil over top during the last 20 minutes.) Remove from pan; cool on rack. Drizzle with ***Confectioners' Glaze:*** Combine 1 cup sifted confectioners' sugar and about 1½ tablespoons milk.

Little Raisin Loaves

Prepare dough as directed in recipe for Glazed Raisin Loaf. Cover and let rise till double (1½ to 2 hours). Punch down; form in 6 balls. Shape in small loaves; place in 6 greased 4½x2⅝x2-inch loaf pans. Cover and let rise in a warm place till almost double (45 to 60 minutes). Bake in a moderate oven (375°) for 20 minutes or till done. Cool and drizzle with Confectioners' Glaze (see the recipe above).

Knead with heel of hands, rocking in a pull-push motion, then folding dough toward you with curved fingers. After each "rock," give dough a quarter turn. Repeat till smooth.

With rolling pin, flatten dough in an oblong—width should be about same as length of pan. Starting at narrow end, roll up dough, sealing well at each turn with tips of fingers.

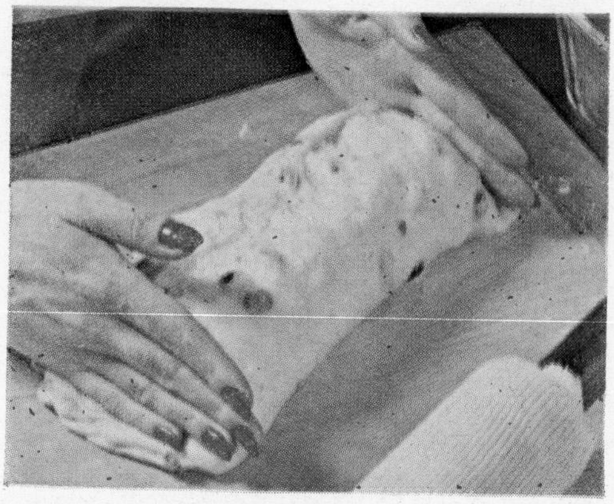

Press down on ends of loaf with edge of hands, making two thin, sealed strips. Be firm—dough will be springy. Fold strips under loaf as you put it in greased pan; end crusts will be smooth.

Raisin-Nut Braid

1 package active dry yeast *or*
 1 cake compressed yeast
¼ cup water
2 cups milk, scalded
½ cup sugar
½ cup shortening
2 teaspoons salt
6½ to 7 cups sifted all-purpose flour
1 cup seedless raisins
1 cup chopped California walnuts

Soften active dry yeast in *warm* water or compressed yeast in *lukewarm* water. Combine milk, sugar, shortening, and salt. Cool to lukewarm. Add about 3 *cups* flour; beat well. Add the softened yeast; stir in raisins and nuts. Add enough remaining flour to make a moderately stiff dough. Turn out on a lightly floured surface and knead till smooth and satiny (about 5 to 8 minutes). Place in a greased bowl, turning once to grease surface. Cover; let double (2 hours).

Punch down. Divide dough into two equal parts. Shape each part into a smooth ball. Cover and let rest 10 minutes. Divide each half of dough in thirds and roll out into strands about 1 inch across and 20 inches long. On a greased baking sheet, lay 3 strands about 1 inch apart. Braid together beginning in the middle and working toward either end to avoid stretching. Repeat with 3 remaining strands on another baking sheet. Cover and let rise in a warm place till double (about 1¼ hours). Bake in a moderate oven (375°) for 20 to 25 minutes.

While still slightly warm, brush tops with ***Confectioners' Icing:*** Slowly add 2 tablespoons milk to 1 cup sifted confectioners' sugar. Stir till smooth. Garnish with candied cherries, if desired. Makes 2 braids.

Raisin-Nut Loaves

Prepare dough as directed in recipe for Raisin-Nut Braid. Cover and let rise in a warm place till double (about 2 hours). Punch down. Divide dough into two equal parts. Shape each part into a smooth ball.

Cover and let rest 10 minutes. Shape each in a loaf and place in 2 greased 9½x5x3-inch loaf pans. Cover and let rise in a warm place till double. Bake in a moderate oven (375°) about 40 minutes. While loaves are slightly warm, brush tops with Confectioners' Icing (see above).

For variety make little loaves

Tiny loaves are made from recipe for Glazed Raisin Loaf

Orange Bread

1 package active dry yeast *or*
 1 cake compressed yeast
¼ cup water
• • •
1¾ cups water
¼ cup orange juice
¼ cup grated orange peel
½ cup sugar
1½ teaspoons salt
3 tablespoons melted shortening
• • •
7½ cups sifted all-purpose flour
1 egg

Soften active dry yeast in ¼ cup *warm* water (110°) or compressed yeast in ¼ cup *lukewarm* water (85°). To the 1¾ cups water, add orange juice, grated orange peel, sugar, salt, and melted shortening. Add 2 *cups* of the flour and mix well. Add egg and the softened yeast. Beat thoroughly. Add the remaining 5½ cups flour or enough to make a moderately soft dough.

Turn out on a lightly floured surface and knead till smooth and elastic (about 5 to 8 minutes). Place dough in a lightly greased bowl, turning once to grease the surface. Cover and let rise in a warm place till double (about 1½ hours).

Punch down. Cover and let rest for 10 minutes. Divide the dough into two equal portions. Shape each into a loaf. Place in two greased 9½x5x3-inch pans. Cover and let rise in a warm place till double (about 1 hour and 15 minutes). Bake loaves in a moderate oven (375°) for about 45 minutes or till done. Brush tops with melted butter for a soft crust. Makes 2 loaves.

Butter Braid

Soften 1 package active dry yeast in ¼ cup warm water. Combine ½ cup butter, 2 tablespoons sugar, 2 teaspoons salt, and 1 cup scalded milk. Cool to lukewarm. Sift 5 to 5½ cups all-purpose flour. Stir in 2 *cups* flour; beat well. Add yeast and 2 eggs; mix well. Add enough remaining flour to make a soft dough. Turn out on floured surface. Knead till smooth (5 to 8 minutes). Place in lightly greased bowl, turning dough once. Cover; let rise till double (1½ hours).

Punch down. Turn out on lightly floured surface; divide in 8 parts; form in balls. Cover; let rest 10 minutes. Shape each ball in a 13-inch strip, 1 inch in diameter. For each braided loaf, place 4 strips side by side on a well-greased baking sheet. Braid without stretching dough, beginning in middle and working toward either end. For a 4-strand braid, throw the strips alternately under and over. Seal ends of strands and tuck under braid. Cover; let rise till very light and puffy (1 hour). Brush with 1 beaten egg. Bake in moderate oven (375°) about 30 to 35 minutes. Makes 2 braids.

Cinnamon Swirl Orange Bread

Soften 1 package active dry yeast in ¼ cup warm water. Mix 1 cup scalded milk, ½ cup sugar, ¼ cup shortening, 1½ teaspoons salt, 1 tablespoon grated orange peel, and ¾ cup orange juice; cool to lukewarm.

Sift 6½ to 7 cups all-purpose flour. Stir in 2 *cups* flour; beat smooth. Stir in yeast and 1 slightly-beaten egg; beat well. Add enough remaining flour to make a soft dough. Turn out on lightly floured surface; knead till smooth (10 minutes). Place in greased bowl, turning dough once. Cover and let rise till double (1¼ hours).

Punch down; divide in half. Cover; let rest 10 minutes. Roll each half in 15x7-inch rectangle, ½ inch thick. Combine ½ cup sugar and 1 tablespoon cinnamon. Spread each rectangle with half the sugar mixture. Sprinkle each with 1 teaspoon water; smooth with spatula. Roll. Seal edge; place sealed edge down in greased 8½x4½x2½-inch loaf pan. Cover; let rise till double (1 hour).

Bake at 350° for 30 minutes. Cool; frost with icing made of 1 cup sifted confectioners' sugar, 1 teaspoon grated orange peel, and 4 teaspoons orange juice.

Cinnamon Swirl Loaf

See this lovely loaf on the cover—

1 package active dry yeast *or*
1 cake compressed yeast
¼ cup water

• • •

2 cups milk, scalded
½ cup sugar
½ cup shortening
2 teaspoons salt
7½ to 8 cups sifted all-purpose flour
2 slightly-beaten eggs
¾ cup sugar
1½ tablespoons cinnamon
Soft butter

Soften active dry yeast in *warm* water or compressed yeast in *lukewarm* water. Combine next 4 ingredients; cool to lukewarm.

Add 3 cups of the flour; mix well. Stir in softened yeast and eggs; beat well. Add enough of remaining flour to make a soft dough. Turn out on lightly floured surface. Knead till smooth (8 to 10 minutes). Place in lightly greased bowl, turning once to grease surface. Cover and let rise in warm place till double (1½ to 2 hours).

Punch down and divide dough in half. Cover and let rest 10 minutes. Roll each half in 15x7-inch rectangle, about ½ inch thick. Mix ¾ cup sugar and the cinnamon. Reserve 2 tablespoons of mixture; sprinkle remainder over dough. Sprinkle 1 teaspoon of water over each; smooth with spatula.

Roll each as for jelly roll, beginning with narrow side. Seal long edge. Place sealed edge down in 2 greased 9½x5x3-inch loaf pans. Let rise till almost double (45 to 60 minutes). Just before baking, brush loaves with soft butter, and sprinkle with remaining cinnamon-sugar.

Bake in moderate oven (375°) 35 to 40 minutes or till done. (If crust browns too fast, cover with aluminum foil last 15 to 20 minutes of baking.) Turn out of pans and cool on rack. Makes 2 loaves.

It's Cinnamon Swirl Orange Bread for scrumptious eating

Sugar 'n spice swirl through the bread and lacy icing adorns the top. Secret: Drizzle icing from a spoon, moving it back and forth like "push-and-pulls" in penmanship. →

BUTTER

California Prune Bread

1 package active dry yeast
¼ cup warm water
1 cup milk, scalded
¾ cup liquid from cooking prunes
2 teaspoons salt
¼ cup sugar
¼ cup shortening
6 to 6¼ cups sifted all-purpose flour
1 cup chopped cooked prunes

Soften yeast in warm water. Combine milk, prune liquid, salt, sugar, and shortening; cool till lukewarm. Add 2 *cups* flour; beat until smooth and elastic. Add softened yeast and prunes; mix. Add remaining flour or enough to make a soft dough. Turn out on a lightly floured surface; knead till smooth, about 10 minutes. Shape in a ball; place in a greased bowl, turning once to grease surface. Cover; let rise till double, 2 hours.

Turn out and divide dough in half; let rest 10 minutes. Shape into 2 loaves. Place in two greased 8½x4½x2½-inch loaf pans. Cover; let rise till double, 50 to 55 minutes. Bake in moderate oven (375°) about 40 to 45 minutes. Turn out of pans while hot. Brush sides and top with butter. Makes 2 loaves.

Health Bread

2 packages active dry yeast
½ cup warm water
1 cup quick-cooking oatmeal
2 teaspoons salt
2 tablespoons shortening
1 cup raisins
2¾ cups boiling water
1 cup bran
¾ cup molasses
1 cup stirred whole-wheat flour
6¾ to 7 cups sifted all-purpose flour

Soften yeast in warm water. Combine next 6 ingredients; cool to lukewarm. Add softened yeast and molasses. Stir in whole-wheat flour and 2 *cups* white flour; beat well. Gradually add enough flour to make a soft dough. Turn out on lightly floured surface; knead till smooth. Place in a greased bowl, turning dough once. Cover; let rise in warm place till double, about 1 hour.

Punch down; divide in half. Cover; let rest 10 minutes. Shape into 2 loaves. Place in 2 greased 9½x5x3-inch loaf pans. Let rise till double, about 45 minutes. Bake in moderate oven (350°) for 55 to 60 minutes.

Dilly Bread

2 tablespoons chopped onion
1 tablespoon butter
1 package active dry yeast
¼ cup warm water
1 cup large-curd cream-style cottage cheese, heated lukewarm
2 tablespoons sugar
2 teaspoons dill seed
1 teaspoon salt
¼ teaspoon soda
1 egg
2½ cups sifted all-purpose flour

Cook onion in butter till tender. Soften yeast in water. Combine in mixing bowl cottage cheese, sugar, onion, dill seed, salt, soda, egg, and softened yeast; mix well. Add enough flour to make a stiff dough, beating well on mixer after each addition. Cover; let rise till double, about 1¼ hours.

Stir down. Turn into well-greased 9½x5x 2-inch loaf pan. Let rise till light, about 40 minutes. Bake in moderate oven (350°) for 50 to 55 minutes. Cover with foil the last 15 minutes. Brush with soft butter and sprinkle with salt. Makes 1 loaf.

Cheese Loaf

1 package active dry yeast
¼ cup warm water
½ cup packaged (shaker top) grated American cheese
2 tablespoons sugar
1 teaspoon salt
2 tablespoons shortening
¾ cup hot water
3 to 3½ cups sifted all-purpose flour
1 egg

Soften yeast in ¼ cup warm water. Combine next 5 ingredients, stirring to dissolve. Cool to lukewarm. Stir in 2 *cups* flour, mixing well. Add yeast and egg; mix well. Add remaining flour or enough to make soft dough. Turn out on lightly floured surface; knead till smooth. Place in lightly greased bowl, turning once to grease surface. Cover; let rise till double, 1¼ hours.

Punch down; divide dough in 2 parts. Cover; let rest 10 minutes. Shape each part in roll 12 inches long. Twist the two rolls together in rope fashion, pinching ends together. Place in greased 9½x5x3-inch loaf pan. Cover; let rise till double, 1½ hours. Bake in moderate oven (375°) for 35 minutes.

Sally Lunn

1 package active dry yeast
¼ cup warm water
1 cup milk, scalded
½ cup butter or margarine
¼ cup sugar
3 eggs
4 cups sifted all-purpose flour
1 teaspoon salt

Soften yeast in water. Cool milk to lukewarm. Add cooled milk and set aside.

Cream butter and sugar; add eggs one at a time, mix well after each. Add flour and salt to creamed mixture alternately with yeast mixture, beating well after each addition. Beat till smooth. Cover; let rise till double, about 1 hour.

Beat down and pour into 2 well-greased 8½x4½x2½-inch loaf pans*. Let rise till double, about 40 minutes. Bake in moderate oven (350°) for 30 minutes or till golden brown and crusty. Serve hot with butter.

*Or use a well-greased 10-inch tube pan, and bake at 350° about 45 minutes.

Parmesan Casserole Bread

1 package active dry yeast *or*
  1 cake compressed yeast
¼ cup water
¼ cup milk, scalded
1½ cups sifted all-purpose flour
1 tablespoon sugar
½ teaspoon salt
⅓ cup butter or margarine
1 beaten egg
½ cup grated Parmesan cheese
2 tablespoons chopped parsley

Soften active dry yeast in *warm* water or compressed yeast in *lukewarm* water. Cool milk to lukewarm. Meanwhile sift flour, sugar, and salt into mixing bowl. With pastry blender or pastry fork cut in butter till mixture resembles coarse meal. Add egg, softened yeast, and milk; beat well. Stir in the cheese and parsley.

Turn into greased 8x1½-inch round pan. Cover with damp cloth and let rise till double, about 40 minutes. Dot with more butter. Bake in moderate oven (375°) 20 to 25 minutes. Cut in pie-shaped wedges.

Offer tempting parsley-flecked wedges of Parmesan Casserole Bread

This tasty cheese bread is so very easy—no kneading and no shaping. It takes only a little over an hour from inspiration to the table. Serve it with cool salads or hot meals, it's sure to make a hit!

Tender Yeast Rolls

Yeast roll basics

Serve light and airy rolls just once, and they'll become a tradition! For success in baking bread and rolls, first choose a basic recipe and master it, then develop any variations you might desire.

• Dough for rolls is softer than for plain bread, as soft as can be handled without sticking to hands or board. Softer dough makes lighter and more tender rolls.

• With increasing amounts of sugar and fat, the action of yeast is retarded; more yeast is often needed for rolls than for loaves.

• Most rolls require only thorough mixing, with little or no kneading.

• Rolls will be crusty if they are placed 1 inch apart when baking.

• Rolls brushed with salad oil or melted fat before baking will have tender crusts. Those brushed with milk or 1 beaten egg diluted with 1 tablespoon milk will have crisp crusts.

• Rolls should be served at once or turned out of pans to allow to cool.

Plain Roll Dough

No kneading! We suggest this easy recipe for the Cloverleaf Rolls or Orange Swirls—

1 package active dry yeast *or*
1 cake compressed yeast
¼ cup water

• • •

¼ cup sugar
¼ cup shortening
1 teaspoon salt
1 cup milk, scalded

• • •

1 slightly-beaten egg
3½ cups sifted all-purpose flour

Soften active dry yeast in *warm* water or compressed yeast in *lukewarm* water. In large bowl, combine sugar, shortening, and salt; stir in hot milk; cool to lukewarm.

Add softened yeast, egg, and 2 *cups* of the flour; beat well. Gradually add remaining flour or enough to make a soft dough. Cover; let rise in a warm place till double (about 1½ hours). Punch down.* Turn out on lightly floured surface. Shape as Cloverleaf Rolls or Orange Swirls (see below). Makes about 24 hot rolls.

*For easier handling, refrigerate the dough for several hours before shaping.

Cloverleaf Rolls

On a lightly floured surface, roll Plain Roll Dough to ¼ inch thick. Cut rounds of dough with a 1¾-inch cutter. Shape in small balls—3 should half-fill a greased muffin cup (see picture on opposite page). Brush each with melted butter. Cover; let double (about 25 to 30 minutes). Bake at 400° for about 10 to 12 minutes. Serve hot.

Orange Swirls

For easier handling of dough, divide Plain Roll Dough in half, and round each piece in a ball. Cover and let rest for 10 minutes. Roll each ball to a 16x8-inch rectangle, a little less than ¼ inch thick.

Prepare filling: Brush each rectangle with 2 tablespoons melted butter. Combine ½ cup sugar, 4 teaspoons grated orange peel, and ½ cup chopped walnuts. Sprinkle *half* of mixture over each rectangle.

Beginning with the long side of the rectangle, roll up jellyroll fashion (see the picture on opposite page); seal the seam. Cut the filled roll of dough in 12 slices, each about 1¼ inches wide.

Place each roll cut side down in a greased muffin cup (see picture on opposite page), first giving bottom of each roll a little poke in the center—this will add height, and make a prettier shape.

Cover and let rolls rise in a warm place till almost double (about 30 to 40 minutes). Bake at 375° for 15 minutes or until done.

Remove rolls from pan. While still warm, frost with ***Orange Icing:*** Blend 2 cups sifted confectioners' sugar, 2 teaspoons grated orange peel, and 3 tablespoons orange juice. Serve warm. Makes 24 rolls.

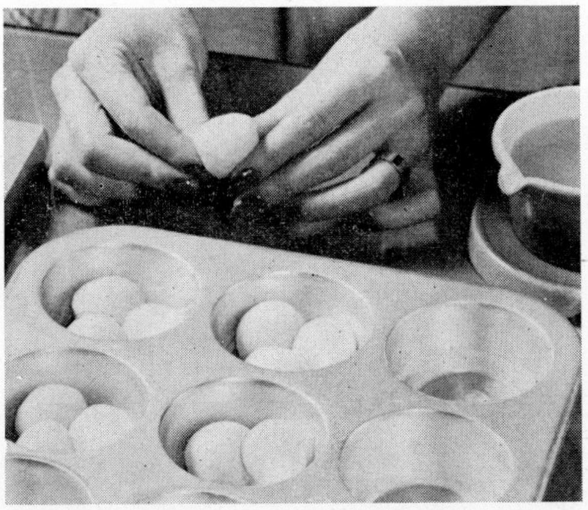

Cloverleaf Rolls: Roll to ¼ inch; cut in 1¾-inch rounds. (Or just pinch off bits of dough.) Shape in balls, pulling edges under.

Orange Swirls: Place each slice cut side down in muffin cup; first giving bottom a little poke in center—adds height, makes prettier shape.

Short-cut Cloverleaves: Place 1 large ball of dough in each muffin cup. Snip the tops crisscross with scissors right in the pan.

Orange Swirls: Roll dough up from long side as for jellyroll; seal seam well. Cut filled roll in 12 slices, each about 1¼ inches wide.

Butter-Pecan Rolls

1 package active dry yeast
¼ cup warm water
1 cup milk, scalded
¼ cup shortening
¼ cup sugar
1 teaspoon salt
3¼ to 3½ cups sifted all-purpose flour
1 beaten egg
1 recipe *each* Filling and Topping

Soften yeast in *warm* water. Combine hot milk, shortening, sugar, and salt; cool to lukewarm. Add 1 *cup* flour; beat well. Beat in yeast and egg. Gradually add remaining flour to form a soft dough, beating well. Brush top lightly with soft shortening; cover dough and let rise in warm place till double (about 1½ to 2 hours).

Punch down; turn out on lightly floured surface. Divide in half. Roll each piece in 12x8-inch rectangle, ⅜ inch thick.

Filling: Brush each with 2 tablespoons melted butter. Combine ½ cup sugar, and 2 teaspoons cinnamon; sprinkle half over each. Start with long side; roll up, jellyroll style; seal. Cut each in eight 1½-inch slices.

Topping: In each of two 9½x5x3-inch loaf pans, mix ½ cup brown sugar, ¼ cup butter, and 1 tablespoon light corn syrup. Heat slowly, stirring frequently till blended. Remove from heat. Sprinkle ⅓ cup pecans in each pan and top with 8 rolls, cut side down. Cover; let rise till double (35 to 45 minutes). Bake in moderate oven (375°) about 25 minutes. Cool 2 or 3 minutes; invert on rack; remove pans. Makes 16.

Rich Roll Dough

For Fantans and Butterhorns—

1 package active dry yeast *or*
  1 cake compressed yeast*
⅓ cup water

• • •

½ cup sugar
½ cup shortening
2 teaspoons salt
⅔ cup milk

• • •

5 to 5¼ cups sifted all-purpose flour
3 slightly-beaten eggs

Soften active dry yeast in *warm* water (110°) or compressed yeast in *lukewarm* water (85°). Combine sugar, shortening, salt, and milk; scald, stirring till shortening melts and sugar dissolves; cool to lukewarm. Add 1½ *cups* of the flour; beat well. Add softened yeast and eggs; beat well. Stir in remaining flour or enough to make a soft dough.

Turn out on floured surface. Knead lightly till smooth and elastic (5 to 8 minutes). Place dough in lightly greased bowl, turning once to grease surface. Cover; let rise in warm place till double (about 3 hours). Punch down. Turn out on lightly floured surface. Shape as Fantans (makes 27) *or* as Butterhorn Rolls (makes 36).

*Rich dough is a slow riser. In a hurry? You can speed up the rising time by using 2 packages active dry yeast or 2 cakes compressed yeast. Then, the first rising (in the bowl) will take about 1½ hours, and the second rising (after shaping the rolls) will take about 50 minutes.

1 Cut each rectangle of dough lengthwise in 6 strips, each 1½-inches wide.

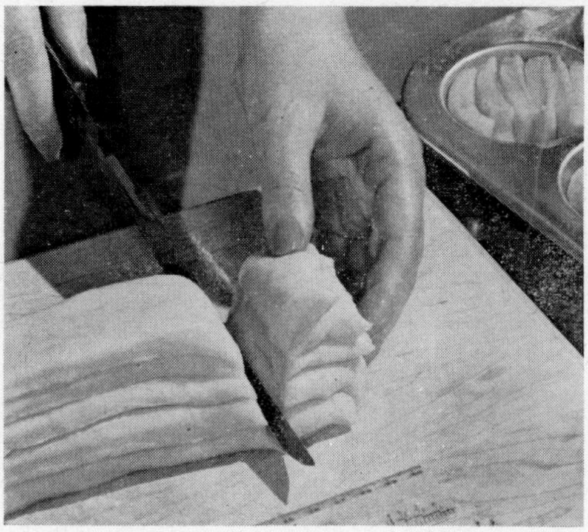

2 Place all 6 strips on top of one another; cut in 1½-inch lengths, making 9 pieces.

3 Grasp wedge at corners of end opposite point and start to roll up away from you.

4 While holding corners of end opposite point, flip the point toward you.

Fantans

Divide Rich Roll Dough in 3 equal pieces and round each in a ball. Cover; let rest 10 minutes. Roll each ball in a 14x9-inch rectangle, about ¼ inch thick. Brush with melted butter or margarine.

Cut each rectangle lengthwise in 6 strips, 1½-inches wide (first picture). Pile all 6 strips on top of one another; cut in 1½-inch lengths, making 9 pieces (second picture). Place cut side down in greased muffin pans. Cover and let rise in warm place till double (about 1 to 1½ hours). Bake in moderate oven (375°) for about 15 minutes or till done. Makes 27 rolls.

Butterhorn Rolls

Divide Rich Roll Dough in 3 equal pieces; round each piece in a ball. Cover; let rest 10 minutes. Roll each to 12-inch circle, about ¼ inch thick. Brush with melted butter. Cut each circle in 12 wedges. To shape, grasp wedge at the corners of end opposite point and start to roll up away from you (third picture). Now flip the point toward you (fourth picture).

Arrange rolls, points down, on greased baking sheets and brush with melted butter. Cover and let rise in warm place till double (about 1 hour). Bake in hot oven (400°) for 10 minutes or till done. Makes 36 rolls.

Refrigerator White Rolls

1 package active dry yeast
¼ cup warm water
• • •
¾ cup milk, scalded
¼ cup shortening
¼ cup sugar
1 teaspoon salt
3 cups sifted all-purpose flour
1 egg

Soften the yeast in warm water. Combine the milk, shortening, sugar, and salt; cool to lukewarm. Add 1 *cup* of the flour; beat well. Beat in yeast mixture and the egg. Add remaining flour; mix well. Place in a greased bowl, turning dough once. Cover; store in refrigerator at least 2 hours or till needed.

About 1½ to 2 hours before serving time, shape dough on well-floured surface. Let rise in warm place till double (about 1¼ hours). Bake in hot oven (400°) 12 to 15 minutes. Makes about 16 medium rolls.

Whole-wheat Rolls

2 packages active dry yeast *or*
  2 cakes compressed yeast
½ cup water
1¾ cups milk, scalded
½ cup sugar
1 tablespoon salt
3 tablespoons shortening
4 cups stirred whole-wheat flour
3 cups sifted all-purpose flour
2 beaten eggs

Soften active dry yeast in *warm* water or compressed yeast in *lukewarm* water. Combine hot milk, sugar, salt, shortening; cool to lukewarm. Add 1 *cup* whole-wheat flour and 1 *cup* all-purpose flour; beat well. Add yeast mixture and eggs. Stir in remaining flour or enough to make soft dough. Place in greased bowl, turning once to grease surface; cover, place in refrigerator.

About 2 hours before serving time, knead lightly on floured surface; form in rolls. Let rise in warm place till double (1½ hours). Bake in hot oven (400°) 15 to 20 minutes. Brush with butter. Makes 4 dozen rolls.

Bran Refrigerator Rolls

2 packages active dry yeast *or*
  2 cakes compressed yeast
1 cup water
• • •
1 cup shortening
¾ cup sugar
1 cup whole bran
2 teaspoons salt
1 cup boiling water
• • •
6½ cups sifted all-purpose flour
2 beaten eggs

Soften active dry yeast in *warm* water (110°) or compressed yeast in *lukewarm* water (85°). Combine shortening, sugar, bran, and salt; add boiling water and stir till shortening melts. Cool to lukewarm. Stir in 1 *cup* flour; add eggs and yeast mixture. Add half the remaining flour and beat well. Add remaining flour and mix well. Place in greased bowl, turning once to grease surface. Cover; chill in refrigerator till ready to use.

Form 2 or 3 balls of dough to fill greased muffin pans half full; or form in rolls, using 1 larger ball of dough for each. Let rise till double (1½ to 2 hours). Bake in hot oven (425°) 15 minutes. Makes 3½ dozen rolls.

Corn-meal Dinner Rolls

1 package active dry yeast
¼ cup warm water
• • •
¼ cup butter or margarine
¼ cup shortening
½ cup sugar
1 tablespoon salt
2 cups scalded milk
• • •
3 cups sifted all-purpose flour
2 beaten eggs
1½ cups corn meal
4½ cups sifted all-purpose flour

Soften yeast in water. Combine next 5 ingredients; cool to lukewarm. Add 3 cups flour, eggs, and yeast mixture. Beat till smooth. Mix in corn meal and 4½ cups flour. Knead 10 minutes. Place in greased bowl, turning dough once. Cover; let rise till double (about 1¾ hours).

Punch down; shape in small balls. Place 2 balls in each greased muffin cup. Brush with melted butter or margarine; cover and let rise till double (about 1 hour). Bake in moderate oven (375°) 15 minutes. Makes 36.

Clothespin Rolls

1 package active dry yeast
¼ cup warm water
½ cup milk, scalded
½ cup shortening
¼ cup sugar
1 teaspoon salt
2½ to 3 cups sifted all-purpose flour
½ cup corn meal
2 eggs

Soften yeast in water. Combine next 4 ingredients: cool to lukewarm. Stir in 1½ cups flour and the corn meal; beat well. Add yeast and eggs; mix well. Add enough flour to make soft dough. Turn out on lightly floured surface; knead till smooth. Place in greased bowl, turning dough once. Cover; let rise in warm place till double (1¼ hours).

Punch down; turn out on lightly floured surface. Shape pieces of dough into ropes about 8 inches long and ¼ inch in diameter. Wrap around greased peg clothespins, pressing gently to seal ends. Place on greased baking sheet; cover; let double (45 minutes). Bake at 375° 10 minutes. Immediately remove clothespins by twisting gently.

Note: Dough may also be formed into 20 pan rolls. Bake pan rolls about 15 minutes.

Cheese Buns

1 package active dry yeast
1¼ cups warm water
2 tablespoons salad oil
1 tablespoon sugar
1 teaspoon salt
2 teaspoons instant onion
¼ teaspoon celery seed
1 egg
1 cup shredded sharp process cheese
3 cups sifted all-purpose flour
Small stuffed green olives, cut crosswise in half

Soften yeast in water. Add next 7 ingredients and 2 *cups* of the flour. Beat vigorously, with electric mixer or by hand till smooth, about 2 minutes. Add remaining flour and continue beating with spoon till smooth, about 1 minute. Cover and let rise till double (30 to 45 minutes).

Beat batter hard, about 50 strokes. Spoon into well-greased deep muffin cups, filling about half full. Press olive half, pimiento side up, in center of each. Cover and let rise till double (15 to 20 minutes). Press olive down slightly, but let top show. Bake in hot oven (425°) for about 10 to 15 minutes, or till lightly browned. Remove from pans and serve warm. Makes 18.

English Muffins

1 package active dry yeast
½ cup warm water
1½ cups milk, scalded
2 tablespoons sugar
2 teaspoons salt
¼ cup shortening
5¾ to 6 cups sifted all-purpose flour

Soften yeast in water. Combine next 4 ingredients; cool to lukewarm. Stir in 2 *cups* flour; beat well. Add yeast; mix. Add enough of remaining flour to make a moderately stiff dough. Turn out on a lightly floured surface; knead till smooth (8 to 10 minutes). Place in lightly greased bowl, turning dough once. Cover; let rise till double (1¼ hours).

Punch down; cover and let rest 10 minutes. Roll to slightly less than ½ inch on lightly floured surface. Cut with a 3-inch round cutter. (Reroll edges.) Cover and let rise till very light (1¼ hours). Bake on top of range on medium hot greased griddle, turn frequently till done, about 30 minutes. Cool thoroughly. Split with a fork, toast on both sides. Serve at once. Makes 2 dozen.

Herb Pan Rolls are easy and speedy, so light and tender. You use just 3 ingredients plus herbs. Simply delicious!

Herb Rolls

Old-fashioned yeast pan rolls made from biscuit mix. Bottom crisp. Top brown!—

1 package active dry yeast
¾ cup warm water
2½ cups packaged biscuit mix
½ teaspoon celery seed
1 teaspoon poultry seasoning

Soften yeast in warm water. Stir in biscuit mix and remaining ingredients; beat vigorously (2 to 3 minutes). Turn out on surface well dusted with biscuit mix. Knead till smooth, about 25 strokes. Roll in a 14x6-inch rectangle, about ¼ inch thick. Cut dough lengthwise in thirds, then crosswise at 2-inch intervals to make 21 squares. Form each square into a ball.

In greased 8x1½-inch round pan, arrange 13 rolls (not quite touching each other) around edge; arrange an inner circle of 8 rolls, leaving a 2-inch hole in center. Cover with damp cloth. Let rise till double (about 1 hour). Bake in hot oven (400°) 15 to 20 minutes or till golden brown. Serve hot.

Penny Rolls

Soften 1 package active dry yeast in ½ cup warm water. Combine ¼ cup sugar, 1 tablespoon salad oil or shortening, 1 teaspoon salt, and ½ cup hot water. Cool to lukewarm. Stir in 1 egg and softened yeast.

Sift 3 to 3¼ cups all-purpose flour. Stir in 2 *cups* flour; on electric mixer, beat at medium speed about 2 minutes. Stir in remaining flour or enough to make a soft dough. Beat vigorously with spoon 3 minutes or till dough is smooth. Scrape down sides of bowl. Cover; let rise till double (1 to 1¼ hours). Stir down in 20 to 25 strokes. Cover tightly and refrigerate overnight.

Turn out on floured surface; use sharp knife to cut in half. Refrigerate other half. Pinch off balls of dough and shape in rolls. Place in greased muffin pans filling ⅓ full. Repeat with remaining dough. Cover; let rise till double (45 to 60 minutes).

Bake at 375° for 10 minutes or till golden. Brush tops with melted butter. Remove from pans and serve at once. Makes 30 small rolls.

Shamrocks or Potato Rolls—they're grand!

Just a few snips of the scissors shape Shamrock Rolls. They're made from hot mashed potatoes. For a soft tender crust brush with butter after they come from the oven. Pass while hot.

1 After the dough has risen, round in a ball. Cover and let rest 10 minutes. Cut the ball in fourths, then cut each fourth in 6 wedges. Form the wedges in smooth little balls.

2 Place balls of dough on greased baking sheet—leave room for rising. For leaves, snip balls almost to center in 3 places. Then snip at midpoint in edge of each leaf. Let rise.

Shamrock Rolls

1 package active dry yeast *or*
 1 cake compressed yeast
¼ cup water
½ cup hot mashed potatoes
¼ cup shortening
¼ cup sugar
1½ teaspoons salt
1 cup milk, scalded
• • •
1 egg
4 to 4½ cups sifted all-purpose flour

Soften active dry yeast in *warm* water, or compressed yeast in *lukewarm* water. Combine potatoes, shortening, sugar, salt, and hot milk. Cool to lukewarm.

Add softened yeast and egg. Stir in 2 *cups* of the flour; beat well. Stir in the remaining flour or enough to make a soft dough. Turn out and knead on lightly floured surface till smooth and elastic, 6 to 8 minutes.

Place in lightly greased bowl, turning once to grease surface. Cover and let rise in a warm place till double, about 1 hour. Punch down. Shape in ball. Cover and let rest 10 minutes. To shape Shamrock Rolls, follow the directions under the pictures on opposite page. Let rolls rise on greased baking sheet till almost double, about 1 hour. Bake in hot oven (400°) about 10 to 12 minutes. Makes 2 dozen rolls.

Batter Rolls

1 package active dry yeast *or*
 1 cake compressed yeast
¼ cup water
½ cup shortening
¼ cup sugar
1 teaspoon salt
1 cup milk, scalded
2 cups sifted all-purpose flour
1 slightly-beaten egg
1¼ cups sifted all-purpose flour

Soften dry yeast in *warm* water (110°) or compressed yeast in *lukewarm* water (85°). Combine shortening, sugar, and salt in a large mixing bowl. Add scalded milk; stir till shortening is melted. Cool to lukewarm.

Start mixer on medium speed (or beat by hand); add 2 cups flour. Beat 1 minute or until gluten strands are practically visible. Stop the mixer. Add softened yeast and egg. Beat batter smooth on medium speed, about ½ minute. Add remaining 1¼ cups flour.

Beat batter at medium speed until smooth, about 2 minutes. Since batter is stiff, you might need to push it away from beaters with a rubber scraper occasionally. Cover dough and let rise till double, about 1 hour. Stir down and beat thoroughly with a wooden spoon. Make into Dinner Rolls or Butterscotch Dainties. For Cinnamon Nut Whirls chill dough overnight.

Dinner Rolls

Prepare batter as directed in Batter Rolls. After batter has risen, stir down. Drop batter by tablespoons into 2¾-inch greased muffin pans, filling them half full. Let rise in warm place till double, about 30 minutes. Bake in hot oven (400°) about 15 minutes.

Butterscotch Dainties

½ recipe Batter Rolls
For each muffin cup:
 1 teaspoon butter or margarine
 2 teaspoons brown sugar
 1 tablespoon light corn syrup

Prepare batter as directed in Batter Rolls. In a small skillet combine butter, brown sugar, and corn syrup; heat slowly, stirring often. Place 2 teaspoons of hot mixture into each cup of a 2-inch muffin pan. Arrange a pecan half over mixture.

After batter has risen, stir down and drop by tablespoons into cups, filling half full. Let rise till double, about 30 minutes. Bake in moderate oven (375°) for 15 to 20 minutes. Cool 2 to 3 minutes; invert on cooling rack; remove pan. One recipe of Batter Rolls makes 36 Butterscotch Dainties.

Cinnamon Nut Whirls

1 recipe Batter Rolls
1 cup sugar
2 teaspoons cinnamon
1 cup finely chopped nuts

Prepare batter as directed in Batter Rolls. Chill batter overnight. When ready to shape, combine sugar, cinnamon, and nuts. Spread mixture on waxed paper. Grease hands; roll dough into 8-inch strands about ½ inch thick. Coat strands with sugar-nut mixture. Coil on a greased baking sheet. Let rise till light, about 30 minutes. Bake in moderate oven (375°) for 15 to 20 minutes. Makes 18.

Puff Pillow Buns

Soften 1 package active dry yeast in 1/4 cup *warm* water or 1 cake compressed yeast in 1/4 cup *lukewarm* water. Pour 1/2 cup scalded milk over 1/3 cup butter or margarine, 1/4 cup sugar, and 1 teaspoon salt. Stir till butter melts. Cool to lukewarm. Add 2 beaten eggs, 1 teaspoon grated lemon peel, and 1 cup sifted all-purpose flour; beat well. Stir in the softened yeast. Add 2 cups sifted all-purpose flour, mixing well. Cover the bowl with a damp cloth and refrigerate dough at least 4 hours or overnight.

When ready to shape dough prepare ***Cream-Cheese Filling:*** Blend two 3-ounce packages softened cream cheese, 1 tablespoon sugar, 1 slightly-beaten egg yolk, and 1/2 teaspoon vanilla. Divide dough in fourths. (Refrigerate unused portion of dough.)

On generously floured surface, roll each portion into 12x8-inch rectangle. With floured knife cut in six 4-inch squares. Place about 2 tablespoons of filling in the center of each square; bring opposite corners to the center, pinching to seal.

Place 2 inches apart on a greased baking sheet. Brush with 1 slightly-beaten egg white. Let rise uncovered in warm place till half again as large (not double), about 20 to 30 minutes. Bake in hot oven (400°) 10 minutes or till done. Serve hot. Makes 2 dozen.

This is one to keep in mind for a special brunch or luncheon

Let your talents show when you serve a colorful and refreshing fruit plate accompanied with oven-fresh Puff Pillow Buns. Your guests will rave about these wonderful feather-light buns with a delicious cream-cheese filling baked in the center. For a beverage serve tall glasses of pink lemonade.

Cranberry Wagon-wheel Rolls

2 packages active dry yeast *or*
2 cakes compressed yeast
⅔ cup water
⅔ cup milk, scalded
½ cup sugar
1¼ teaspoons salt
⅓ cup shortening
4 to 4½ cups sifted all-purpose flour
Cranberry-Apple Filling

Soften active dry yeast in *warm* water or compressed yeast in *lukewarm* water. Combine milk, sugar, salt, and shortening; stir till sugar dissolves. Add 2 *cups* of the flour and beat till smooth; stir in yeast and remaining flour to make a soft dough.

Turn out on a lightly floured surface; knead till smooth and satiny, about 8 to 10 minutes. Place dough in a greased bowl, turning once to grease surface. Cover and let dough rise in a warm place till double, takes about 1½ hours.

Punch down; divide and form into 2 balls; let rest 10 minutes. Divide each ball into about 8 pieces and form each of these into a bun. Place each bun about 2 inches apart on a greased baking sheet; flatten slightly. Cover and let rise in a warm place till double. Make an indentation in each bun, leaving ½-inch edge around roll. Fill this indentation with Cranberry-Apple Filling.

Bake in moderate oven (375°) for 15 to 20 minutes or until done. Remove from baking sheet immediately and sprinkle with confectioners' sugar if desired.

Cranberry Apple-Filling: Mix together 1 cup chopped fresh cranberries, 1 cup minced apples, ½ cup sugar, and 1 teaspoon cinnamon.

Double-decker Coffee Strips

1 package active dry yeast *or*
1 cake compressed yeast
¼ cup water
¼ cup milk, scalded
¼ cup sugar
½ teaspoon salt
2¼ cups sifted all-purpose flour
¼ cup shortening
1 beaten egg
Prune Filling
Confectioners' Icing

Soften active dry yeast in *warm* water or compressed yeast in *lukewarm* water. Cool milk to lukewarm and stir into yeast mixture. Mix together ¼ cup sugar, salt, and flour. Cut in shortening till it resembles coarse corn meal. Add the egg. Stir flour and sugar mixture into the yeast-milk mixture; mix thoroughly.

Place in a greased bowl, turning once to grease surface. Cover and let rise in warm place till double, about 1½ to 2 hours. Punch down and turn out on lightly floured surface. Roll into a rectangle 14x12-inches and place on greased baking sheet.

For *Prune Filling:* Mix together 1½ cups chopped cooked prunes, 3 tablespoons sugar, ½ teaspoon grated lemon peel, and 3 tablespoons lemon juice. Spread this mixture lengthwise over ½ the dough. Fold dough over filling and seal the other 3 edges. Cover and let rise in warm place till double, about 1 hour. Bake in moderate oven (350°) 15 to 20 minutes. When cool frost with Confectioners' Icing and slice in strips.

Cinnamon Circles

1 package active dry yeast
½ cup warm water
1 cup milk, scalded
½ cup sugar
½ cup shortening
1¼ teaspoons salt
5½ cups sifted all-purpose flour
2 eggs
1 teaspoon lemon extract
½ cup soft butter or margarine
1 cup sugar

Soften yeast in water. Combine next 4 ingredients; mix well. Cool to lukewarm. Add 2 *cups* flour and beat well. Add eggs; mix well. Beat in softened yeast and lemon extract. Add remaining flour to make a soft dough. Turn out and knead on a lightly floured surface till smooth and satiny. Place in lightly greased bowl, turning once to grease surface. Cover and let rise till double.

Roll dough to about ⅛ inch on lightly floured surface. Spread with ⅓ of the butter, sprinkle with ⅓ of the sugar. Fold over and roll to ⅛ inch. Repeat this spreading, folding, and rolling process twice more. Combine ½ cup sugar and 1 tablespoon cinnamon. Sprinkle half the mixture over dough. Roll as for jelly roll.

Cut dough in ½-inch slices. Place on greased baking sheet. Flatten with palm of hand. Sprinkle remaining cinnamon-sugar on top. Decorate with walnuts or pecans. Let rise till almost double. Bake in hot oven (400°) about 12 minutes. Makes 30 to 36.

Nut Crusty Twists

Soften 1 package active dry yeast in ¼ cup *warm* water or 1 cake compressed yeast in ¼ cup *lukewarm* water. Combine 1 cup scalded milk, ½ cup sugar, ½ cup shortening, and 1½ teaspoons salt; cool to lukewarm. Add softened yeast and 2 beaten eggs. Mix well. Stir in about 5 cups sifted all-purpose flour to make rather soft dough. Turn out on lightly floured surface; knead till smooth. Place in greased bowl, turning once to grease surface.

Cover; let rise till double (1½ hours). Punch down. Roll dough in pencil-size strips, about 10 inches long. Dip in milk, then sugar; roll in chopped walnuts. Twist each into figure 8. Place on greased baking sheet and let double. Bake in hot oven (400°) 15 minutes, or till done. Makes 3 dozen.

Coffeetime Twists

1 package active dry yeast *or*
  1 cake compressed yeast
¼ cup water
¾ cup buttermilk
3 tablespoons sugar
1 teaspoon salt
2 tablespoons shortening
¼ teaspoon soda
3 cups sifted all-purpose flour
1 slightly-beaten egg
2 tablespoons soft butter
⅓ cup brown sugar
1 teaspoon cinnamon

Soften active dry yeast in *warm* water or compressed yeast in *lukewarm* water. Heat buttermilk to lukewarm; combine with sugar, shortening, salt, and soda. Add 1 cup flour; beat smooth. Add yeast and egg; beat well. Stir in remaining flour. Turn out on lightly floured surface; knead till smooth.

Roll into 24x6-inch rectangle, ¼-inch thick; spread with butter. Combine brown sugar and cinnamon, sprinkle over lengthwise half of the dough; fold other half over to make long, narrow rectangle. Cut into 24 1-inch strips.

To form rolls, hold strip at both ends and twist in opposite directions. Place on greased baking sheet; let rise in warm place till light (about 1 hour). Bake in moderate oven (375°) 12 to 15 minutes. Makes 24.

While warm, frost with Icing: Combine 1 cup sifted confectioners' sugar, 2 tablespoons milk, and ¼ teaspoon vanilla.

Cherry Yeast Rolls

1 package active dry yeast
¼ cup warm water
½ cup milk, scalded
¼ cup sugar
¼ cup butter or margarine
1 teaspoon salt
3 eggs
4 to 4½ cups sifted all-purpose flour
1 recipe Cherry Filling

Soften yeast in water. Combine next 4 ingredients; stir till sugar dissolves and butter melts. Cool to lukewarm. Stir in eggs and yeast mixture. Stir in about 2 *cups* of the flour; beat well. Add remaining flour (or enough to make a soft dough). Turn out on lightly floured surface; knead till smooth, about 5 minutes. Divide in 2 portions. Shape each in a smooth ball; cover and let rest 10 minutes. Roll each ball in 12x8-inch rectangle. Spread lengthwise half of each rectangle with Cherry Filling.

Fold each rectangle in half lengthwise and cut crosswise in 12 strips. Twist each strip two or three times; arrange on greased baking sheet. Cover; let rise till double, about 35 minutes. Bake in hot oven (400°) about 10 minutes or till done. Makes 24.

While hot, ice with ***Confectioners' Frosting:*** Blend 1½ cups sifted confectioners' sugar, dash salt, ½ teaspoon vanilla, and 2 to 2½ tablespoons milk; beat smooth. Brush on with pastry brush for smooth glaze.

Cherry Filling

1 1-pound can (2 cups) pitted tart
  red cherries
. . .
¼ cup sugar
2 tablespoons cornstarch
Dash salt
Few drops red food coloring
¼ cup sugar
Few drops almond extract

Drain cherries, reserving ⅓ cup juice. Finely chop cherries; drain again. In saucepan, combine ¼ cup sugar, cornstarch, and salt. Stir in reserved cherry juice. Add few drops red food coloring. Heat, stirring constantly, till mixture comes to boiling. Add ¼ cup sugar; cook and stir till clear and thick. Remove from heat; stir in drained, chopped cherries and almond extract. Cool to room temperature. Makes about 1⅓ cups filling.

These tender rolls are fragrant with fresh orange peel on the inside and Orange Icing on top.

Orange Bowknots

They're so airy and light they almost fly away. Try them and you'll agree—

1 package active dry yeast *or*
1 cake compressed yeast
¼ cup water
1 cup milk, scalded
½ cup shortening
⅓ cup sugar
1 teaspoon salt
5 to 5½ cups sifted all-purpose flour
2 beaten eggs
2 tablespoons grated orange peel
¼ cup orange juice
Orange Icing

Soften dry yeast in *warm* water or compressed yeast in *lukewarm* water. Combine hot milk, shortening, sugar, and salt. Cool to lukewarm. Stir in about 2 *cups* of the flour and beat well. Add eggs; mix well. Stir in softened yeast. Add orange peel, juice, and remaining flour (or enough to make a soft dough). Cover; let rest 10 minutes.

Turn out on a lightly floured surface. Knead till smooth and elastic (about 8 to 10 minutes). Place dough in a lightly greased bowl, turning once to grease surface.

Cover dough and let rise in a warm place till double (about 2 hours). Punch down; cover and let rest 10 minutes.

Roll dough in 18x10-inch rectangle, ½-inch thick. Cut strips 10 inches long and ¾-inch wide. Roll each strip back and forth lightly under your fingers; loosely tie in knot. Arrange on a greased baking sheet. Cover and let rise in a warm place till double (about 45 minutes). Bake in a hot oven (400°) for 12 minutes. Makes 24.

Ice with ***Orange Icing:*** Blend 1 teaspoon grated orange peel, 2 tablespoons orange juice, and 1 cup sifted confectioners' sugar.

Orange Spirals

Prepare dough and let rise as for Orange Bowknots. Punch down; cover and let rest 10 minutes. Divide dough in half. Roll each to 12x9-inch rectangle, ¼-inch thick, and spread with ***Orange Filling:*** Combine ½ cup sugar, ½ cup chopped walnuts, 1 tablespoon grated orange peel, ¼ cup melted butter.

Roll each half of dough as for jellyroll; seal edge; cut in 1-inch slices. Place cut side down in greased muffin pans. Cover; let rise till double (45 to 60 minutes). Bake at 400° for 12 minutes. Makes 24.

Delicious Yeast Coffeecakes

Apricot Bubble Balls

1 package active dry yeast *or*
1 cake compressed yeast
¼ cup water

• • •

½ cup milk, scalded
⅓ cup sugar
⅓ cup shortening
1 teaspoon salt
3¾ to 4 cups sifted all-purpose flour
2 beaten eggs

• • •

¼ cup melted butter or margarine
¾ cup sugar
1 teaspoon cinnamon
⅔ cup apricot or pineapple preserves
¾ cup finely chopped California walnuts

Soften active dry yeast in *warm* water (110°) or compressed yeast in *lukewarm* water (85°). Combine scalded milk, ⅓ cup sugar, shortening, and salt; cool to lukewarm. Stir in 1 *cup* of the flour; beat well. Add softened yeast and eggs. Add remaining flour, or enough to make a soft dough. Mix thoroughly and place in a greased bowl, turning once to grease surface. Cover and let rise till double, about 2 hours.

Punch down and let rest 10 minutes. Divide dough into 20 pieces and form into balls. Roll each ball in melted butter or margarine. Combine sugar and cinnamon, roll ball in mixture. Place a layer of 10 balls in a well-greased 10-inch tube pan. Place a spoonful of the preserves between each ball, and sprinkle with half the nuts; repeat with second layer. Cover and let rise in warm place till double, about 45 minutes.

Bake in a moderate oven (350°) about 30 to 35 minutes. Cool about 8 minutes; invert pan and remove ring. Makes 1 coffeecake.

Have a baking day at home

← Pictured (top to bottom) are Apricot Bubble Balls, Double-decker Coffee Strips, Cranberry Wagon-wheel Rolls, Pineapple Crisscross Coffeecake, Cherry Lattice Coffeecake, and Jeweled Banana Bread. (See index listing.) Cheap luxury!

Pineapple Crisscross Coffeecake

It has pineapple and coconut on the inside and crunchy almonds on top—

2 packages active dry yeast *or*
2 cakes compressed yeast
½ cup water
¾ cup milk, scalded
½ cup sugar
2 teaspoons salt
¼ cup shortening
5 to 5¼ cups sifted all-purpose flour
2 eggs
1 teaspoon grated lemon peel

• • •

3 tablespoons melted butter
Pineapple-Coconut Filling
1 slightly-beaten egg white
½ cup slivered blanched almonds, toasted

Soften active dry yeast in *warm* water (110°) or compressed yeast in *lukewarm* water (85°). Combine scalded milk, sugar, salt, and shortening in bowl; cool to lukewarm. Add about 2 *cups* of the flour and mix well. Add softened yeast, eggs, and lemon peel and mix well. Add remaining flour or enough to make a soft dough. Turn out on a lightly floured surface. Cover and let rest 10 minutes. Knead till smooth and satiny, about 8 minutes. Place in a greased bowl, turning once to grease surface. Cover and let rise till double, about 1¾ hours.

Punch down and divide dough into 3 portions and let rest 10 minutes. Roll each portion into a 12x8-inch rectangle and place on a greased baking sheet. Brush dough with melted butter and spread the Pineapple-Coconut Filling lengthwise down the center third of the dough. With scissors make cuts 2 inches in from the side at 1-inch intervals along edges of dough. Alternately fold strips over filling in herringbone fashion. Cover and let rise till double, 45 minutes.

Brush top with egg white and sprinkle with almonds. Bake in moderate oven (350°) about 25 to 30 minutes. Makes 3 coffeecakes.

Pineapple-Coconut Filling: Mix together 1½ cups drained crushed pineapple, 1 cup toasted shredded coconut, ½ cup brown sugar, and ¼ teaspoon cinnamon. Spread on coffeecake.

Ribbon Loaf

1 package active dry yeast *or*
 1 cake compressed yeast
¼ cup water
• • •
½ cup milk, scalded
¼ cup sugar
1 teaspoon salt
¼ cup shortening or salad oil
2½ cups sifted all-purpose flour
1 beaten egg

Soften active dry yeast in *warm* water or compressed yeast in *lukewarm* water. Combine milk, sugar, salt, and shortening, stirring to melt shortening. Cool till lukewarm. Add enough flour to milk mixture to make a thick batter. Add egg; beat well. Stir in softened yeast. Add remaining flour to make a soft dough. Knead on lightly floured surface till smooth and satiny. Place in lightly greased bowl, turning once to grease surface. Cover; let rise till double (1½ hours).

Round into ball; let rest, covered, 10 minutes. On lightly floured board, roll out into 12x15-inch rectangle; brush with melted butter or margarine. Combine ½ cup sugar and 1 teaspoon cinnamon; sprinkle half of mixture on dough. Fold dough in thirds to make 4x15-inch strip; cut in 10 equal slices. Coat bottom of 8½x4½x2½-inch loaf pan generously with butter or margarine; sprinkle with remaining cinnamon-sugar mixture. Put strips of dough, cut side down, close together in pan. Cover; let rise in warm place till almost double (about 45 minutes). Bake in moderate oven (350°) 35 to 40 minutes. Turn out immediately. Makes 1 loaf.

Prune Coffee Braid

1 package active dry yeast
¼ cup warm water
¾ cup milk, scalded
¼ cup sugar
2 teaspoons salt
¼ cup shortening
3 to 3¾ cups sifted all-purpose flour
1 tablespoon grated lemon peel
1 slightly-beaten egg
• • •
Prune Filling
2 tablespoons melted butter
2 tablespoons sugar
½ teaspoon cinnamon

Soften yeast in water. Combine next 4 ingredients; stir till sugar and salt dissolve. Cool to lukewarm. Add about 1 *cup* flour; beat smooth. Stir in lemon peel, egg, and yeast; beat well. Add enough flour to make soft dough. Turn out on floured surface; knead till smooth. Place in greased bowl; turning dough once. Cover; let double.

Punch down, let rest 10 minutes. Divide dough in half; divide each half in 3 portions. Roll out a portion to form 12x4-inch rectangle. Spread with 3 tablespoons Prune Filling; roll and seal edge. Place on greased baking sheet. Repeat with two more portions. Braid 3 strips together; seal ends. Make second braid in same way. Brush braids with melted butter; sprinkle with combined sugar and cinnamon. Let rise about 45 minutes. Bake at 350° for 25 to 30 minutes. Makes 2.

Prune Filling: Mix 1 cup chopped cooked prunes, 2 tablespoons sugar, 1 tablespoon lemon juice, and ¼ cup chopped walnuts.

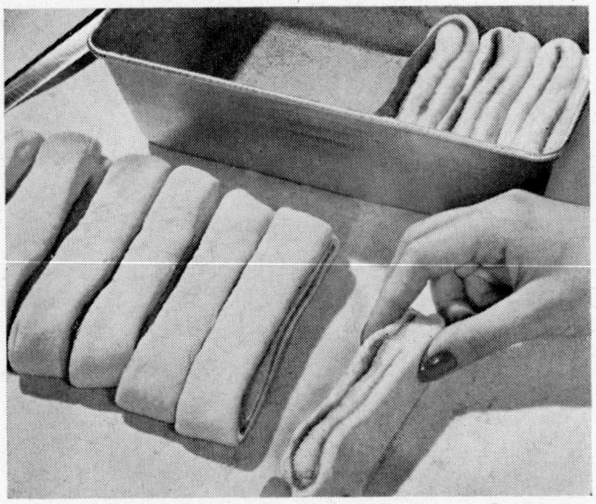

Place strips of dough, cut side down, close together in prepared 8½x4½x2½-inch loaf pan.

Cross rolls in center. Braid first one end, then the other. Seal rolls together at each end.

Prune-Nut Braid

2 packages active dry yeast
½ cup warm water
½ cup milk, scalded
½ cup sugar
1 teaspoon salt
½ cup shortening
4½ to 5 cups sifted all-purpose flour
2 eggs
• • •
1 recipe Prune-Nut Filling
1 recipe Lemon Confectioners' Icing

Soften yeast in water. Combine next 4 ingredients; cool to lukewarm. Stir in 2 *cups* flour. Add eggs; mix well. Stir in yeast. Add remaining flour to make soft dough. Knead on floured surface till smooth. Place in lightly greased bowl, turning once. Cover; let rise till double. Punch down; divide and round into 2 balls. Cover; let rest 10 minutes.

For the braid, roll out one of the balls on lightly floured surface to make 8x14-inch rectangle. Place on greased baking sheet. Spread Prune-Nut Filling down center. On each side, cut 4 gashes at equal intervals, 2½ inches long. Crisscross strips from each side, tucking in end of last one. Cover; let double. Bake at 375° for 20 minutes.

Frost with Lemon Confectioners' Icing. Use remaining ball of dough to make the Butterfly Rolls or Spicy Twists.

Lemon Confectioners' Icing

Mix ½ cup confectioners' sugar with 1 tablespoon lemon juice and 1 tablespoon soft butter till of spreading consistency.

Prune-Nut Filling

Combine 1 cup chopped prunes (if hard, soak before chopping), ½ cup finely chopped apples, ⅓ cup chopped California walnuts, ¼ cup sugar, and 1 tablespoon lemon juice.

Butterfly Rolls

Use half of dough from recipe for Prune-Nut Coffee Braid; roll in 8x16-inch rectangle, ¼-inch thick on lightly floured surface. Brush with melted butter. Sprinkle with mixture of ½ cup sugar and ½ teaspoon cinnamon. Roll as for jelly roll; seal edge. Cut in 1-inch slices. Place, sealed edge down, on baking sheet.

With handle of knife, press crosswise at center to form deep groove. Cover; let double. Bake in moderate oven (375°) for 10 to 12 minutes. Makes 16 rolls.

Spicy Twists

Use half of dough from recipe for Prune-Nut Braid; roll in 8x16-inch rectangle (about ¼ inch thick) on lightly floured surface. Brush with melted butter or margarine. Sprinkle with mixture of ½ cup sugar and ½ teaspoon cinnamon.

Fold dough in half lengthwise and cut in strips 1 inch wide. Pick up each by ends, and twist in opposite directions. Place on greased baking sheet; press ends to seal. Cover and let rise in warm place till double. Bake in moderate oven (375°) for 10 to 12 minutes. Brush with Lemon Confectioners' Icing, if desired. Makes 16 twists.

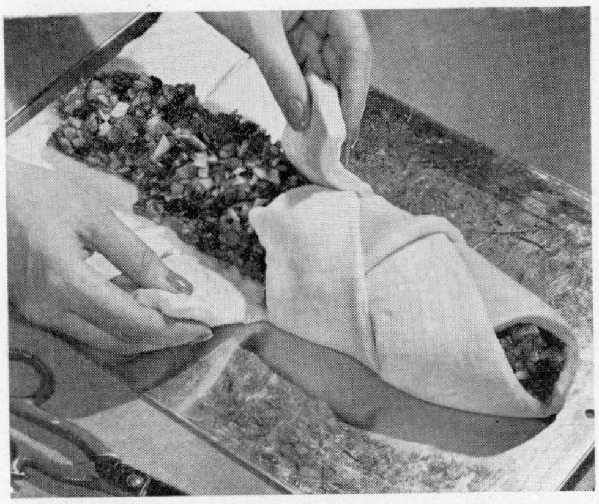

Cut gashes as directed above. Crisscross strips from each side, tucking in end of last one.

Pick up each strip of dough by the ends, then twist in opposite directions as shown.

How to shape daisy coffeecake

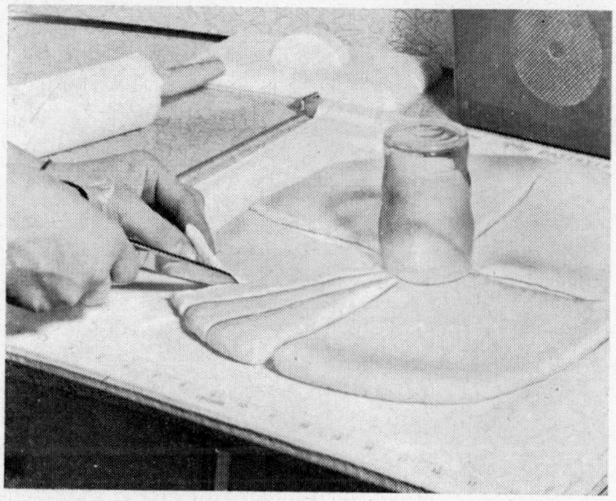

1 On lightly floured surface or greased baking sheet, roll dough to a 14-inch circle. Place a glass in center, cut circle in 4 sections. Cut each section in 5 strips, 20 in all.

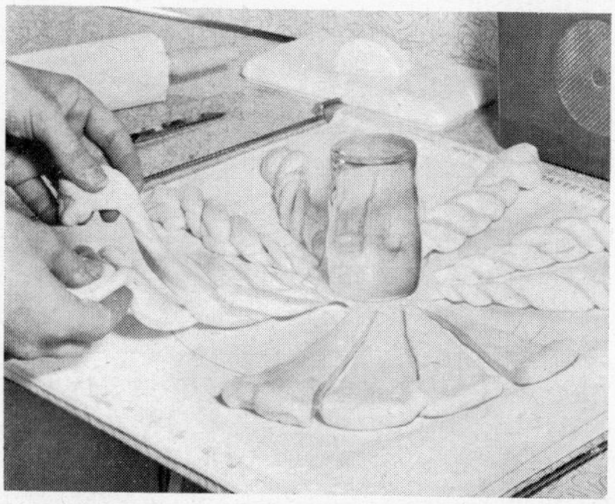

2 Take 2 strips that are side by side and crisscross these together; pinch the ends to seal. Continue around the circle.

Apricot Daisy Coffeecake

1 package active dry yeast *or*
1 cake compressed yeast
¼ cup water
½ cup milk, scalded
¼ cup butter or margarine
2 tablespoons sugar
1 teaspoon salt
3 to 3½ cups sifted all-purpose flour
2 beaten eggs

• • •

Apricot jam
1 cup sifted confectioners' sugar
1½ tablespoons milk
¼ teaspoon vanilla

Soften active dry yeast in *warm* water or compressed yeast in *lukewarm* water. Combine milk, butter, sugar, and salt; cool to lukewarm. Add 1 *cup* of the flour; beat well. Stir in softened yeast and eggs; add enough flour to make a moderately stiff dough.

Turn out on lightly floured surface. Knead till smooth and satiny, about 8 to 10 minutes. Place in a greased bowl, turning once to grease surface. Cover and let rise in warm place till double, about 1¼ hours.

Punch down; let rest 10 minutes. Shape as directed under the pictures. Let rise in warm place till almost double, about 45 minutes. Bake in moderate oven (375°) about 25 minutes or till golden. While still warm, spoon 1 teaspoon apricot jam into center of each daisy.

To match picture, drizzle coffeecake with *Confectioners' Icing:* Combine confectioners' sugar, 1½ tablespoons milk, and vanilla. Beat icing till smooth.

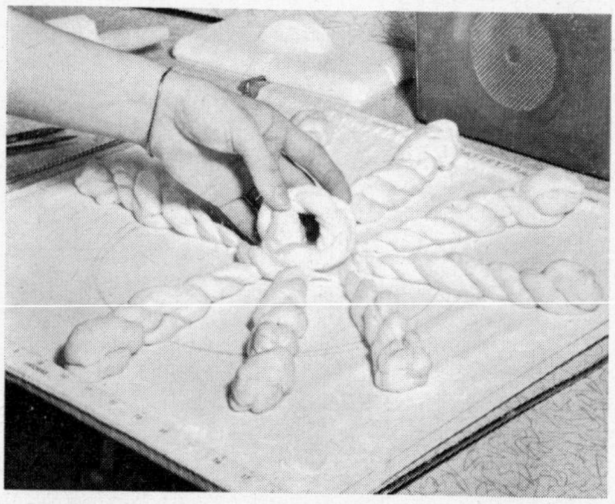

3 Remove the glass from the center of dough. Coil one of the crisscrossed pairs loosely in a circle and place in the spot where the glass has been. This forms the center daisy.

4 Bring each of remaining sets up loosely around center to form daisies. Place each loosely around center coil. When finished it will resemble a bouquet of daisies, 10 in all.

A flower to delight—Apricot Daisy Coffeecake swirled with icing

Swedish Tea Ring

A dainty bread for which Swedish cooks are famous—

1 package active dry yeast *or*
  1 cake compressed yeast
¼ cup water
¾ cup milk, scalded
⅓ cup sugar
1 teaspoon salt
⅓ cup shortening
4 to 4½ cups sifted all-purpose flour
2 eggs

• • •

Raisin Filling
  2 tablespoons melted butter or margarine
  ½ cup sugar
  2 teaspoons cinnamon
  ½ cup seedless raisins

Soften active dry yeast in *warm* water (110°) or compressed yeast in *lukewarm* water (85°). Combine scalded milk, sugar, salt, and shortening. Cool to lukewarm. Stir in about 2 *cups* of the flour. Add eggs; beat well. Stir in softened yeast. Add remaining flour or enough to make a soft dough.

Turn out on a lightly floured surface; knead till smooth and elastic. Place in a greased bowl, turning once to grease surface. Cover and let rise in a warm place till double (about 1½ hours).

Punch down and let rise till double (about 1 hour). Divide dough in half; round into 2 balls. Cover and let dough rest, 10 minutes. On lightly floured surface, roll one half into 9x13-inch rectangle, ¼ inch thick.

For *Raisin Filling:* Spread dough with 1 tablespoon melted butter or margarine. Combine sugar, cinnamon, and seedless raisins; spread half on dough. Roll as for jelly roll. Seal long edge. Shape in ring, seam side down, on greased baking sheet; seal ends of ring. With scissors snip ⅔ of the way to center at 1½-inch intervals. Turn each section slightly to one side. Repeat shaping and filling other half of dough.

Cover and let double (45 minutes). Bake at 375° for 25 to 30 miuutes. Remove from oven. Makes 2 tea rings.

Immediately brush with warm, light corn syrup and sprinkle inner edge of ring with about ¼ cup chopped California walnuts. Or, for a satin finish, brush with melted butter or margarine. Or, to match cover, drizzle with thin confectioners' icing and circle with red and green maraschino cherries.

Danish Coffee Ring

A tasty coffee ring chock-full of raisins and nuts. It's spiced just right with mace. Make one large ring or, if you prefer, make two small rings—freeze one for later—

1 package active dry yeast *or*
  1 cake compressed yeast
¼ cup water

• • •

½ cup milk, scalded
¼ cup shortening
¼ cup sugar
½ teaspoon salt

• • •

1 slightly-beaten egg
½ teaspoon vanilla
1 teaspoon grated lemon peel
2½ to 3 cups sifted all-purpose flour

• • •

2 tablespoons butter, melted
½ cup raisins
½ cup slivered almonds, toasted
⅓ cup sugar
½ teaspoon mace *or*
  1½ teaspoons cinnamon

Soften active dry yeast in *warm* water (110°) or compressed yeast in *lukewarm* water (85°). Combine scalded milk, shortening, ¼ cup sugar, and salt. Cool to lukewarm. Add the egg, vanilla, lemon peel, and 1 *cup* of the flour; beat well. Stir in softened yeast; mix well. Add remaining flour or enough to make a moderately soft dough.

Turn out on a lightly floured surface; knead till smooth and elastic. Place in a greased bowl, turning once to grease surface. Cover and let rise in warm place till double, about 1½ hours. Punch down. Cover and let rest about 10 minutes. Roll to 21x7-inch rectangle, about ¼ inch thick.*

Brush dough with melted butter. Combine raisins, almonds, ⅓ cup sugar and mace; spread on dough. Roll as for jelly roll; seal the long edge. Shape in ring, seam side down, on a greased baking sheet. With scissors, snip almost to center at 1-inch intervals. Pull sections apart and twist slightly. Cover and let rise in a warm place till double, about 50 minutes.

Bake coffee ring in moderate oven (375°) for 20 minutes or till done. Frost with Icing: Mix 1 cup sifted confectioners' sugar, 4 teaspoons milk, ½ teaspoon vanilla, and dash salt. Makes 1 large ring.

*To make 2 small rings, divide dough in half; roll each piece to a 13x6-inch rectangle. Shape and bake as above.

Thumbprint Coffeecake

- 1 package active dry yeast
- ¾ cup warm water
- 2½ cups packaged biscuit mix
- ¼ cup whipping or light cream, or evaporated milk
- ⅓ cup brown sugar
- ¼ teaspoon cinnamon

Soften yeast in water. Stir in biscuit mix; beat vigorously 2 to 3 minutes. Turn out on surface well dusted with biscuit mix. Knead till smooth, about 25 strokes.

Butter sides and bottom of 8-inch round pan, then sprinkle with sugar. Place dough in pan, pressing out so it touches sides. Cover with damp cloth. Let rise till double.

With thumb, punch deep holes in dough every 2 inches, leaving 1¼-inch margin around edge of pan. Fill these "wells" with cream. Sprinkle brown sugar and cinnamon over dough. Bake at 400° for 15 to 20 minutes. If desired, top holes with red jelly.

Cherry Lattice Coffeecake

- 1 package active dry yeast *or* 1 cake compressed yeast
- ¼ cup water
- ⅔ cup butter
- ⅓ cup sugar
- 1 teaspoon salt
- 4 beaten eggs
- 4 cups sifted all-purpose flour
- ¾ cup light cream
- Cherry Filling

Soften dry yeast in *warm* water or compressed yeast in *lukewarm* water. Cream together butter, ⅓ cup sugar, and salt. Reserve 2 tablespoons of beaten eggs for use later and add remaining eggs to creamed mixture; beat well. Stir in flour alternately with softened yeast and light cream. Mix, but do not beat. Set aside 1 cup of dough and spread the remainder in 2 well-greased 9-inch square pans. Cover with *Cherry Filling:* Combine ½ cup *each* of softened butter, chopped blanched almonds, sugar, and cherry preserves. Mix well.

For lattice, blend ¼ cup sifted flour into reserved dough. Divide into 12 parts; roll each between floured hands to make 9-inch strips. Arrange 6 strips in lattice pattern over Cherry Filling in each pan. Brush strips with reserved beaten egg. Cover; let rise till double. Bake in moderate oven (375°) 20 to 25 minutes. Makes 2 coffeecakes.

Apricot-Date Coffeecake

- 1 package active dry yeast *or* 1 cake compressed yeast
- ¼ cup water
- ½ cup milk, scalded
- 2 tablespoons butter
- ¼ cup sugar
- ½ teaspoon salt
- 2¾ to 3¼ cups sifted all-purpose flour
- 1 slightly-beaten egg
- ½ cup canned apricot filling
- ½ cup chopped dates

Soften active dry yeast in *warm* water or compressed yeast in *lukewarm* water. Combine scalded milk, butter, sugar, and salt; cool to lukewarm. Add 1 *cup* flour, beat smooth. Add yeast and egg, beat well. Stir in enough flour to make soft dough.

Turn out on lightly floured surface; knead until smooth and elastic. Place dough in a greased bowl, turning once to grease surface. Cover and let rise in warm place till double (1¼ hours). Punch down; divide in half and let rest 10 minutes.

Roll half the dough in 9x7-inch rectangle ½ inch thick. Spread half the apricot filling down center third of dough; sprinkle with half the dates. Fold sides over so they meet at the center of the filling; seal.

Place dough, seam side down on greased baking sheet. Snip strips 1 inch wide almost to center on both sides of coffeecake. Turn each strip on its side. Repeat with remaining dough and filling. Cover and let rise till double (45 minutes). Bake in moderate oven (350°) about 15 minutes. Makes 2.

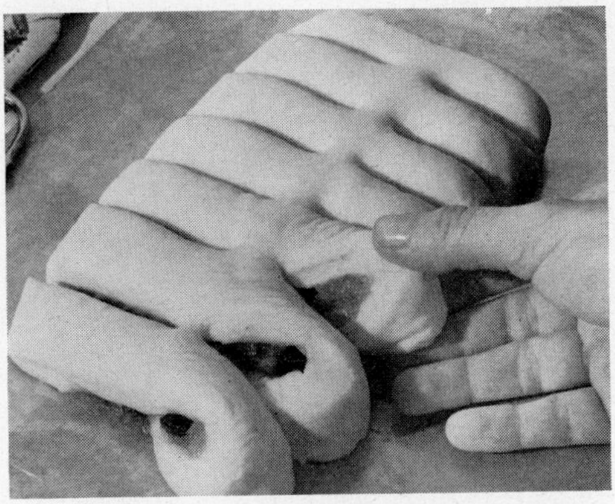

Place coffeecake sealed edge down on a greased baking sheet. Snip edges nearly to the center with shears and turn each strip on its side.

Truly regal in beauty—
It's Sunburst Coffeecake

The secret is in the shaping; just follow directions below. Surprise inside—it's full of plump raisins, candied cherries, and citron bits. For pretty finishing touch, drizzle the top with icing and circle with crown of halved cherries.

Cut dough in half; divide each half into 12 balls; roll each between hands to form 8-inch rolls. Place 6 rolls, twisted in a horseshoe shape, around 4-inch circle in center of pan.

Form the remaining 6 rolls in O-shapes; join seamed ends at center of circle, allowing rounded end to overlap the first layer of horseshoe shapes at a point in between the petals.

Sunburst Coffeecake

2 packages active dry yeast
½ cup warm water
½ cup sugar
¼ cup shortening
2 teaspoons salt
¾ cup scalded milk
5 to 5¼ cups sifted all-purpose flour
2 eggs
1 cup raisins
¾ cup chopped candied cherries
¼ cup chopped candied citron

Soften yeast in water. Combine next 4 ingredients; cool to lukewarm. Add 2 cups flour, and mix well. Add yeast and eggs; beat well. Add fruit and enough flour to make a soft dough. Turn out on lightly floured surface; knead till smooth (10 minutes). Place in greased bowl, turning dough once. Cover and let rise till double (1½ hours).

Punch down; turn out on lightly floured surface. Cover and let rest 10 minutes. Divide dough in half; then divide each half into 12 equal pieces. With hands, roll each piece into a column 8-inches long and ¾ inch in diameter. On a baking sheet arrange 6 of the pieces in a U-shape around a 4-inch circle with ends toward the center. Make the remaining 6 pieces into oval shapes and arrange over the U-shapes, with ends joining in center. Let rise till double (1 hour). Bake at 350° for 25 minutes or till done. Drizzle with Confectioners' Icing.

Orange Lattice Coffeecake

Soften 1 package active dry yeast in ¼ cup *warm* water. Cream together ⅔ cup butter, ⅓ cup sugar, and 1 teaspoon salt; add 4 beaten eggs; beat well. Stir in 4 cups sifted all-purpose flour alternately with softened yeast and ¾ cup light cream. Mix well, *but do not beat.* Reserve 1 cup dough. Spread remainder in 2 well-greased 9x9x2-inch pans; cover with *Orange Filling:* Combine ⅔ cup *each* soft butter, chopped blanched almonds, sugar, and orange marmalade.

For lattice, blend ¼ cup sifted all-purpose flour into reserved dough; divide in 12 parts. Roll each between floured hands to make 9-inch strip. Arrange 6 strips, lattice fashion, over filling in each pan; brush strips with beaten egg. Cover and let rise in warm place till almost double, 45 to 60 minutes. Bake at 375° for 20 to 25 minutes. Makes 2.

Flaky Danish Crescent

1 package active dry yeast
¼ cup *warm* water
2 cups sifted all-purpose flour
1 tablespoon sugar
½ teaspoon salt
½ cup chilled butter or margarine
¼ cup milk, scalded
1 slightly-beaten egg yolk
Meringue
½ cup chopped almonds or pecans

Soften yeast in water. Sift together dry ingredients; cut in butter till some of the mixture is like corn meal and some the size of peas. Mix cooled milk and egg yolk; add with yeast to flour, stirring to make a soft dough. Cover; chill few hours, or overnight.

Halve dough (keep half chilled). On floured surface, roll one piece in 12x9-inch rectangle, about ⅛ inch thick. Reserve 2 tablespoons Meringue for glaze; spread dough with *half* of remainder. Sprinkle with *half* the nuts. Roll as for jellyroll (start at the the long side). Seal edges and ends.

Place roll, seam down, on baking sheet. Shape in crescent; flatten slightly. Repeat with remaining dough. Cover; let rise till double. Brush with reserved Meringue. Garnish with additional almonds, thinly sliced. Bake at 375° for about 20 minutes.

Meringue: Fold ½ cup sugar and 1 teaspoon cinnamon into 1 stiff-beaten egg white.

Fruit-filled Tea Ring

Soften 1 package active dry yeast in ¼ cup *warm* water. Combine ½ cup scalded milk, 3 tablespoons shortening, 3 tablespoons sugar, and 1 teaspoon salt; cool to lukewarm. Sift 2½ to 2¾ cups all-purpose flour; add 1 cup to milk mixture; beat well. Add softened yeast, 1 beaten egg, and ½ teaspoon vanilla. Mix in remaining flour or enough to make a soft dough. Knead lightly on floured surface. Place in greased bowl, turning once. Cover; let rise till double.

Roll to 13x9-inch rectangle, ¼-inch thick. Brush with melted butter; spread evenly with *Fruit Filling:* Mix ¼ cup sugar, 1 teaspoon cinnamon, ½ cup chopped walnuts, and ½ cup chopped candied fruits and peel.

Roll lengthwise; seal edge. Shape in a ring on greased baking sheet. With scissors, snip almost to center at 1-inch intervals. Pull sections apart and twist slightly. Let double. Bake at 375° about 20 minutes.

Streusel Coffeecake

1 package active dry yeast *or*
  1 cake compressed yeast
¼ cup water
1 cup milk, scalded
¼ cup sugar
¼ cup shortening
1 teaspoon salt
3½ cups sifted all-purpose flour
1 egg
• • •
Streusel Topping:
  1 cup sifted all-purpose flour
  ½ cup brown sugar
  ½ cup granulated sugar
  1 teaspoon cinnamon
  ½ cup butter or margarine
  ¼ cup finely chopped nuts
• • •
  1½ teaspoons vanilla

Soften active dry yeast in *warm* water (110°) or compressed yeast in *lukewarm* water (85°). Combine milk, sugar, shortening, and salt; cool to lukewarm. Add 1 *cup* of the flour; beat well. Beat in softened yeast and egg. Gradually add remaining flour to form soft dough, beating well. Cover and let rise in warm place till double (1½ to 2 hours). Turn out on lightly floured surface; divide in thirds. Pat each third evenly into greased 8x1½-inch round cake pan or baking dish.

Make Streusel Topping: Combine flour, sugars, and cinnamon; cut in butter till crumbly. Add nuts. Sprinkle ⅓ of topping over each coffeecake. Cover; let rise in warm place till double (30 to 45 minutes). Bake in moderate oven (375°) about 20 minutes or till done. *Immediately* drizzle ½ teaspoon vanilla over each coffeecake. Serve warm.

Golden Bubble Ring

2 packages active dry yeast *or*
  2 cakes compressed yeast
½ cup water
• • •
½ cup milk, scalded
½ cup shortening
½ cup sugar
1 teaspoon salt
4 to 4½ cups sifted all-purpose flour
2 beaten eggs
Melted butter or margarine
¾ cup sugar
1 teaspoon cinnamon

Soften active dry yeast in *warm* water, or compressed yeast in *lukewarm* water. Combine milk, shortening, ½ cup sugar, and salt. Cool to lukewarm. Add 1 *cup* flour; beat well. Add yeast mixture and eggs. Beat smooth. Mix in remaining flour, or enough to make a soft dough. Knead on lightly floured surface till smooth and elastic (8 to 10 minutes). Place in greased bowl, turning once to grease surface. Cover; let rise in warm place till double (1 to 1¼ hours). Punch down. Cover; let rest 10 minutes.

Shape into about 28 balls, golf-ball size. Roll each in melted butter, then in mixture of ¾ cup sugar and cinnamon. Arrange in well-greased 9-inch tube pan. Sprinkle with any remaining sugar mixture. Let rise in warm place till double (about 1 hour).

Bake in moderate oven (350°) about 35 to 40 minutes. Cool in pan 15 to 20 minutes. Invert on rack; remove ring from pan.

Dutch Apple Coffeecake

1 package active dry yeast
¼ cup water
⅔ cup milk, scalded
¼ cup shortening
⅓ cup sugar
½ teaspoon salt
2¼ cups sifted all-purpose flour
2 slightly-beaten eggs
½ cup seedless raisins
Apple Topping:
  2 tablespoons melted butter
  4 cups sliced pared tart apples
  ⅓ cup sugar
  1 teaspoon cinnamon
  ½ teaspoon nutmeg

Soften active dry yeast in warm water. Combine scalded milk, shortening, sugar, and salt; cool to lukewarm. Stir in 1 *cup* of the flour. Add softened yeast and eggs; beat well. Add the raisins and remaining flour; beat thoroughly. Cover and let rise in a warm place till almost double (1 hour).

Place in a greased 9x13-inch pan. Prepare Apple Topping: Brush top with melted butter. Arrange apple slices over batter. Sprinkle apple slices and batter with combined cinnamon, sugar, and nutmeg. Let rise till light (about 30 minutes).

Bake in a moderate oven (350°) for 30 to 35 minutes or till done. Serve warm.

Another time omit the Apple Topping. Instead, brush the coffeecake with 2 tablespoons melted butter and sprinkle with ¼ cup granulated sugar and ½ cup chopped California walnuts.

Delectable Doughnuts

Dough for doughnuts should be as soft as can be handled. A soft dough is easier to roll when well chilled. Cut doughnuts with a floured cutter and let stand 15 minutes.

Fry in deep, hot fat (375°); if fat is too hot, doughnuts will not be baked through; if too cool, they will be fat-soaked. Don't fry too many at one time—fat temperature will cool down too rapidly.

Turn doughnuts only once while frying, usually as soon as they rise to the top. Drain on paper towels. Shake in paper sack in granulated or confectioners' sugar. Or glaze with a thin confectioners' icing.

Raised Doughnuts

1 package active dry yeast *or*
  1 cake compressed yeast
¼ cup water
• • •
¾ cup milk, scalded
¼ cup shortening
¼ cup sugar
1 teaspoon salt
1 egg
3½ to 3¾ cups sifted all-purpose flour

Soften active dry yeast in *warm* water (110°) or compressed yeast in *lukewarm* water (85°). Combine milk, shortening, sugar and salt; cool to lukewarm. Add 1 *cup* of the flour; beat well. Add softened yeast and egg; mix. Add enough of remaining flour to make soft dough. Turn out on lightly floured surface; knead till smooth and satiny (about 8 minutes). Place in greased bowl, turning once to grease surface. Cover and let rise till double (about 1¼ hours). Punch down. Let rise again till double (about 55 minutes).

Roll out dough ⅓ inch thick. Cut with floured doughnut cutter. Let rise till very light (30 to 40 minutes).

Fry in deep hot fat (375°) till browned. Drain on paper towels. While warm dip doughnuts in granulated sugar or glaze with Orange Glaze. Makes about 1½ dozen.

Orange Glaze

Add 1 teaspoon grated orange peel and 3 tablespoons orange juice to 2 cups sifted confectioners' sugar. Mix till smooth.

Best Cake Doughnuts

4 beaten eggs
⅔ cup sugar
⅓ cup milk
⅓ cup shortening, melted
3½ cups sifted all-purpose flour
3 teaspoons baking powder
¾ teaspoon salt
1 teaspoon cinnamon
½ teaspoon nutmeg

Beat eggs and sugar till light; add milk and cooled shortening. Sift together dry ingredients; add to first mixture and mix well. Chill dough thoroughly.

On lightly floured surface, roll dough ⅜ inch thick. Cut with floured cutter; let stand 15 minutes. Fry in deep, hot fat (375°) until brown, turning once. Drain on paper towels. While warm, shake in sack containing ½ cup sugar and 1 to 2 teaspoons cinnamon, if desired. Makes 1½ to 2 dozen.

Twists. Roll dough ¼ inch thick. Cut strips ¾ inch wide. Twist or form in knots. Fry in deep hot fat (375°). Drain. Makes 30.

New Orleans Square Doughnuts

1 cake compressed yeast
¼ cup lukewarm water
¾ cup milk, scalded
¼ cup shortening
¼ cup sugar
1 teaspoon salt
1 egg
About 3½ cups sifted all-purpose flour

Soften yeast in lukewarm water. Combine milk, shortening, sugar and salt; cool to lukewarm. Add 1 *cup* of the flour; beat well. Add softened yeast and egg; mix. Add enough of remaining flour to make soft dough. Turn out on lightly floured surface; knead till smooth (about 8 minutes). Place in greased bowl, turn once to grease surface. Cover; let rise till double (1¼ hours). Punch down. Let rise again till double (55 minutes).

Roll out dough to 14x10-inch rectangle ⅓ inch thick. Cut in 2-inch squares. Let rise till light (30 to 40 minutes). Fry in deep hot fat (375°) about 4 minutes, turning once. Drain. While warm, dip in sugar. Makes 36.

Take your choice from a variety of doughnuts We show New Orleans Square Doughnuts, Fluffy Potato Doughnuts, Coconut Cake Doughnuts, Fruited Doughnut Balls, Filled Doughnuts and Crullers. Serve with mugs of hot cider.

Fluffy Potato Doughnuts

3 eggs
1⅓ cups sugar
½ teaspoon vanilla
1 cup mashed potatoes, cooled*
2 tablespoons melted shortening
4 cups sifted all-purpose flour
6 teaspoons baking powder
2 teaspoons nutmeg
1 teaspoon salt
½ cup milk

Beat eggs with sugar and vanilla till light. Add potatoes and shortening. Sift together dry ingredients; add alternately with milk to potato mixture, beating well. Chill 3 hours.

Roll out half of dough at a time, keeping other half chilled. Roll on floured surface to ⅜ inch thick. Cut with floured 1½-inch doughnut cutter; chill 15 minutes.

Fry in deep hot fat (375°) about 3 minutes or till brown, turning once; drain. Dip in sugar. Makes 2 to 2½ dozen.

*Cook 2 medium potatoes; mash with butter and milk to make light and fluffy.

Coconut Cake Doughnuts

2 eggs
½ cup sugar

• • •

¼ cup milk
2 tablespoons melted shortening
  or salad oil
2⅓ cups sifted all-purpose flour
2 teaspoons baking powder
½ teaspoon salt
½ cup flaked coconut

Beat eggs with sugar till light; add milk and cooled shortening. Add sifted dry ingredients and coconut; stir just till blended. Chill mixture several hours.

Roll on lightly floured surface to ½ inch thick. Cut out doughnuts with doughnut cutter. Fry in deep hot fat (375°) till brown; turn and brown other side (about 1 minute per side). Drain on paper towel. Sprinkle with sugar. Makes 1 dozen doughnuts.

Crullers

2 packages active dry yeast *or*
  2 cakes compressed yeast
½ cup water
½ cup milk, scalded
⅓ cup sugar
1½ teaspoons salt
¼ cup shortening
3¼ to 3¾ cups sifted all-purpose flour
1 slightly-beaten egg

Soften dry yeast in *warm* water or compressed yeast in *lukewarm* water. Mix milk, sugar, salt, and shortening; stir till shortening melts; cool to lukewarm. Add 1 *cup* of the flour; beat well; add egg and softened yeast. Add enough of remaining flour to make a moderately soft dough.

Knead on lightly floured surface about 8 minutes. Place in greased bowl, turning once to grease the surface. Cover and let rise till double, about 1 to 1½ hours. Punch down, let rise again till double. Punch down and let rest 10 minutes.

On lightly floured surface roll into 12x9-inch rectangle, ½ inch thick. Cut in half crosswise; cut each half into 12 strips. Roll each strip under hands to make 10-inch strip; twist for crullers. Cover; let rise about 45 minutes or till almost doubled in size.

Fry in deep hot fat (375°) about 2 minutes, turning once; drain. Brush with confectioners' icing to glaze. Makes 2 dozen.

Filled Doughnuts

2 packages active dry yeast *or*
  2 cakes compressed yeast
½ cup water
¾ cup milk, scalded
⅓ cup shortening
¼ cup sugar
1 teaspoon salt
2 eggs
4½ to 5 cups sifted all-purpose flour
18 prunes
¼ cup sugar

Soften the active dry yeast in *warm* water, compressed yeast in *lukewarm* water. Combine milk, shortening, ¼ cup sugar, and salt; stir till shortening is dissolved. Cool to lukewarm. Add yeast, eggs, and 2 *cups* flour; beat well. Add enough remaining flour to make soft dough. Turn out on lightly floured surface and knead till smooth and elastic, about 8 to 10 minutes. Place in a greased bowl, turning to grease surface. Cover; let rise till double, about 50 minutes.

Meanwhile, cook prunes according to package directions, adding ¼ cup sugar at beginning of cooking. Cool; halve, pit.

Cut dough in half for easy handling. Roll ⅜-inch thick; cut with a 2½-inch round cutter. Place a prune half in each round of dough; fold dough over prune and seal edges; cover and let rise in warm place till double, 20 minutes.

Fry in deep hot fat (375°) till golden, about 1 minute on each side. Drain on paper towel. Roll in sugar. Makes 3 dozen.

Fruited Doughnut Balls

2 cups sifted all-purpose flour
½ teaspoon soda
¼ teaspoon salt
2 beaten egg yolks
½ cup sugar
½ cup sour milk
2 tablespoons orange juice
½ cup finely chopped pecans
¼ cup chopped raisins
¼ cup finely chopped dates
1 teaspoon grated orange peel

Sift together flour, soda, and salt. Combine next 4 ingredients; stir into dry ingredients. Add nuts, fruits, and peel. Stir to blend.

Drop by teaspoons into deep hot fat (350°) and fry 4 to 5 minutes or till brown on all sides, turning once. Drain on paper towel. Roll in sugar. Makes 2 dozen.

SANDWICH
CROISSANTS
PANE COMUNE

Foreign and Holiday Breads

Borrow these breads from faraway lands—each delightfully different. And for holiday fare choose from a variety of festive loaves—all yours for the baking.

In Rome you can window-shop for bread

← You'll be amazed at the great variety—round loaves, long loaves, hard rolls, and bread sticks. Folks often select a few freshly baked crusty rolls and enjoy them with a cup of fancy Italian coffee or hot chocolate at a near-by sidewalk cafe.

Foreign breads

Italian bread know-how

• For light loaves and rolls, take care not to flatten or drive air out when slashing tops before baking—be extra gentle if bread has already risen. *Sharp* knife helps!

• For crackled top crust, cool baked loaves, rolls, and bread sticks in a draft. You can hear crust crackle.

• Eat Italian breads while fresh. Because they are made with water and have little or no fat, they dry out fast. However, bread sticks are dandy keepers.

Italian Bread, American

1 package hot-roll mix
⅔ cup warm water
2 cups slightly-beaten egg whites
½ teaspoon salt
• • •
Yellow corn meal

In large mixing bowl, soften yeast from hot-roll mix in *only* ⅔ *cup warm* water. Reserve 1 tablespoon egg white for glaze (omit the egg called for on package); stir remaining egg white into softened yeast. Add salt and the roll mix; blend well.

Turn out on generously floured surface (use ¼ cup all-purpose flour); knead 7 minutes or so, working in *all* the flour to form *very* stiff dough that is smooth and satiny. Place in lightly greased bowl, turning once to grease top. Cover and let rise in warm place till double (about 1 hour).

Turn dough out on lightly floured surface. Shape, tapering ends, in 1 long narrow loaf (12 inches) or in 2 shorter loaves. Place on greased baking sheet sprinkled with corn meal. Cover and let rise in warm place till double (about 30 to 45 minutes). Add 1 tablespoon water to reserved egg white; brush over tops and sides of loaves.

With sharp knife, gently make lengthwise cut, ½- to ¾-inch deep, down center of loaf. (Place large shallow pan on lower rack of oven; fill with boiling water.) Bake at 375° for 15 minutes; brush with egg white, bake 15 to 20 minutes longer or till done.

Italian Bread (*Pane Italiano*)

The crust is wonderfully crisp, although perhaps not as thick as if it had been baked in an Italian brick oven—

2 packages active dry yeast *or*
2 cakes compressed yeast
2½ cups water
1 tablespoon salt
7¼ to 7¾ cups sifted all-purpose flour
• • •
Yellow corn meal
1 slightly-beaten egg white

In large mixing bowl, soften active dry yeast in *warm* water or compressed yeast in *lukewarm* water. Stir in 2 *cups* of the flour; beat well. Add salt. Then stir in *about 4½ cups* of the remaining flour. (Dough should be stiffer than for ordinary bread.)

Turn out on lightly floured surface. Cover; let rest 10 minutes. Knead *15 to 25 minutes* or till very elastic, kneading in remaining *¾ to 1¼ cups* flour. (The longer kneading time develops gluten more, makes a more typical Italian bread.) Place dough in lightly greased bowl, turning once to grease surface. Cover; let rise in warm place till double (about 1½ hours). Punch down; let rise again till double (about 1 hour). Turn out on lightly floured surface. Divide in half and form each part in ball. Cover and let dough rest 10 minutes.

Shape (directions at end of recipe). Place on baking sheets sprinkled with corn meal (gives crunchy bottom crust). Add 1 tablespoon water to egg white; brush over top and sides of loaves. Cover with damp cloth, but don't let it touch dough. (Make tent by placing cloth over tall tumblers.) Let rise in warm place till double (1 to 1½ hours). (When ready to bake, place large shallow pan on lower rack of oven; fill with boiling water. This makes crust crisper.)

Bake large loaves (Long, Plump, or Round) in moderate oven (375°) till light brown, about 20 minutes; brush again with egg-white mixture. Bake about 20 minutes longer or till nicely browned and done. Cool.

Bake small breads (Individual Loaves and Hard Rolls) in hot oven (400°) 15 minutes. Brush again with egg-white mixture. Bake 10 to 15 minutes longer. Cool.

Recipe makes 2 Long Loaves; *or* 2 Plump Loaves; *or* 2 Round Loaves; *or* 8 Individual Loaves; *or* 12 Hard Rolls.

Long Loaves: Roll each half of dough in 15x12-inch rectangle, 1/4-inch thick. Beginning at long side, roll up tightly, sealing well as you roll (see picture). Taper ends. Place each loaf diagonally, seam side down, on baking sheet prepared as in recipe. With *sharp* knife, make diagonal cuts 2 1/2 inches apart (1/8- to 1/4-inch deep). Follow recipe to brush, rise, bake.

Plump Loaves: Roll each half of dough in 15x8-inch rectangle, a little less than 1/2 inch thick. Roll up tightly, beginning at short side, sealing well as you roll. Taper ends by rolling under hands till loaf measures 10 to 11 inches in length. Place loaves seam side down on prepared baking sheet—see recipe. Brush and let rise as in recipe. Then, with sharp knife gently make lengthwise cut, 1/2- to 3/4-inch deep, down center of loaf. Bake as in recipe.

Round Loaves: Place the two balls of dough on large baking sheet prepared as above. With *sharp* knife score loaves, making 4 shallow cuts, 1 inch apart, across top, then making 4 crosswise cuts. Follow recipe to brush, rise, bake.

Individual Loaves: Cut each half of dough in quarters, making 8 pieces. Round each in ball. Cover and let rest 10 minutes. Shape each in small loaf, twisting and pulling ends to taper. (Loaf should measure about 6 inches in length.) Place 2 to 3 inches apart on prepared baking sheet—see recipe. Press down ends of loaves. Follow recipe to brush and let rise. Then, with *sharp* knife gently make 3 shallow cuts diagonally across top of each loaf. Bake as in recipe.

Hard Rolls: Divide each ball of dough in half; cut each half in thirds, making 12 pieces in all. Shape each in oval or round roll; place about 2 inches apart on prepared baking sheet—see recipe. Follow recipe to brush and let rise. Cut shallow crisscross in top of each. Bake as in recipe.

Plump Loaves. Shape Long Loaves the same way. Roll up dough as for jelly roll (start at narrow side for plumps, at long side for longies). Seal dough at end of each turn.

Round Loaves. With *sharp* knife, score top: Make 4 parallel cuts across top of loaf, then make 4 crosswise cuts. Score marks should be shallow. They'll spread as loaves rise.

Individual Loaves. Divide dough in 8 parts and round in balls. Roll each under hands until oval, pulling and rolling ends to taper. These little loaves measure 6 inches.

Oil Rolls
(*Panini All'olio*)

Beautiful, shiny rolls you'll be proud of! Softer, less crisp-crusted than the Hard Rolls. (Use the olive oil and malt, and you'll think you're in Rome!)—

1 package active dry yeast *or*
  1 cake compressed yeast
1 cup water

• • •

2 tablespoons sugar or
  baker's malt
1½ teaspoons salt
¼ cup olive oil or salad oil
3¼ to 3½ cups sifted
  all-purpose flour

• • •

1 slightly-beaten egg

In large mixing bowl, soften active dry yeast in *warm* water or compressed yeast in *luke-warm* water. Add sugar, salt, and oil; stir to dissolve sugar. Gradually add 3 *cups* of the flour (or enough to make soft dough).

Turn out on floured surface. Cover and let rest 10 minutes. Knead till smooth and elastic (8 to 10 minutes) kneading in remaining ¼ *to* ½ *cup* flour. Place in a lightly greased bowl, turning dough once to grease surface. Cover and let rise in a warm place till double (1½ to 1¾ hours). Turn out on a lightly floured surface; form in a ball. Cover and let rest 10 minutes.

Shape: (directions at end of recipe). Place rolls about 3 inches apart on greased baking sheet. Add 1 tablespoon of water to egg; brush over tops and sides of rolls.

Cover dough with damp cloth, but don't let it touch the dough. (Make tent by placing the cloth over tall tumblers.) Let rise in a warm place till double (about 45 to 60 minutes). (When ready to bake, place a large shallow pan on bottom rack of the oven; fill with boiling water.) Bake rolls in a moderate oven (375°) for about 20 minutes or till done. Delicious served warm or cool. Makes 12 rolls.

Note: For a glossier crust, brush the rolls again with the egg mixture after first 10 minutes of baking.

Rose Rolls: Divide dough in 12 equal pieces and shape in balls. Place 3 inches apart on greased baking sheet. Brush and let rise. Then, with scissors, carefully snip a circle in the top of each roll, cutting ¼ inch deep. Make 5 cuts radiating from the circle.

Bowknots: Divide dough in 12 equal balls; Roll each to pencil-like strand 9 inches long, ½ to ¾ inch in diameter. Form in loose knot. Place 2 to 3 inches apart on greased baking sheet. Brush, let rise.

Double Crescents: Roll dough to 23x 12-inches. Brush with melted butter. Cut in half lengthwise to make two long strips. Cut one strip in 12 triangles, 3½ inches at base and 6 inches on sides (see A in sketch below). Cut remaining strip lengthwise in half; then crosswise in thirds (each section is almost 8x3 inches); cut each section in half diagonally (see B in diagram below).

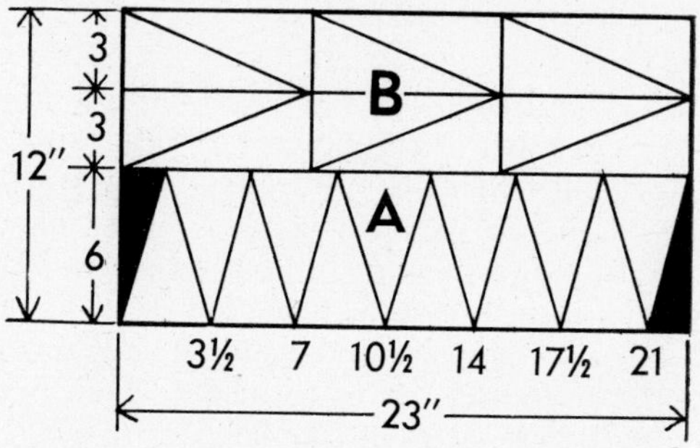

First roll larger triangles (A's) into crescents: (Stretch triangles back to original size if dough has shrunk.) Begin with narrow side, and roll each up loosely toward point. Place point down, 3 inches apart on greased baking sheets. Curve ends slightly. Roll the other triangles (B's) to make spirals. Again begin with narrow side, and roll each up loosely keeping straight edge even so spirals will be larger at one end than at other. Stand spirals (B's), large end up against outer curve of crescents. (Lightly moisten with water the place where crescents and spirals meet so they'll stick together; lean top of spiral over crescent.) Brush the rolls with egg mixture and let rise.

Taralli (Twists): Roll dough in 18x12-inch rectangle. Brush with melted butter; sprinkle with anise seed. Cut lengthwise in 12 strips 1½ inches wide. Holding a wooden spoon by the bowl, turn spoon while wrapping strip of dough loosely around handle. (Don't stretch the dough.) Push twisted dough off handle; bring ends together to form wreath. Place 2 or 3 inches apart on greased baking sheet. Brush with egg mixture; sprinkle with more anise seed. Let rise.

To divide dough for the Rose Rolls or Bowknots (below), cut the ball of risen dough into 12 equal parts. First cut in quarters, then cut each quarter of dough in thirds.

Here are breads right from "the old country." Good long kneading gives Italian breads the typical light texture and wonderful flavor. The dough should be so stiff that you have to knead in the last cup of flour. Our recipe for Oil Rolls gives lots of shapes—try them all!

Rose Rolls. Shape in balls. Place on greased baking sheet. Cover; let double. With scissors, snip circle (¼ inch deep) in top of each roll. Gently make 5 cuts radiating from circle.

Double Crescents. Make crescent from each A triangle. Place on greased baking sheet; curve ends. Make spiral from each B triangle. Press spiral, large end up, to crescent.

Bowknots. Make 9-inch strands by rolling each piece of dough back and forth under hands, stretching and smoothing as you go. Form strand in *loose* knot. Cover; let rise.

Taralli. To twist, hold wooden spoon by the bowl and turn spoon while wrapping strip of dough loosely around handle. Then gently slip twisted dough from handle. Press ends together.

Italian Bread Sticks (*Grissini*)

So nice and crisp, they break with a snap. (Napoleon was a grissini fan, had them sent from Torino. He called this bread "petit baton de Turin.")—

1 package active dry yeast *or*
1 cake compressed yeast
¾ cup water

• • •

1 tablespoon sugar
1½ teaspoons salt
2 tablespoons olive oil *or* salad oil
1 egg yolk

• • •

2¼ to 2½ cups sifted all-purpose flour

• • •

1 slightly-beaten egg white

In a large bowl, soften active dry yeast in *warm* water (110°), or compressed yeast in *lukewarm* water (85°).

Stir in sugar, salt, olive oil or salad oil, and egg yolk. Add 2¼ *cups* of the flour (or enough to make a soft dough). Turn dough out on a lightly floured surface. Cover and let rest 10 minutes. Knead till smooth and elastic (about 5 to 8 minutes).

Place dough in a lightly greased bowl, turning once to grease surface. Cover and let rise in a warm place till double (about 1½ to 2 hours). Punch dough down. Cover tightly and refrigerate at least 4 hours or overnight before shaping.

Turn out on lightly floured surface and divide dough in 12 equal parts. Roll each piece of dough under hands to form pencil-like strand, 14 to 16 inches long and about ½ inch in diameter. Smooth each strand as you work. Place about 2 inches apart on a greased baking sheet. Add 1 tablespoon water to egg white; brush mixture over sticks.

Let rise uncovered in a warm place till double (45 to 60 minutes). Brush again with the egg-white mixture and sprinkle with coarse salt, if desired. (Place large shallow pan on lower rack of the oven; fill with boiling water.) Bake bread sticks in a hot oven (425°) for about 12 to 15 minutes or till sticks are crusty and brown.

Note: If you prefer bread sticks with hard crisp centers, bake them in a hot oven (400°) for about 18 to 20 minutes.

Kolache (Old-world Fruit Buns)

A bit of the old-world with a modern twist—

1 package active dry yeast *or*
1 cake compressed yeast
¾ cup water

• • •

2 tablespoons sugar
2 tablespoons melted butter or margarine, cooled
2½ cups packaged biscuit mix
Cherry preserves *or*
Prune Filling:
¾ cup chopped stewed prunes
¼ teaspoon grated lemon peel
1 tablespoon lemon juice
1 tablespoon sugar

Soften active dry yeast in *warm* water (110°) or compressed yeast in *lukewarm* water (85°). Add 2 tablespoons sugar, the butter, and biscuit mix; beat vigorously 2 to 3 minutes. Turn out on surface well-dusted with biscuit mix. Knead till smooth and elastic, about 25 strokes.

Shape in twelve 2-inch balls. Place about 3 inches apart on greased baking sheet. Flatten slightly. Make a deep depression in the center of each; fill with cherry preserves or Prune Filling. Cover filled buns with damp cloth. Let rise in a warm place till almost double, about 1 to 1½ hours. Bake in hot oven (400°) for 10 minutes or until done. Dust with confectioners' sugar. Serve while hot. Makes 12.

Prune Filling: Combine chopped stewed prunes, grated lemon peel, lemon juice, and 1 tablespoon sugar; mix well.

Indian Puris

2 tablespoons shortening
2 cups sifted all-purpose flour
½ teaspoon salt
½ cup grated process cheese
½ to ⅔ cup water

Cut shortening into flour and salt. Add cheese. Stir in water to make a soft dough. Turn out on floured surface and knead for about 10 minutes. Let rest 10 minutes.

Roll *very thin* on lightly floured surface to a 16x10-inch rectangle. Cut in 2½-inch circles. Fry in deep hot fat (385°) till puffed and golden brown, 2 to 3 minutes, turning once. (A perfect Puri resembles a fragile bubble.) Drain on paper towels. Serve warm with a curry. Makes about 25.

Saffron-Lemon Tea Bread

2 cups sifted all-purpose flour
2 teaspoons baking powder
½ teaspoon salt
¼ teaspoon soda
½ cup shortening
¾ cup sugar
⅛ teaspoon powdered saffron
2 teaspoons grated lemon peel
2 eggs
⅔ cup water
2 tablespoons lemon juice

Sift together the flour, baking powder, salt, and soda. Cream shortening, sugar, saffron, and lemon peel till fluffy. Beat in eggs, one at a time. Combine water and lemon juice and add alternately with the dry ingredients to the creamed mixture, beginning and ending with the dry ingredients.

Turn into 3 well-greased 5½x3x2¼-inch loaf pans. Bake in a moderate oven (350°) about 35 minutes. Cool in pans for 10 minutes. Turn out onto wire rack to finish cooling. Spread slices with softened cream cheese or butter for tea sandwiches. Makes 3 loaves.

Cinnamon Fantan Buns

1 package active dry yeast *or*
1 cake compressed yeast
¼ cup water
½ cup milk, scalded
¼ cup sugar
¼ cup shortening
1 teaspoon salt
3 cups sifted all-purpose flour
1 egg
2 tablespoons melted butter
⅓ cup chopped California walnuts
½ cup sugar
1½ teaspoons cinnamon

Soften active dry yeast in *warm* water or compressed yeast in *lukewarm* water. Combine milk, ¼ cup sugar, shortening, and salt; stir. Cool to lukewarm. Add 1 *cup* flour; mix well. Stir in softened yeast and egg; beat well. Add 2 *cups* flour (or enough to make a soft dough). Cover; let rest 10 minutes.

Turn out on a lightly floured surface and knead till smooth and satiny (about 8 minutes.) Place in lightly greased bowl, turning once to grease surface. Cover; let rise in a warm place till double (about 1½ hours). On a lightly floured surface, form in a ball. Cover and let rest 10 minutes.

Roll out in 20x10-inch rectangle. Brush with 2 tablespoons melted butter or margarine. Combine chopped walnuts, ½ cup sugar, and the cinnamon; sprinkle over dough. Roll up, starting at long side. Cut in eight 2½-inch lengths. *Without cutting all the way through*, snip each in thirds. Place on greased baking sheet; spread thirds to form fan. Cover; let rise till almost double (about 25 minutes). Bake in moderate oven (350°) for 12 to 15 minutes or till done.

Danish Kringle

¾ cup butter
¼ cup sifted all-purpose flour

• • •

1 package active dry yeast
¼ cup *warm* water
1 beaten egg
¾ cup milk, scalded and cooled to lukewarm
3 tablespoons sugar
1 teaspoon salt
3 to 3½ cups sifted all-purpose flour
Raisin Filling
Almond Topper

Cream butter with ¼ cup flour; roll between sheets of waxed paper to 10x4-inch rectangle. Chill. Soften yeast in *warm* water. Combine egg, cooled milk, sugar, salt, and softened yeast; stir in flour to make a soft dough. On a floured surface, roll dough to a 12-inch square; place chilled butter in center; overlap sides of dough atop butter. Turn dough ¼-way around, then roll dough to 12-inch square.

Repeat folding and rolling twice more. Wrap in waxed paper. Chill 30 minutes. Roll to 24x12-inch rectangle. Cut lengthwise in 2 strips; spread each with Raisin Filling and roll as for jelly roll, starting with long side. Moisten the edges; seal. Stretch each to 30-inch length without breaking. Place seam sides down on a greased baking sheet, shaping in an oval with ends meeting. Flatten to ½ inch with a rolling pin. Add Almond Topper. Cover; let rise till double, 25 minutes. Bake at 375° for 25 to 30 minutes. Makes 2.

Almond Topper: Brush Kringles with a beaten egg; sprinkle with mixture of ¼ cup sugar and ½ cup halved almonds.

Raisin Filling: Add 1 teaspoon ground cardamom to ¼ cup soft butter; gradually stir in 2 cups sifted confectioners' sugar. Blend in 2 tablespoons cream; add 1 cup light seedless raisins and mix.

You can make several different shapes from just one dough. For an extra treat some are filled with Almond Filling.

Danish Pastry

This delicate pastry takes time but is well worth every minute you spend—

1½ cups butter *or*
  1 cup butter and ½ cup margarine
⅓ cup sifted all-purpose flour

• • •

2 packages active dry yeast *or*
  2 cakes compressed yeast
½ cup water
¾ cup milk, scalded
¼ cup sugar
1 teaspoon salt
1 beaten egg
4 cups sifted all-purpose flour

Cream butter with ⅓ cup flour. Pat or roll butter mixture between 2 sheets of waxed paper to form a 12x6-inch rectangle. *Chill thoroughly.* Soften active dry yeast in *warm* water or compressed yeast in *lukewarm* water. Combine milk, sugar, and salt. Cool to lukewarm. Add yeast and egg. Mix well. Add 4 cups flour; or enough to make soft dough.

Turn out and knead on lightly floured surface until smooth and glossy, about 5 minutes. Roll dough in a 14-inch square on lightly floured surface. Place the thoroughly chilled butter mixture on half the dough. Fold over other half of dough, sealing edges well with heel of hand.

Roll dough on lightly floured surface in a 20x12-inch rectangle. Fold in thirds so that you will have 3 layers. (If butter softens, chill after each rolling.) Roll again into a 20x12-inch rectangle. Repeat the folding and rolling 2 more times. Chill ½ hour after last rolling.

Shape as shown in the pictures. Place the rolls on ungreased baking sheet. Let rise in a warm place till almost double, about 1 hour. Bake in very hot oven (450°) about 8 minutes. If desired, brush tops immediately with Confectioners' Icing. Serve warm. Makes about 3 dozen pastries.

Almond Filling

¼ cup butter or margarine
¼ cup sugar
¼ cup ground blanched almonds

Thoroughly cream together butter and sugar. Add ground almonds and mix well. Use only 1 *level teaspoon* filling on each roll.

Confectioners' Icing

Light cream
2 cups sifted confectioners' sugar
1 teaspoon vanilla
Dash salt

Add sufficient light cream to confectioners' sugar to make of spreading consistency. Add vanilla and salt. Mix until smooth.

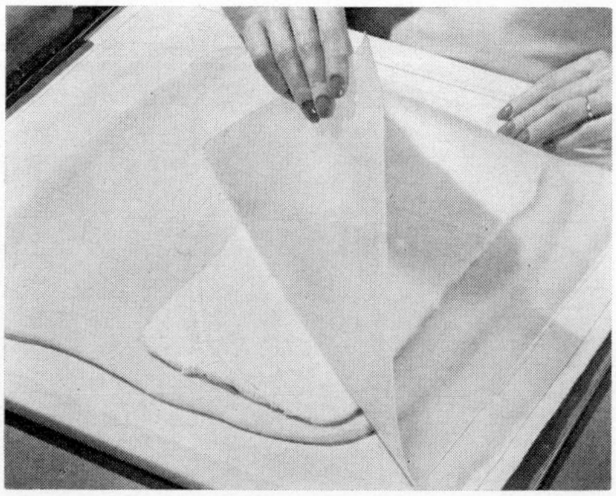

1 Cream butter and flour; roll between sheets of waxed paper in 12x6-inch rectangle; chill. Prepare dough; roll in 14-inch square. Peel top sheet from butter; put butter on half of dough; remove other sheet.

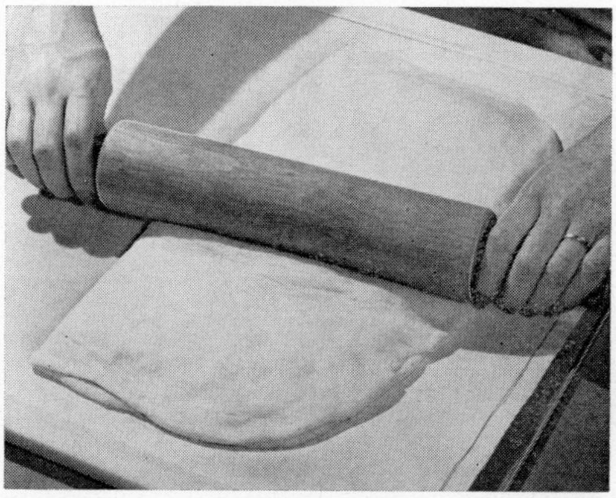

2 Fold the dough in half over the butter-covered layer. Seal the edges of dough together tightly by pressing down with heel of your hand. Roll the dough in a 20x12-inch rectangle on a lightly floured surface.

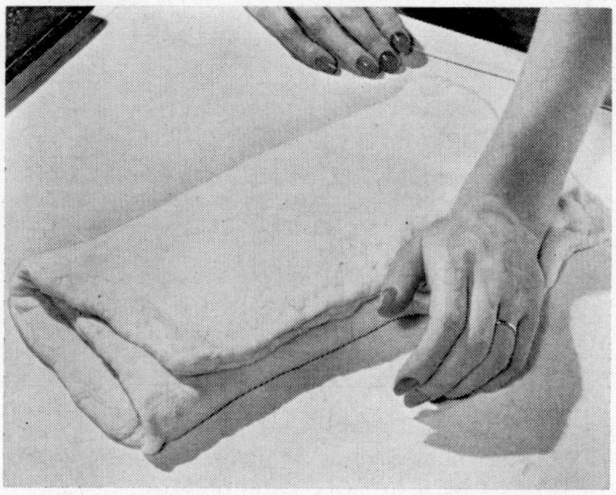

3 Fold dough in thirds. Seal edges together with heel of hand. Roll again in 20x12-inch rectangle. Repeat folding and rolling 2 more times. Chill ½ hour after last rolling. If butter softens, chill dough after each rolling.

4 Almond Fans: Use ⅓ of dough. Roll to 12x 8-inches. Cut in 4x2-inch pieces. Place Almond Filling in center of each; fold lengthwise. Seal edges tightly; curve slightly. Snip side opposite sealed edge at 1-inch intervals.

5 Twists: Use ⅓ of dough. Roll in 12x-7inch rectangle (about ¼ inch thick). Cut in strips 6 inches long, ¾ inch wide. Hold ends of strip; twist in opposite directions. Form strip into a circle, knot, figure-8, or snail shape.

6 Baby Bunting Rolls: Roll ⅓ of dough in 12x9-inch rectangle. Cut in 3-inch squares. Place 1 level teaspoon Almond Filling in center of each. Fold opposite corners to center; overlap edges, sealing to prevent unfolding.

A favorite from Germany A rich loaf chock full of fruits, nuts, and peels—that's our German Stollen. As shown here, it's all dressed up for the holidays, but it's sure to be a hit any time of year.

Swedish Almond Braid

- 1 package active dry yeast *or* 1 cake compressed yeast
- ¼ cup water
- 1 cup milk, scalded
- ¾ cup sugar
- ½ cup softened butter
- 1 teaspoon salt
- 5¼ to 5½ cups sifted all-purpose flour
- 1 egg yolk
- ¾ teaspoon almond extract
- 1 slightly-beaten egg white
- ¼ cup sugar
- ¼ cup slivered almonds

Soften active dry yeast in *warm* water (110°) or compressed yeast in *lukewarm* water (85°). Combine milk, ¾ cup sugar, butter and salt; stir till butter is melted and sugar is dissolved; cool. Stir in *2 cups* of the flour and beat well. Add egg yolk, softened yeast, almond extract, and enough of the remaining flour to make a soft dough.

Turn out on a lightly floured surface and knead till smooth and elastic, about 8 to 10 minutes. Place dough in a lightly greased bowl, turning once to grease surface. Cover; let rise till almost double, about 2 hours.

Punch down and divide into 6 equal parts; form into balls. Cover and let rest 10 minutes. Roll each ball into a ropelike strip about 12 inches long. Form into 2 braids, starting at the center and braiding toward each end. Tuck under the ends.

Place in 2 greased 8½x4½x2½-inch loaf pans. Cover; let rise in a warm place till almost double. Brush tops of loaves with egg white. Sprinkle with ¼ cup sugar and the slivered almonds. Bake in a moderate oven (350°) about 40 to 55 minutes. Makes 2.

German Stollen

1 package active dry yeast *or*
  1 cake compressed yeast
¼ cup water

• • •

1 cup milk, scalded
½ cup butter or margarine
¼ cup sugar
1 teaspoon salt
¼ teaspoon ground cardamom
4 to 4½ cups sifted
  all-purpose flour
1 slightly-beaten egg
1 cup seedless raisins
¼ cup currants
¼ cup chopped mixed candied fruits
2 tablespoons grated orange peel
1 tablespoon grated lemon peel
¼ cup chopped blanched almonds
Glaze

Soften active dry yeast in *warm* water (110°) or compressed yeast in *lukewarm* water (85°). Combine milk, butter, sugar, salt, and cardamom; cool to lukewarm. Stir in 2 *cups* of the flour; beat well. Add the softened yeast and egg; beat well. Stir in fruits, peels, and nuts. Add enough of the remaining flour to make a soft dough.

Turn out on a lightly floured surface. Knead till smooth and elastic (about 8 to 10 minutes). Place in a greased bowl, turning once to grease surface of dough. Cover and let rise in a warm place till double (about 1¾ hours). Punch down; turn out on a lightly floured surface. Divide in 3 equal parts. Cover; let rest 10 minutes.

Roll each of the 3 parts to a 10x6-inch rectangle. Without stretching, fold the long side over to within 1 inch of the opposite side; seal edge. Place on greased baking sheets. Cover and let rise in a warm place till almost double (about 1 hour). Bake in a moderate oven (375°) for 15 to 20 minutes or till golden brown. While warm, brush with Glaze. Makes 3 loaves.

To match picture, top Stollen with additional pieces of candied fruits. *Or*, if desired, make holly leaves and berries from citron and bits of cut-up candied cherries. Another time, make flowers, using halves of blanched almonds for the petals, a bit of red candied cherry for the center, with citron or bit of green candied cherry for leaves.

Glaze: Combine 1 cup sifted confectioners' sugar, 2 tablespoons hot water, and ½ teaspoon butter. Brush over Stollen.

Almond Horns

Served at Lüchow's in New York City as a fitting climax to a hearty meal. Like a Danish pastry with almond filling—you'll wonder how anything could taste so good!—

¼ pound soft butter (½ cup or 1 stick)
½ cup sugar
5 slightly-beaten eggs
2 packages active dry yeast *or*
  2 cakes compressed yeast
⅓ cup water

• • •

⅔ cup milk, scalded
5½ to 6 cups sifted all-purpose flour

• • •

¼ pound butter (½ cup or 1 stick),
  firm, but not brittle-cold
Almond Filling
1 slightly-beaten egg yolk
1 tablespoon water
Sliced almonds

Thoroughly mix the soft butter, sugar, and eggs. Soften active dry yeast in *warm* water or compressed yeast in *lukewarm* water. Cool milk to lukewarm, then stir into egg mixture along with the softened yeast. Last, add enough flour to make a soft dough, mixing well. Refrigerate 3 hours to chill.

On lightly floured surface, roll dough to a 14-inch square, about ½ inch thick. Now roll in remaining butter this way: Dot the butter over *half* the dough, then fold other half of dough over butter-dotted area; seal edges. Now roll the dough to a 20x12-inch rectangle, ¼ inch thick; fold in thirds; seal edges and repeat this step 3 more times, chilling dough after each rolling if it softens. Put the dough back in refrigerator until next day (or until well chilled).

Next day, divide dough in fourths. On lightly floured surface, roll each piece to a 15-inch circle, about ⅛ inch thick. Cut each circle into 6 wedges. Along side opposite point, put about 1 tablespoon Almond Filling; roll up, going toward point. Place point down on greased baking sheet. Cover; let rise in a warm place till almost double, about 30 to 45 minutes. Just before placing in oven, brush tops of horns with a mixture of 1 slightly-beaten egg yolk mixed with 1 tablespoon water. Sprinkle with almonds. Bake at 350° for 20 to 25 minutes or till done. Serve warm. Makes 2 dozen.

Almond Filling: Combine ½ pound (1 cup) almond paste, ⅔ cup sugar, and 1 egg. Mix ingredients thoroughly.

Kugelhoff

1 package active dry yeast
¼ cup *warm* water
½ cup milk, scalded
¼ cup butter
½ cup sugar
2 eggs
2½ cups sifted all-purpose flour
1 teaspoon salt
½ cup golden seedless raisins
1 teaspoon grated lemon peel
1 tablespoon melted butter
3 tablespoons fine dry bread crumbs
Blanched whole almonds

Soften yeast in *warm* water. Cool milk to lukewarm. In mixing bowl, cream butter and sugar till light; add eggs, one at a time, beating after each. Add yeast and milk. Sift together flour and salt; add to creamed mixture. Beat at medium speed on mixer till smooth, 2 minutes. Stir in raisins and lemon peel. Cover; let rise till double (2 hours).

Meanwhile prepare a 1½-quart Turk's Head Mold: Brush liberally with butter; sprinkle with bread crumbs, coating well. Arrange almonds in a design in bottom of mold. Stir down batter; spoon carefully into mold. Let rise till almost double (1 hour). Bake at 350° for 25 minutes or till done. Cool 10 minutes. Remove mold.

Savarin a l'orange

1 package active dry yeast
¼ cup *warm* water
¼ cup milk, scalded
8 teaspoons sugar
⅓ cup melted butter
½ teaspoon salt
About 2 cups sifted all-purpose flour
2 beaten eggs
Orange Syrup
Marmalade Glaze
Creme

Soften yeast in water. Combine next 4 ingredients; cool to lukewarm. Add about ¾ *cup* flour to make a thick batter. Add yeast and eggs; mix well. Add enough remaining flour to make a stiff batter. *Beat thoroughly* till smooth, about 5 minutes. Cover; let double (1 hour). Stir down; turn into a well-greased and floured 5-cup ring mold. Let rise till almost double. Bake at 350° for 20 to 25 minutes. Cool 5 minutes; remove mold.

Immediately prick Savarin in several places and drizzle with Orange Syrup. Let stand 30 minutes, basting frequently to soak well. Brush entire surface with Marmalade Glaze. Trim top with orange sections and blanched almonds. Fill center with Creme.

Orange Syrup: Combine ½ cup *each* sugar, water, and orange juice. Add 1 tablespoon orange peel, cut in thin slivers (white part removed). Cook mixture 5 minutes. Cool to lukewarm. Drizzle warm syrup over Savarin, soaking well.

Marmalade Glaze: Heat and stir ¾ cup orange marmalade; sieve. Use as directed.

Creme: Combine 1 cup whipping cream, 1 tablespoon confectioners' sugar, and 1 teaspoon vanilla. Whip till peaks form.

Serve impressive Kugelhoff

← Your guests will marvel at the beauty of this elegant molded bread. Slightly sweet and subtly flavored with lemon—it's the perfect choice with coffee or tea.

Jule Kaga

1 package active dry yeast
¼ cup *warm* water
½ cup butter
½ cup sugar
1 teaspoon salt
½ teaspoon ground cardamom
1 cup milk, scalded
4½ to 5 cups sifted all-purpose flour
1 slightly-beaten egg
½ cup seedless raisins
½ cup citron, diced
½ cup candied cherries, chopped

Soften yeast in *warm* water. Combine butter, sugar, salt, cardamom and milk; cool to lukewarm. Add 2 *cups* flour; beat well. Add softened yeast, egg, and fruits. Add enough remaining flour to make soft dough. Turn out on a lightly floured surface, knead till smooth (8 to 10 minutes). Shape dough in a ball. Place in a lightly greased bowl, turning once to grease surface. Cover; let rise till double (about 2½ hours).

Punch down. Turn out on a lightly floured surface; divide into 2 parts; form into balls. Cover; let rest 10 minutes. Shape into 2 round loaves; place on greased baking sheets. Cover; let rise till double (1½ hours). Glaze: Beat 1 egg yolk slightly, then add 2 tablespoons sugar and 2 tablespoons water. Mix well and brush over loaves before baking. Bake at 350° for 30 minutes or till done.

Savarin Chantilly

1 package active dry yeast *or*
1 cake compressed yeast
¼ cup water
½ cup milk, scalded
⅓ cup soft butter or margarine
¼ cup sugar
½ teaspoon salt
• • •
2 cups sifted all-purpose flour
1 egg
Savarin Syrup
Apricot Glaze
Creme Chantilly

Soften active dry yeast in *warm* water or compressed yeast in *lukewarm* water. To hot milk, add butter, sugar, and salt; stir till butter melts. Cool to lukewarm. Stir in ½ *cup* of the flour. Beat in egg and softened yeast. Add remaining flour. Beat vigorously 5 to 7 minutes. Cover; let rise in warm place till double (about 1¼ hours).

Stir down batter and spoon into well-greased 6-cup ring mold. Cover; let rise till almost double (about 45 minutes). Bake in moderate oven (350°) 35 minutes or till done and top is nicely browned. Cool 5 minutes and remove from mold.

Prick top of Savarin in several places and gradually drizzle with Savarin Syrup; let stand about 30 minutes, basting frequently to soak well. Now brush entire surface with warm Apricot Glaze. Trim top with blanched almonds, candied cherries, citron. At serving time, fill center with Creme Chantilly. Makes 14 servings.

Savarin Syrup: Combine 1 cup sugar and 2 cups water; bring to boiling. Remove from heat and cool to lukewarm. Stir in ½ cup kirsch, rum, or cognac.

Apricot Glaze: Heat and stir one 12-ounce jar (about 1¼ cups) apricot preserves; sieve. Brush over Savarin.

Creme Chantilly: Whip 2 cups whipping cream with 2 tablespoons confectioners' sugar and 2 teaspoons vanilla.

Serve Savarin Chantilly

This rich airy cakelike-bread is served as a feast-day dessert in France. A delicious syrup soaks through it, then it's topped with a glaze and trimmed with fruit and nuts.

Delicious Crepes Frangipane C'est magnifique!

Once you taste these delectable pancakes you are sure to agree that they are truly the "best you have ever eaten." These light and delicate crepes are filled with a rich Almond Cream Filling, brushed with melted butter and topped with grated unsweetened chocolate and confectioners' sugar. For certain, they're a treat in any language.

Crepes Frangipane (Crepes with Almond Cream Filling)

These fragile dessert pancakes boast a flurry of grated unsweetened chocolate atop. You can stow filled crepes in the refrigerator till time to heat and serve—

Crepes:

⅓ cup sifted all-purpose flour
1 tablespoon sugar
Dash salt
1 egg
1 egg yolk
¾ cup milk
1 tablespoon butter or margarine, melted

Measure ingredients into a blender container or mixing bowl; blend or beat with an electric or rotary beater until smooth. Refrigerate several hours or till thick. Heat a heavy 6-inch skillet till a drop of water will dance on the surface.

Grease lightly and pour in 2 tablespoons of batter. Lift skillet off the heat and tilt from side to side till the batter covers the bottom evenly. Return skillet to heat and cook till underside of crepe is lightly browned (about 1½ minutes). To remove, invert skillet over paper towels. Cook the remaining crepes the same way, just on one side for about 1½ minutes. Makes 10 crepes.

Almond Cream Filling:

1 cup sugar
¼ cup all-purpose flour
1 cup milk

• • •

2 eggs
2 egg yolks

• • •

3 tablespoons butter or margarine
2 teaspoons vanilla
½ teaspoon almond extract
½ cup ground toasted blanched almonds

Mix sugar and flour. Add milk; cook and stir till thick, then continue cooking and stirring 1 or 2 minutes longer. Beat the eggs and the egg yolks slightly; stir some of the hot mixture into the eggs and then return it to the hot mixture.

While stirring, bring just to a boil and remove from heat. Stir in remaining ingredients. Cool to room temperature. (Chill if not to be used promptly.)

To serve: Spread about 2 tablespoons of Almond Cream Filling on unbrowned side of each crepe; roll up and place folded side down in a buttered 13x9x2-inch baking dish. Brush the crepes with melted butter and heat in a moderate oven (350°) for about 20 to 25 minutes or till hot. Sprinkle tops of crepes with grated unsweetened chocolate and sift confectioners' sugar over all. Serve warm with whipped cream. Makes about 5 servings (10 crepes).

Homemade French Bread It makes grand eating with soups, salads, or casseroles. Our recipe will make two long loaves or a dozen "Shorties."

French Bread

Soften 2 packages active dry yeast in ½ cup *warm* water. Sift 7 to 7½ cups all-purpose flour. Combine 1 tablespoon salt and 2 cups lukewarm water; beat in 2 *cups* of the flour. Blend in softened yeast; stir in 4 to 4½ *cups* of the flour, or enough to make a soft dough. Turn out on lightly floured surface. Cover; let rest 10 minutes. Knead till smooth and elastic, 5 to 8 minutes, working in the remaining 1 *cup* of flour.

Place in lightly greased bowl, turning dough once. Cover; let rise till double (about 1½ hours). Punch down; let rise till double again (about 1 hour).

Punch down. Turn out on lightly floured surface and divide in 2 portions. Cover; let rest 10 minutes. Roll each portion into 15x12-inch rectangle. Roll tightly, beginning at long side, sealing well. Taper ends.

Place each loaf diagonally, seam side down, on greased baking sheet that has been sprinkled with corn meal. With sharp knife, gash tops diagonally every 2½ inches, ⅛ to ¼ inch deep. Beat 1 egg white just till foamy; add 1 tablespoon water. Brush mixture over tops and sides of loaves.

Cover with damp cloth, but don't let it touch loaves (drape cloth over inverted tall glasses). Let double (about 1½ hours). Bake at 375° till light brown, about 20 minutes. Brush again with egg-white mixture. Bake about 20 minutes longer. Cool. Makes 2.

French-bread Shorties

Prepare 1 recipe French Bread. After second rising, punch down. Turn out on lightly floured surface and divide into 12 parts. Cover and let rest 10 minutes. Roll each portion into 6x5-inch rectangle. Roll each one up tightly, beginning at the long side, sealing seam well. Place loaves, seam side down, on greased baking sheet that has been sprinkled with corn meal.

With sharp knife, gash tops diagonally every 1½ inches, ⅛- to ¼-inch deep. Brush tops and sides with mixture of egg white and water. Cover with damp cloth, but don't let it touch the breads (drape cloth over inverted tall glasses). Let double, about 1 hour. Bake at 375° for 15 minutes. Brush again with egg-white mixture. Continue baking about 15 to 20 minutes longer or till well-browned and done. Cool. Makes 1 dozen.

Follow the how-to pictures below for tips on baking French bread

1 When dough has rested 10 minutes, then work in the last cup of flour. Sprinkle the flour on the board and knead it in. Continue kneading till the dough is firm and elastic.

2 After second rising, divide dough in half. Roll each to a 15x12-inch rectangle. Start at one long side and roll dough tightly. Seal dough well at the end of each complete turn.

3 Grease two baking sheets, dust with corn meal. Place a loaf cater-corner on each. Cut diagonal gashes, 2½ inches apart and ⅛ to ¼-inch deep. Brush with egg white mixture.

4 After 20 minutes' baking, open the oven and again brush the tops and sides of loaves with egg-white-water mixture. For a cracked crust, cool the baked bread in a draft.

5 For individual loaves, divide dough in 12 parts after second rising. Roll each in 6x5-inch rectangle; roll up tightly. Place on greased baking sheet dusted with corn meal. Gash tops.

6 Shorties (the French call them *petits pains*) are also brushed with the egg-white-water mixture. Remember to brush them again while baking to give glossy finish and crisp crust.

Bake Brioche—light as a feather

Brioche

Soften 1 package active dry yeast in ¼ cup *warm* water. Scald ½ cup milk; cool to lukewarm. Thoroughly cream ½ cup butter, ⅓ cup sugar, and ½ teaspoon salt. Add milk. Sift 3¼ cups all-purpose flour. Add 1 *cup* of the flour to creamed mixture. Add yeast, 3 beaten eggs, and 1 beaten egg yolk; beat well. Add remaining flour; beat 5 to 8 minutes longer. Cover; let double (2 hours). Stir down; beat well. Cover with foil; refrigerate overnight. Stir down; turn out on lightly floured surface. Divide dough in fourths. Follow shaping directions under the pictures. Cover; let rise till double (1 hour). Combine 1 slightly-beaten egg white and 1 tablespoon sugar; brush tops. Bake in a moderate oven (375°) for 15 minutes or till done. Serve warm. Makes 24.

Follow these easy directions for shaping pretty, puffy Brioche

1 Set aside one-fourth of dough. Cut remaining 3 pieces in half and form each piece in 4 balls (24 in all). Tuck under cut edges.

2 Place large balls in greased muffin pans. Cut reserved dough into 4 wedges, divide each into 6 smaller pieces. Shape in 24 balls.

3 With your thumb or a knife handle, poke indentation in top of each large ball in muffin cups. Holes will hold the small balls.

4 Brush holes slightly with water; press small ball into each indentation. Let rise; brush tops with egg white-sugar mixture. Bake.

Dainty crescent rolls Croissants are buttery-rich and so very flaky, almost like puff pastry. They are best served warm from the oven, but they can be reheated in a roll warmer or a very slow oven.

Croissants

1½ cups butter
⅓ cup sifted all-purpose flour
2 packages active dry yeast
½ cup *warm* water
¾ cup milk, scalded
¼ cup sugar
1 teaspoon salt
1 beaten egg
3¾ to 4 cups sifted
  all-purpose flour
1 egg yolk
1 tablespoon milk

Cream butter with ⅓ cup flour. Roll mixture between waxed paper to 12x6-inches. Chill 1 hour or longer. Soften yeast in water. Combine next 3 ingredients; cool to lukewarm. Add yeast and egg; mix well. Add 3¾ *cups* flour or enough to make soft dough. Knead on floured surface 5 minutes. Roll to 14-inch square. Place *chilled* butter on one half; fold over other half; seal edges. Roll to 20x12-inches; seal edges.

Fold in thirds so you have 3 layers. (If butter softens, chill after each rolling.) Roll to 20x12-inches again. Fold and roll twice more; seal edges. Fold in thirds to 12x7-inches. Chill 45 minutes. Cut dough crosswise in fourths. Roll each fourth (keep remainder chilled) to 22x7-inches, paper-thin. Cut in 10 pie-shaped wedges, 4 inches at base and 7 inches long (you'll have an extra ½-wedge on each end; put together).

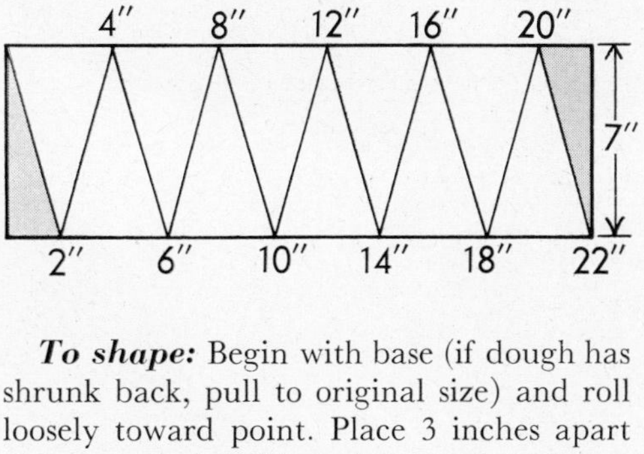

To shape: Begin with base (if dough has shrunk back, pull to original size) and roll loosely toward point. Place 3 inches apart on ungreased baking sheet, point down; curve ends. Cover; let double, 30 to 45 minutes. Beat egg yolk with milk; brush on rolls. Bake at 375° for 12 to 15 minutes. Makes 40.

Happy Holiday Breads

Hot Cross Buns

2 packages active dry yeast *or*
 2 cakes compressed yeast
½ cup water
• • •
¼ cup milk, scalded
½ cup salad oil or melted shortening
⅓ cup sugar
¾ teaspoon salt
3½ to 4 cups sifted all-purpose flour
½ to 1 teaspoon cinnamon
3 beaten eggs
⅔ cup currants

Soften active dry yeast in *warm* water or compressed yeast in *lukewarm* water. Combine milk, salad oil, sugar, and salt; cool to lukewarm. Sift together 1 *cup* of the flour and the cinnamon; stir into milk mixture. Add eggs; beat well. Stir in softened yeast and currants. Add remaining flour (or enough to make a soft dough), beating well.

Cover dough with damp cloth and let rise in a warm place till double (about 1½ hours). Punch down and turn out on a lightly floured surface. Roll or pat to ½ inch thick. Cut dough in rounds with a floured 2½-inch biscuit cutter.

Shape buns with fingers and place on a greased baking sheet, about 1½ inches apart. Cover and let rise in a warm place till almost double (about 1 hour). If desired, snip *shallow* cross in each bun with *sharp* scissors or knife. Brush tops with 1 slightly-beaten egg white. (You'll have some left over—save it to use in the frosting.)

Bake in a moderate oven (375°) for 15 minutes or until lightly browned. Remove buns to rack to cool slightly. For frosting, add vanilla and about ¾ cup sifted confectioners' sugar to the remaining egg white. Pipe frosting crosses on while buns are warm. Serve while warm. Makes about 2 dozen.

Traditional Easter breads

← Anise Loaf is centered with a bright red egg. Easter Basket Bread nests hard-cooked eggs. In back are Lemon Buns, Cardamom Bread and Hot Cross Buns.

Anise Loaf

1 package active dry yeast
¼ cup water
½ cup milk, scalded
⅓ cup sugar
¼ cup butter
½ teaspoon salt
¼ teaspoon oil of anise
6 drops oil of cinnamon
2¾ to 3 cups sifted all-purpose flour
1 egg
1 uncooked egg in shell, tinted with
 red food coloring
1 slightly-beaten egg
1 tablespoon water
2 tablespoons sesame seed

Soften yeast in *warm* water. Pour scalded milk over sugar, butter, and salt; stir till butter melts. Cool to lukewarm. Stir in flavorings. Add 1 *cup* of the flour; mix well. Stir in 1 egg and softened yeast; beat well. Add remaining flour (or a little more or less to make a soft dough). Turn out on lightly floured surface. Knead till smooth and elastic (8 to 10 minutes). Place in a lightly greased bowl, turning once. Cover; let rise in a warm place till double (about 1¼ hours).

Punch down. Let rise till almost double (1 hour). Turn out on a lightly floured surface and divide dough in thirds; form in balls. Cover; let rest 10 minutes. Roll each part under hands to form strand 16 inches long, tapering ends. Line up, 1 inch apart, on greased baking sheet. Braid loosely without stretching, beginning in middle, working toward either end. Pinch ends together. Tuck tinted uncooked egg, large end up, in center of braid. Cover; let rise till almost double (40 minutes). Combine beaten egg and water; brush over braid; sprinkle with sesame seed. Bake at 375° for 25 minutes.

Cardamom Bread

Follow recipe for Anise Loaf, but omit the anise and cinnamon. Instead, add 1½ to 2 teaspoons ground cardamom or 1 teaspoon crushed cardamom to the milk mixture. Just before baking, brush braid with milk and sprinkle with 2 tablespoons sugar (omit egg-water mixture and sesame seed).

Here we show you how you can fashion Easter Basket Bread and Lemon Buns. Children and grown-ups alike will love them. You can see all these gay holiday breads pictured on page 65. Just adorn the tops with candy decorettes for a festive touch and you're all set for the Easter Bunny!

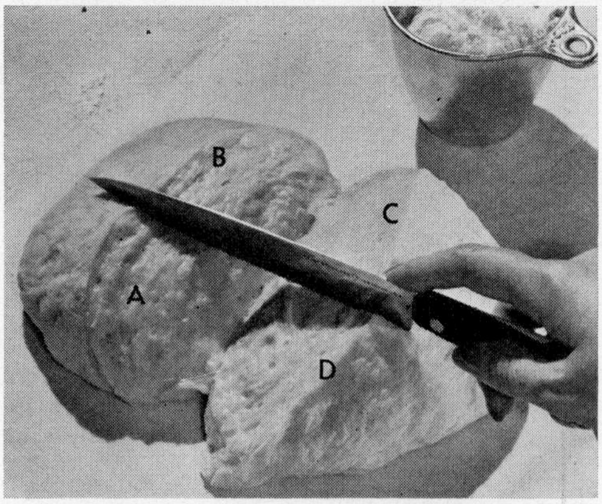

1 Divide dough into 4 equal parts. Use A, B, and C for Easter Basket Bread. Set aside D for Lemon Buns and the crisscrosses.

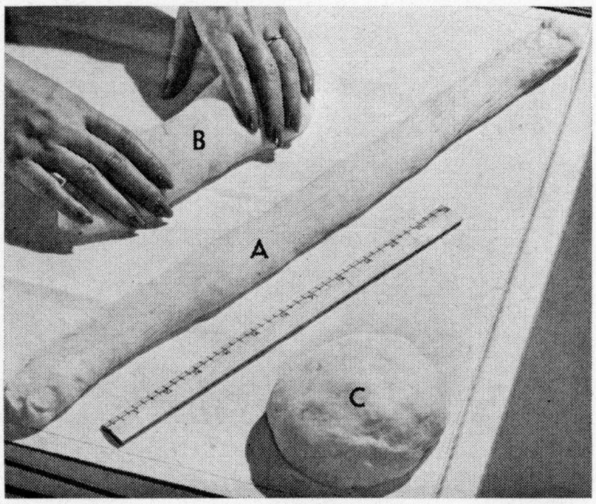

2 Easter Basket Bread starts out as a braid. Roll A, B, and C into strands, each 20 inches long. Stretch and smooth as you go.

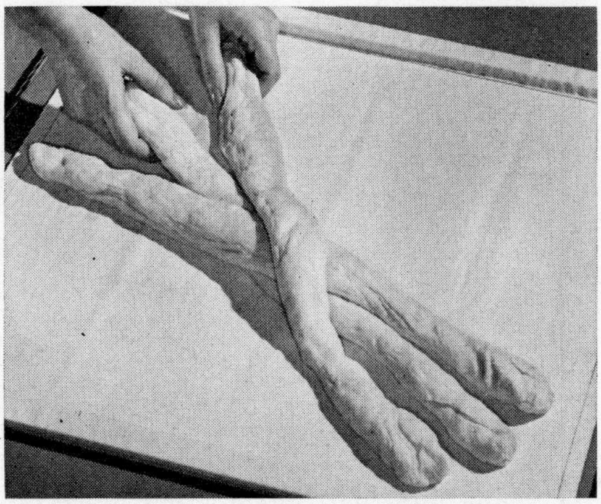

3 Line up 3 strands, 1 inch apart. Braid loosely and without stretching from center toward each end. Taper ends; pinch to seal.

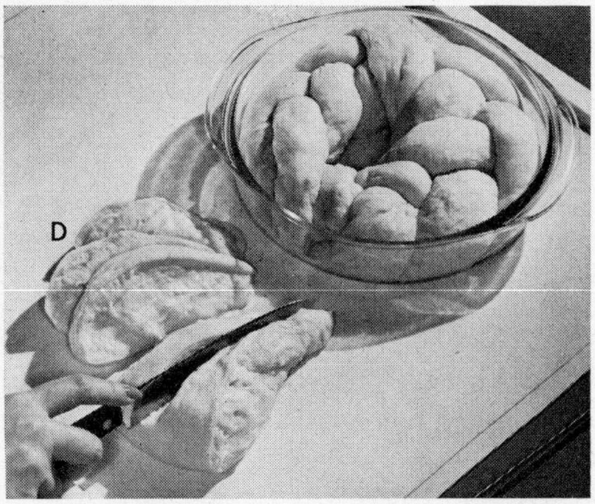

4 Fit braid into greased dish or pan. Divide D into 5 equal parts. Shape 4 sections in rounds. Save the remaining for crisscrosses.

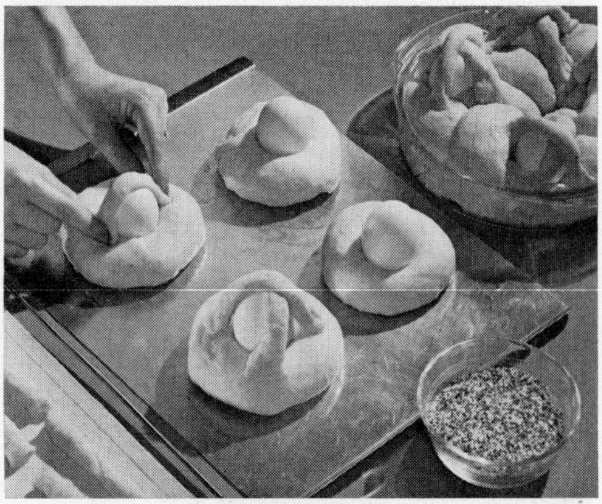

5 Divide remaining dough in 4 pieces. Roll each in 16-inch strip; cut in 4-inch lengths. Cross 2 strips over each egg; seal.

Easter Basket Bread and Lemon Buns

1 package active dry yeast *or*
  1 cake compressed yeast
¼ cup water
• • •
¾ cup milk, scalded
1 package lemon pudding
¼ cup butter, margarine, or shortening
½ teaspoon salt
4 to 4½ cups sifted all-purpose flour
3 beaten eggs
8 uncooked eggs in shell
1 beaten egg
1 tablespoon water
Candy decorettes

Soften active dry yeast in *warm* water or compressed yeast in *lukewarm* water. Pour scalded milk over pudding mix, butter, and salt. Stir till butter melts and pudding dissolves; cool to lukewarm. Add 1½ *cups* of the flour and mix well. Stir in softened yeast and 3 beaten eggs; beat well. Gradually add remaining flour (or a little more or less to make a soft dough). Turn out on lightly floured surface. Knead till smooth and elastic (8 to 10 minutes). Place in lightly greased bowl, turning once. Cover; let rise till double (about 1¼ hours).

Punch down; let rise again till almost double (45 to 60 minutes). Turn out on lightly floured surface and divide dough in fourths; form in balls. Cover; let rest 10 minutes. Shape 3 parts into strands, each 20 inches long; braid. Fit braid into greased 9x1½-inch round pan*. (Dough will almost fill pan.) Tuck 4 uncooked eggs into braid to match picture, page 64.

Divide remaining piece of dough in 5 parts. Shape 4 of these in round buns and place on greased baking sheet. Press an egg in center of each. Divide remaining dough in 4 equal parts. Roll each in pencil-like strip, 16 inches long. Cut in 4-inch strips. Crisscross 2 strips over each egg in *buns* and in *braid*, pressing ends gently into dough. Cover and let rise till almost double (about 45 minutes). Brush all with mixture of beaten egg and water; sprinkle with decorettes. Bake in moderate oven (375°)* for about 25 to 30 minutes for *Easter Basket* and about 15 minutes for *Buns*. Makes 1 Easter Basket Bread plus 4 Lemon Buns.

*If using an 8½x1½-inch round ovenware cake dish, bake the Easter Basket Bread at 350° about 30 to 35 minutes.

Easter Nest Coffeecake

Soften 1 package active dry yeast in ¼ cup *warm* water. Scald ½ cup milk; stir in ¼ cup shortening, ¼ cup sugar, and 1 teaspoon salt; cool to lukewarm. Add 1 *cup* sifted all-purpose flour; beat smooth. Add yeast and 1 slightly-beaten egg; beat well. Add 2 *cups* sifted all-purpose flour (or enough for soft dough). On floured surface, knead till smooth and elastic (8 to 10 minutes). Place in a greased bowl, turning once to grease surface. Cover; let double (1 hour).

Punch down; divide in thirds. Cover; let rest 10 minutes. Shape a *third* of the dough in 6 "eggs"; place close together in center of greased baking sheet. For nest, shape remaining dough in two 26-inch ropes; twist together. Coil around eggs; seal ends. Cover; let rise till double (1 hour). Bake in a moderate oven (375°) for 15 to 20 minutes. Cool. Frost with Confectioners' Icing; sprinkle the eggs with candy decorettes and the nest with green shredded coconut.

Cherry-Nut Loaf

1 package active dry yeast
¼ cup *warm* water
¼ cup sugar
¾ teaspoon salt
2 tablespoons shortening
½ cup milk, scalded
2½ cups sifted all-purpose flour
1 egg, beaten
¼ cup chopped maraschino cherries
½ cup chopped California walnuts

Soften yeast in water. Combine sugar, salt, shortening, and scalded milk. Cool to lukewarm. Add 2 *cups* of the flour; beat vigorously. Add softened yeast and egg; beat well. Add enough remaining flour to make a soft dough. Turn out on a lightly floured surface and knead till smooth and elastic (5 to 8 minutes). Place in a greased bowl, turning once to grease the surface. Cover; let rise in a warm place till double.

Turn dough out on a lightly floured surface and roll into a rectangle. Sprinkle with the cherries and nuts. Knead into dough. Form into a round loaf, 6 inches in diameter. Place on a greased baking sheet. Cover and let rise till double. Bake in a moderate oven (375°) for about 20 minutes. Let cool. Frost with Confectioners' Icing and garnish with cherries or cut gumdrops.

Easter breads that will surely delight everyone

Fun to make, but even more fun to eat. The whole family will want to help you shape these cute Hopping Bunnies. Serve atop bed of green shredded coconut, surrounded by candy eggs. For special dinner bread try our Easter Braid.

Easter Braid

1 package active dry yeast *or*
  1 cake compressed yeast
¼ cup water
• • •
1 cup milk, scalded
½ cup sugar
2 teaspoons salt
½ cup softened butter, margarine, or
  shortening
4½ to 5 cups sifted all-purpose flour
2 beaten eggs
2 teaspoons grated lemon peel
¼ teaspoon mace (optional)
1 cup dark or light raisins
• • •
Sugar Glaze

Soften active dry yeast in *warm* water or compressed yeast in *lukewarm* water. Combine milk, sugar, salt, and butter. Cool to lukewarm. Stir in about 2 *cups* of the flour; add eggs and mix well. Stir in softened yeast. Add lemon peel, mace, the raisins, and remaining flour to make a soft dough.

Turn out on a lightly floured surface and knead till smooth and elastic (about 8 to 10 minutes). Place in a lightly greased bowl, turning once to grease surface. Cover and let rise in a warm place until double (about 1½ hours). Punch down.

Divide and round the dough into 2 balls, one for each loaf. Cover and let rest for 10 minutes. For each loaf: Divide one of the balls in fourths. Shape 3 parts into strands 12 inches long, tapering the ends. Line up the strands 1 inch apart on a lightly greased baking sheet. Braid loosely without stretching the dough, beginning in the middle, and working toward either end. Seal ends well.

Divide remaining dough in thirds. Shape in strands 8 to 9 inches long, tapering the ends. Braid loosely and place atop the large braid, tucking ends of small braid into large one. Cover and let rise in a warm place till double. Bake in moderate oven (350°) about 25 to 30 minues. While warm, spread with Sugar Glaze. Makes 2 braided loaves.

Sugar Glaze

To 2 cups sifted confectioners' sugar, add ¼ cup hot water and 1 teaspoon butter or margarine; mix till well blended. Use as is to brush over warm Hopping Bunnies, or thin with a teaspoon or so more hot water to drizzle over warm Easter Braid.

Hopping Bunnies

1 package active dry yeast
¼ cup water
1 cup milk, scalded
⅓ cup sugar
½ cup shortening
1 teaspoon salt
5 to 5½ cups sifted all-purpose flour
2 beaten eggs
¼ cup orange juice
2 tablespoons grated orange peel
• • •
Sugar Glaze

Soften yeast in *warm* water. Combine next 4 ingredients. Cool till lukewarm. Stir in 2 *cups* flour; beat well. Add eggs; mix well. Stir in yeast. Add orange juice and peel and remainder of flour to make a soft dough. Turn out on a lightly floured surface and knead till smooth and elastic (about 5 to 10 minutes). Place dough in a lightly greased bowl, turning once to grease the surface. Cover and let rise till double (about 2 hours). Punch down. Cover; let rest 10 minutes. To shape: On lightly floured surface roll dough in rectangle ½-inch thick. Cut dough in strips about ½-inch wide and roll between hands to smooth. Shape in bunnies.

For curlicue bunnies: For each you'll need a 10-inch strip of dough for the body and a 5-inch strip for the head. On a lightly greased baking sheet, make a loose swirl of the strip for body. Swirl strip for head and place close to body (they'll "grow" together as dough rises). For ears, pinch off 1½-inch strips and roll between hands till smooth and cigar-shaped. Let point make tip of ear; snip off opposite end and place ear next to head. Pinch off a bit of dough and roll in ball for tail. Let the bunnies rise until almost double before baking.

For twist bunnies: For each, you'll need a 14-inch strip of dough. On lightly greased baking sheet, lap one end of strip over other to form a loop; now bring end that's underneath up over top end, letting one end extend to each side to make ears. Pat tips of ears to shape in point. Roll small ball of dough for tail; place atop dough at bottom of loop. Let bunnies almost double before you put them in the oven.

After shaping, cover; let rise till nearly double, 45 to 60 minutes. Bake in a moderate oven (375°) 12 to 15 minutes. Frost while warm with Sugar Glaze. Makes about 30.

Sugarplum Bread

A delicious fruit-filled holiday favorite. Try the variations—they're each a treat.

2 packages active dry yeast *or*
 2 cakes compressed yeast
⅓ cup water

• • •

1 cup milk, scalded
½ cup sugar
¼ cup shortening
1½ teaspoons salt

• • •

5 to 5¼ cups sifted all-purpose flour
2 beaten eggs
½ teaspoon vanilla
¼ teaspoon nutmeg
½ cup chopped mixed fruits and peels
1 cup seedless raisins

Soften active dry yeast in ⅓ cup *warm* water or compressed yeast in ⅓ cup *lukewarm* water. Combine scalded milk, sugar, shortening and salt. Cool to lukewarm. Stir in about 1½ *cups* of the flour. Beat vigorously. Add eggs; beat well. Stir in the softened yeast, vanilla, and nutmeg. Add the chopped fruits and peels, then enough remaining flour to make a soft dough. Turn dough out on a well-floured surface.

Knead till smooth and elastic, about 6 to 8 minutes. Place the dough in a lightly greased bowl, turning once to grease the surface. Cover and let rise in a warm place till double, about 2 hours. Punch down. Divide the dough in half. Cover the dough and let rest 10 minutes. Make half of dough into Baby Sugarplums; half into Little Sugarplum Loaves.

Baby Sugarplums: Divide half of the dough in sixths. Shape each piece into 6 balls. Place in greased muffin pans. Cover and let rise in a warm place till almost double, 45 minutes to an hour. Bake in a moderate oven (350°) for about 20 minutes or till done. To match picture: Drizzle the top of each with Confectioners' Icing and trim each with a perfect walnut half.

A gift that is sure to please

← Remember your friends at holiday time with a festive loaf of bread. Lucky are the carolers who are invited in for oven-warm Sugarplums made in a variety of shapes.

Little Sugarplum Loaves: Divide half of the dough in fourths. Shape each piece in a loaf. Place in four greased 4½x3x2-inch loaf pans. Cover and let rise in a warm place till almost double. Bake in moderate oven (350°) for 20 to 25 minutes or till done. To match picture: Drizzle the tops with Confectioners' Icing and trim each loaf with red and green candied cherries.

Sugarplum Ring

1 recipe Sugarplum Bread

• • •

⅔ cup sugar
1 teaspoon cinnamon
½ cup chopped California walnuts

• • •

⅓ cup melted butter or margarine

Prepare dough as directed for Sugarplum Bread. Let double (2 hours). Punch down; divide in half. Cover; let rest 10 minutes.

For Sugarplum Ring, pinch off balls of dough about 1¼ inches in diameter. Combine the sugar, cinnamon, and chopped walnuts. Dip tops of balls in melted butter or margarine, then in the sugar mixture. Place balls in layers in 2 greased 5½ cup ring molds. Cover and let rise till double. Bake in a moderate oven (350°) about 20 to 25 minutes. Cool slightly before removing from the pans. Serve warm. Makes 2.

Confectioners' Icing

Add sufficient milk or cream to 2 cups sifted confectioners' sugar to make of spreading consistency. Add 1 teaspoon vanilla and a dash of salt. Mix well.

Sugarplum Round Loaves

Prepare dough as directed for Sugarplum Bread substituting 1 teaspoon grated lemon peel for the vanilla and nutmeg. Cover and let rise in a warm place till almost double (about 2 hours). Punch down and divide dough in half. Cover and let rest 10 minutes.

Shape dough in 2 balls. Place balls on greased baking sheets and pat tops to flatten slightly. Cover and let rise again in a warm place till double (about 2 hours). Bake in a moderate oven (350°) for about 30 minutes. Makes 2 round loaves.

To match picture: Frost with Confectioners' Icing. Circle with red candied cherries and slivers of green candied cherries.

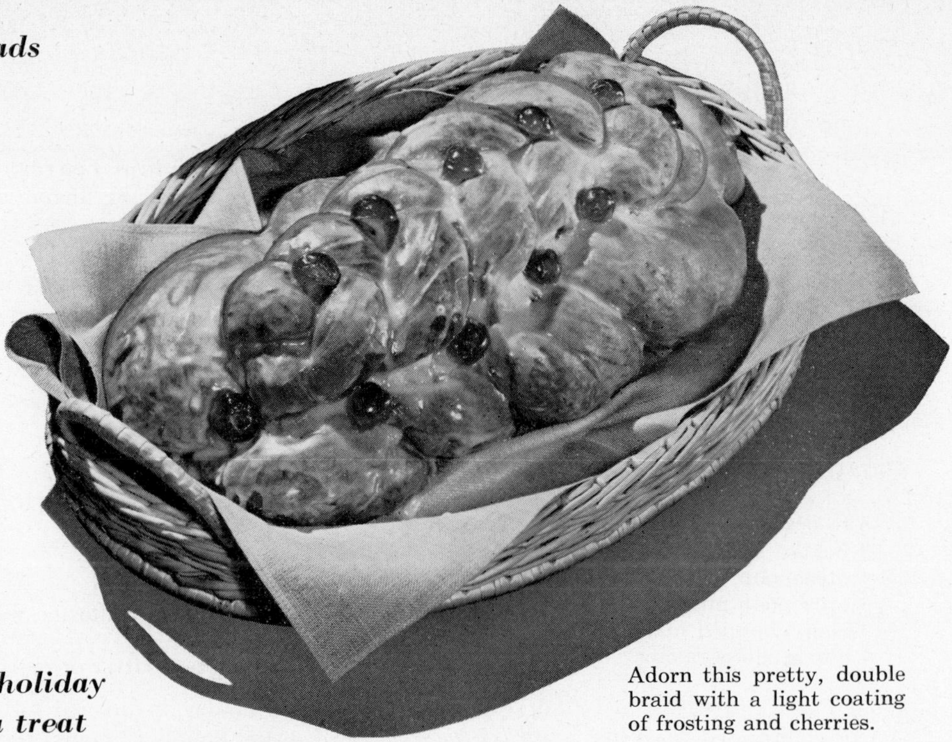

Happy-holiday Braid, a treat

Adorn this pretty, double braid with a light coating of frosting and cherries.

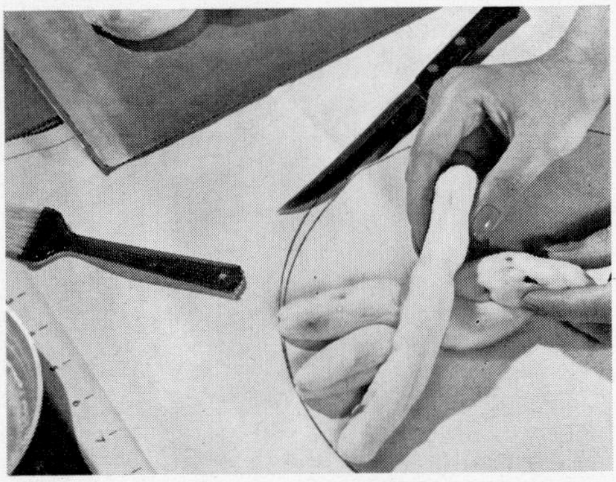

1 It's easy to get a professional look by shaping a loaf like this if you start to braid dough from the center and work toward both ends. Braid loosely without stretching.

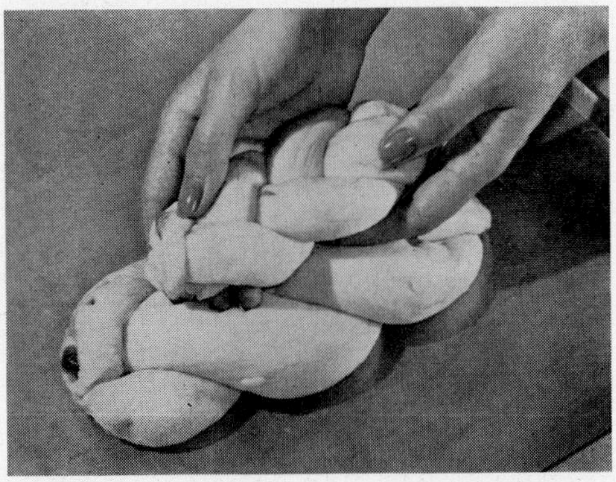

2 Seal the ends of each braid by pinching firmly. Place the small braid pickaback on big one, tucking ends of top braid into the braid below. Cover and let double. Bake.

Happy-holiday Braid

Loaf shaping takes a little of your time, but the results make it well worth the effort. Your reward: the prettiest loaf of all—

Prepare dough as directed in the Sugarplum Bread recipe (see preceding page). Cover and let rise in a warm place until almost double, about 2 hours. Punch down and divide the dough in half. Cover and let rest 10 minutes. Set aside one half.

Divide one half of dough in fourths. Shape three parts into strands 10 inches long. Line them up about 1 inch apart on a greased baking sheet. Braid loosely without stretching the dough, beginning in the middle and working toward either end. Seal ends well.

Divide the other fourth of the dough in three parts. Shape each part in strand 8 inches long. Braid loosely without stretching the dough, again beginning in the middle and working toward either end.

Place smaller braid atop the larger braid. Tuck the ends of the smaller braid into the large braid. Repeat the shaping with the remaining half of dough.

Cover dough and let rise in a warm place till almost double. Bake braid in moderate oven (350°) for about 25 to 30 minutes or until done. Makes 2 braids.

While braid is still slightly warm decorate with swirls of Confectioners' Icing. To match the picture above, trim the top with candied cherry halves.

Merry Christmas Wreath

1 package active dry yeast *or*
  1 cake compressed yeast
¼ cup water
1 cup milk, scalded
¼ cup sugar
¼ cup shortening
1 teaspoon salt
1 well-beaten egg
3½ cups sifted all-purpose flour

Soften active dry yeast in *warm* water or compressed yeast in *lukewarm* water. Combine milk, sugar, shortening and salt. Cool to lukewarm. Add softened yeast and egg. Gradually stir in flour to form a soft dough; beat vigorously. Cover; let rise in a warm place till double, about 2 hours.

Grease a 10-inch ring mold; spread bottom with *Sugar-Fruit Topping:* Melt 2 tablespoons butter or margarine; add 2 tablespoons light corn syrup and ½ cup brown sugar. Place halved candied cherries, cut side up, and almonds on sugar mixture. Shape dough in small balls; roll in melted butter; place 2 rows deep in pan. Let double. Bake in a hot oven (400°) 20 to 25 minutes. Loosen; turn out quickly. Serve warm.

Mince Coffee Circle

2 cups sifted all-purpose flour
¾ cup sugar
2½ teaspoons baking powder
½ teaspoon salt
⅓ cup shortening
1 slightly-beaten egg
½ cup milk
¾ cup moist mincemeat
• • •
Confectioners' Icing

Sift dry ingredients together. Cut in the shortening till the mixture resembles coarse oatmeal. Combine egg, milk, and mincemeat. Add to dry ingredients, mixing just until the flour is moistened. Spoon the mixture into a well-greased 9-inch ring mold, filling it ⅔ full. Bake in a moderate oven (375°) for 25 to 30 minutes.

Frost with *Confectioners' Icing* while warm but not hot: Combine 2 tablespoons butter with 1 cup sifted confectioners' sugar. Add just enough cream to make mixture of a spreading consistency. Add a dash salt. Mix thoroughly. Drizzle atop the warm coffee circle. If desired, trim top with candied red and green cherries and pecan halves.

Mince Coffee Circle

For those who favor the taste of mincemeat, this bread is top-notch! A quick and easy-to-make coffeecake with moist mincemeat flavor baked through. Great partner with hot coffee.

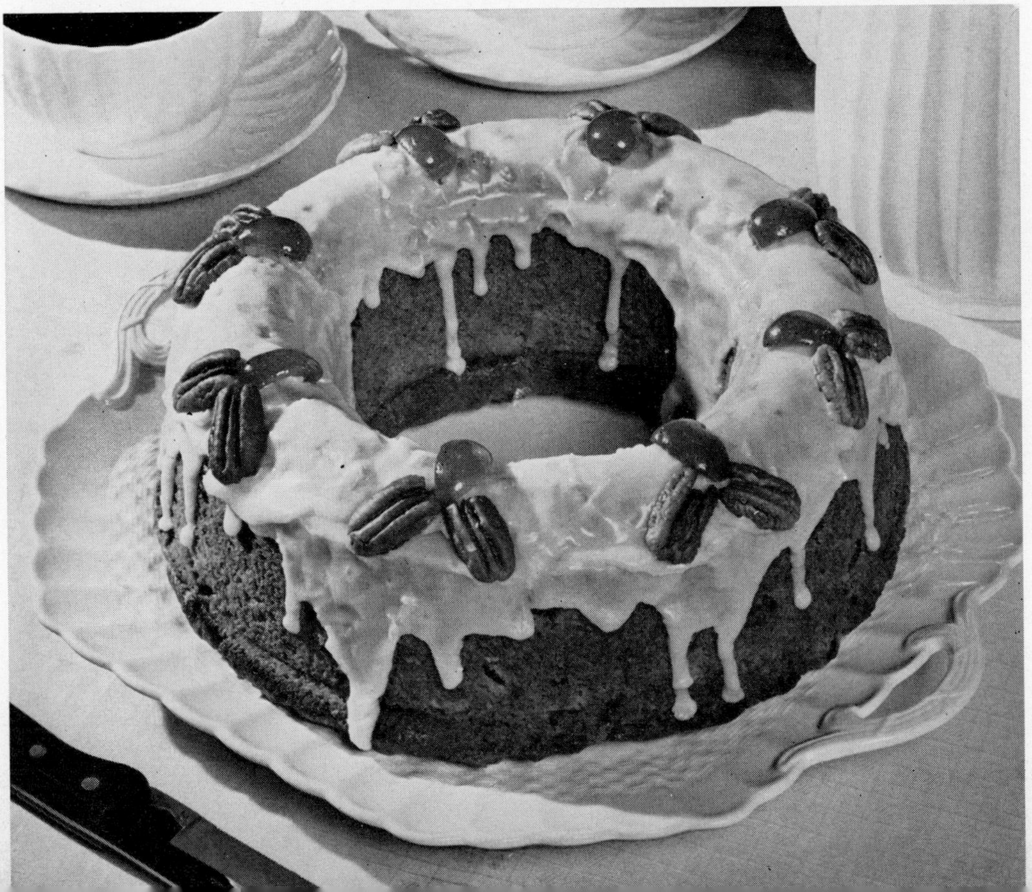

Sugar Tree, sweet 'n good

Cinnamon-roll Tree, pretty

Cherry Puff Tree, gay and snow-capped

Basic Sweet Dough

Start with this dough and bake a variety of Christmas breads—

2 packages active dry yeast *or*
 2 cakes compressed yeast
½ cup water

• • •

¾ cup milk, scalded
¼ cup shortening
½ cup sugar
2 teaspoons salt

• • •

4¾ cups sifted all-purpose flour
1 teaspoon grated lemon peel

• • •

2 well-beaten eggs

Soften active dry yeast in *warm* water (110°) or compressed yeast in *lukewarm* water (85°). Combine scalded milk, shortening, sugar, and salt. Cool to lukewarm. Stir in 2 *cups* flour and lemon peel; beat till smooth. Add softened yeast and well-beaten eggs; mix thoroughly. Add the remaining flour; mix to a soft dough.

Turn out and knead on a lightly floured surface until smooth and elastic, about 6 to 8 minutes. Place dough in a lightly greased bowl, turning once to grease surface. Cover and let rise in a warm place till double. Punch down. Shape as desired.

Tiny Christmas Trees and Wreaths

Make it a tradition at your house. Sweet little breads to hang on your tree, one for every member of the family—

Use ½ recipe of Basic Sweet Dough. Roll the dough with your hands into long, slim ropes ½ inch thick. Cut the ropes into ½ inch bits. Roll each into small balls and arrange on a greased baking sheet.

For trees: Cut a paper pattern of a triangle 3 inches high with a 4¼-inch base. Mark corners of the triangle on baking sheet. Line up the balls in rows 5-4-3-2-1; use 2 balls for the trunk of the tree.

For wreaths: Draw around a small glass and place the balls around the circle. Bake in a moderate oven (350°) for 20 minutes. Decorate each tiny bun, using confectioners' sugar frosting in a pastry tube. Top each bun with a red cinnamon candy if desired. Makes 5 trees and 4 wreaths.

Sugar Tree

Use ¼ recipe Basic Sweet Dough for each tree. Divide into 4 equal parts. Roll each part into a long strand, ½ inch thick. Brush with melted butter. On a piece of waxed paper, combine ⅓ cup sugar and 2 teaspoons grated orange peel. Spread evenly on paper and roll each strand in mixture.

Twist each strand; then pinch the four together to make one long strand. On a greased baking sheet, draw a triangular outline of a tree 8 inches tall and 6 inches at the base. Starting at tip of tree, swirl dough back and forth making a tree. Twist a small piece of dough to make a 2-inch trunk. Cover and let rise in a warm place until double. Bake at 350° for 25 minutes. If desired, decorate with bits of candied cherries.

Cinnamon-roll Tree

Use ¼ recipe Basic Sweet Dough for each tree. Roll on lightly floured surface to 13x5x½-inch rectangle. Brush with melted butter or margarine. Sprinkle with ⅓ cup sugar mixed with 1 teaspoon cinnamon. Roll as for jellyroll and cut into 17 ¾-inch slices. Arrange the slices, cut side down, on greased baking sheet in form of a tree—8 inches tall and 6 inches at base.

Place 1 slice for top; just below this, and overlapping slightly, place 2 slices; then a row of 3 slices; 4 slices, 5 slices. Use the 2 end pieces for the trunk. Cover and let rise in a warm place till double. Bake in a moderate oven (350°) for about 25 minutes. While still hot, brush lightly with butter and sprinkle with granulated sugar.

Toppings for your breads

For glazing: Mix 1 cup sifted confectioners' sugar, 2 tablespoons milk, and a drop of vanilla. Brush lightly over breads and arrange decorations before frosting dries.

For drizzling: Mix 1 cup sifted confectioners' sugar, 5 teaspoons milk or orange juice, and a drop of vanilla. Pour over bread in a thin stream from lip of small pitcher.

For decorating: Thoroughly cream 2 tablespoons butter or margarine. Gradually add 1 cup confectioners' sugar. Mix in 2 teaspoons milk and beat well. Add ½ teaspoon vanilla and a dash of salt. Mix well and put in pastry tube. Decorate breads.

Poinsettia Coffeecake

Use ½ recipe Basic Sweet Dough for each poinsettia. Roll ½ inch thick on lightly floured surface to form rectangle 16x12 inches. Brush with melted butter or margarine. Mix 3 tablespoons sugar and ½ cup of mixed candied fruits and peels *or* finely chopped candied cherries and sprinkle over dough. Roll as for jellyroll; seal edge.

With a sharp knife, snip off ends; cut roll *diagonally* in nine ½-inch pieces. Reserve the end pieces for the center of the poinsettia. Place slices, cut side down, on greased baking sheet. Arrange in a circle, pointed ends out, each slice overlapping slightly. Put end pieces in center. Cover and let rise in a warm place until double. Bake in moderate oven (350°) for 25 minutes or till done. When slightly cool, *glaze* with confectioners' sugar frosting and decorate center with grated orange peel.

Cherry Puff Trees

1 package active dry yeast
¼ cup warm water
1 cup milk, scalded
½ cup shortening
¼ cup sugar
1 teaspoon salt
3¾ cups sifted all-purpose flour
2 well-beaten eggs
1 cup chopped candied cherries

Soften yeast in warm water. Combine scalded milk, shortening, sugar, and salt. Cool to lukewarm. Stir in 2 *cups* of the flour; beat till smooth. Add eggs and yeast. Mix well. Beat in remaining flour to make a very thick batter. Beat 1½ minutes or till smooth. Cover; let rise till double, about 1 hour.

Add cherries; stir down. On greased baking sheets, mark 3 triangles, each 8 inches tall, and 6 inches wide, using rubber spatula. Drop batter by teaspoons within marked triangles—one spoonful at top, two for second row, and so on, ending with sixth row of six spoonfuls. Add two spoonfuls for "trunk." Let rise till double, about 1 hour.

Bake at 375° for 15 minutes or till lightly browned. When slightly cooled, brush with Orange Glaze. If desired, trim with clusters of halved candied cherries. Makes 3 trees.

Orange Glaze: Mix 1 cup sifted confectioners' sugar, 5 teaspoons orange juice, and ½ teaspoon vanilla. Beat smooth.

Quick Breads

Simple and speedy—delicious breads that go good anytime. Here are pancakes and waffles for dessert or breakfast; hot muffins for luncheon go-with; and tasty coffeecakes and nut loaves. They disappear quickly—better have plenty on hand.

A pretty table set for afternoon tea

← It's time for tea with a grand array of delectable breads to make it complete. We show sugar-topped Blueberry Tea Muffins that boast a gentle hint of orange; moist slices of Glazed Lemon Nut Bread; and golden wedge-shaped Tea Scones. For an extra-special touch serve butter in fancy ways—whipped, or in pretty balls, curls or roses. See index listing.

Biscuits and Muffins

Biscuit tips

Light, tender, and flaky—you just can't beat the melt-in-your-mouth goodness of biscuits. So easy to make, biscuits can be whipped together just before a meal and served hot from the oven.

To make praiseworthy biscuits every time, follow the standard mixing procedure: Sift together dry ingredients, then cut in the shortening with a pastry blender or blending fork till the mixture resembles coarse crumbs. (The yellow or brown flecks that appear on baked biscuits are caused by uneven distribution of leavening.)

Make a well in the dry ingredients; add the milk all at once. Stir quickly with a fork *only till dough follows fork around bowl.* Turn dough onto lightly floured surface. (Dough will be soft.) Knead gently 10 to 12 strokes (½ minute). This blends ingredients, assures tall, plump biscuits, and develops desired flakiness. Pat dough out lightly, or roll evenly to ½ inch.

Dip biscuit cutter in flour; then cut dough straight down (without twisting). Bake on ungreased baking sheet. For crusty biscuits, place ¾ inch apart on baking sheet without sides. For soft sides, place close together in shallow baking pan. For browner crust, brush with milk or light cream before baking. Cut biscuits may be stored in refrigerator 30 to 60 minutes before baking.

Biscuits Supreme

2 cups sifted all-purpose flour
4 teaspoons baking powder
½ teaspoon salt
½ teaspoon cream of tartar
2 teaspoons sugar
½ cup shortening
⅔ cup milk

Sift together first 5 ingredients; cut in shortening till mixture resembles coarse crumbs. Add milk all at once; stir only till dough follows fork around bowl. Turn out on lightly floured surface; knead gently ½ minute. Pat or roll ½ inch thick; cut with biscuit cutter. Bake on ungreased baking sheet at 450° for 10 to 12 minutes. Makes 16.

Biscuits Supreme Variations

For these fix-ups, follow recipe for Biscuits Supreme, inserting changes as noted—

Coffeetime Treats: Roll dough ¼ inch thick; spread with softened butter or margarine. Sprinkle with sugar and cinnamon, or brown sugar and chopped nuts. Roll as for jelly roll; cut in ½-inch slices. Bake.

Orange Quickies: Dip cube of loaf sugar into orange juice; then press into center of each biscuit before baking.

Jiffy Snacks: Roll dough ¼ inch thick; spread with softened butter or margarine. Sprinkle with grated cheese and chopped pimiento or crisp, crumbled bacon. Roll as for jelly roll; cut in ½-inch slices. Bake.

Savory Biscuits: Sift ½ teaspoon sage and ¼ teaspoon dry mustard with the dry ingredients. Stir in 1¼ teaspoons caraway seeds with the liquid ingredients. Knead, roll, and bake as for Biscuits Supreme.

Baking-powder Biscuits

2 cups sifted all-purpose flour
3 teaspoons baking powder
½ teaspoon salt
¼ cup shortening
⅔ to ¾ cup milk

Mix and bake biscuits according to picture directions on the opposite page. (For crusty biscuits, bake ¾ inches apart; for soft sides, bake close together.) Makes 16.

Drop Biscuits: Increase milk to 1 cup. Drop from teaspoon onto greased baking sheet. Bake as directed above.

Whole-wheat Biscuits: Substitute 1 cup whole-wheat or graham flour for 1 cup sifted all-purpose flour; mix with sifted dry ingredients. Increase salt to ¾ teaspoon.

Buttermilk Biscuits: Sift ¼ teaspoon soda with dry ingredients. Increase shortening to ⅓ cup; substitute buttermilk for the milk. Mix and bake as directed.

1 Cut shortening into dry mixture till like coarse crumbs. Make well; add milk. Stir quickly just till dough follows fork around bowl.

2 Turn onto lightly floured surface. (Dough will be soft.) Knead gently with heel of hand 10 or 12 strokes. Roll or pat ½ inch thick.

3 Dip biscuit cutter in flour; cut dough straight down—no twisting. Bake on ungreased baking sheet at 450° 12 to 15 minutes.

Tea Scones

2 cups sifted all-purpose flour
2 tablespoons sugar
3 teaspoons baking powder
½ teaspoon salt
6 tablespoons butter
1 slightly-beaten egg
½ cup milk

Sift together dry ingredients. Cut in butter till mixture resembles coarse crumbs. Add egg and milk, stirring only till dough follows fork around bowl. Turn out on floured surface; knead gently about 15 times. Cut the dough in half. Shape each half into a ball and pat or roll a round about ½ inch thick and 6 inches in diameter; cut into 8 wedges like a pie.* Place the wedges on an ungreased baking sheet without allowing the sides to touch. Brush with slightly beaten egg. Bake at 425° about 12 to 15 minutes or to deep golden brown. Makes 16.

*Or cut circle into 6 wedges. Makes 12.

Oatmeal Drop Biscuits

Sift together 1 cup sifted all-purpose flour, 3 teaspoons baking powder, ¾ teaspoon salt; cut in ¼ cup shortening till mixture resembles coarse crumbs. Stir in 1 cup quick cooking oatmeal. Combine 1 beaten egg, 2 tablespoons honey, ½ cup milk; add all at once to dry mixture, stirring just to moisten. Drop by heaping teaspoonfuls on baking sheet. Bake at 425° 10 minutes. Makes 12.

Pecan Tea Biscuits

1¾ cups sifted all-purpose flour
3 tablespoons sugar
2 teaspoons baking powder
½ teaspoon salt
¼ cup shortening
1 beaten egg
¾ cup milk
½ cup chopped pecans
2 tablespoons sugar
½ teaspoon cinnamon

Sift first 4 ingredients together; cut in shortening till mixture resembles coarse crumbs. Combine egg and milk; add all at once to dry mixture, stirring just to moisten. Stir in pecans. Drop by heaping teaspoonfuls on greased baking sheet. Combine 2 tablespoons sugar and cinnamon; sprinkle over. Bake at 425° about 10 minutes. Makes 36.

Dixie Corn-meal Biscuits

1½ cups sifted all-purpose flour
1 tablespoon sugar
2 teaspoons baking powder
¾ teaspoon salt
½ teaspoon soda
• • •
½ cup corn meal
¼ cup shortening
1 slightly-beaten egg
¾ cup dairy sour cream
1 tablespoon sesame seed
2 tablespoons butter or margarine

Sift together first 5 ingredients; stir in corn meal. Cut in shortening till mixture resembles coarse crumbs. Add egg and sour cream; mix just till dough follows fork around bowl. Turn out on lightly floured surface; knead gently ½ minute. Roll or pat to about ¼ inch and cut with floured 2½-inch biscuit cutter. Crease just off center with back of knife; fold over so top overlaps. Seal edges. In skillet, lightly brown sesame seed in butter; brush over biscuits.

Bake on ungreased baking sheet at 425° for 10 minutes or till done. Makes about 24.

Cheese-bottom Biscuits

1 5-ounce jar cheese spread with bacon
⅓ cup soft butter or margarine
2 cups packaged biscuit mix

Mix cheese spread and butter; spread evenly over bottoms of two 8x1½-inch round pans or one 13x9x2-inch pan. Prepare biscuit mix according to package directions for rolled biscuits, using a tiny 1-inch cutter. Place biscuits on cheese. Bake at 400° for 15 to 20 minutes. Serve hot. Makes 5 dozen.

Tomato-Cheese Biscuits

2 cups packaged biscuit mix
¾ cup shredded sharp process American cheese
⅔ cup tomato juice
Melted butter or margarine
Celery seed

Combine biscuit mix and cheese. Add juice all at once; mix and knead according to package directions. Roll a little less than ½ inch thick. Cut with a 1¾-inch biscuit cutter. Place on ungreased baking sheet. Brush with butter; sprinkle with celery seed. Bake at 450° for 10 to 15 minutes. Makes 30.

Onion Biscuits

Delicious. Onion is added to the biscuit batter —delectable flavor bakes in—

¼ cup finely chopped onion
1 tablespoon shortening
• • •
1½ cups sifted all-purpose flour
1½ teaspoons baking powder
½ teaspoon salt
½ teaspoon celery seed
¼ cup shortening
1 slightly-beaten egg
⅓ cup milk

Cook onion in 1 tablespoon shortening till tender but not brown. Sift together the sifted flour, baking powder, and salt; stir in celery seed. Cut in shortening till mixture resembles coarse crumbs. Add onion, egg, and milk all at once and stir just till dough follows fork around bowl.

Turn out on lightly floured surface and knead gently ½ minute. Pat or roll ½ inch thick. Cut with floured 1¾ inch cutter. Bake on ungreased baking sheet in hot oven (425°) 12 minutes or till done. Makes 12.

Cinnamon-petal Biscuits

2 cups sifted all-purpose flour
3 tablespoons sugar
4 teaspoons baking powder
½ teaspoon cream of tartar
½ teaspoon salt
• • •
½ cup shortening
⅔ cup milk
2 tablespoons butter or margarine, melted
⅓ cup sugar
2 teaspoons cinnamon

Sift together dry ingredients; cut in shortening till mixture resembles coarse crumbs. Add milk all at once; stir only till dough follows fork around bowl. Turn out on lightly floured surface; knead gently ½ minute.

Roll to 16x12-inch rectangle, ¼ inch thick; brush with butter. Combine ⅓ cup sugar and cinnamon; sprinkle over surface. Cut in eight 12x2-inch strips. Make two stacks of 4 strips each. Cut each stack in six 2-inch squares.

Grease muffin pans or line with paper bake cups. Pressing layers together slightly, place each square, cut side down, in pans. Bake in hot oven (425°) 10 to 12 minutes or till done. Makes 1 dozen biscuits.

Muffin Magic

So easy to make and fun to serve—muffins can be dainty or jumbo size, plain or dressed up. Best served warm with lots of butter.

The secret for making light tender muffins is to stir only a few strokes—the batter *should* look lumpy. If the batter is overbeaten, the muffins will have dull crusts with peaks on top, and they will be coarse, tough, and full of tunnels. *Perfect* muffins are light and tender, have a moist crumb, straight sides and a slightly rounded top with a rough, shiny, golden brown crust.

"Standard" and "biscuit" methods are the most common muffin methods used.

"Standard" method: Sift dry ingredients into bowl; make well in the center. Combine egg, milk, and salad oil or melted shortening. (Cool melted shortening slightly.) Add to dry ingredients all at once. Stir quickly *only till dry ingredients are moistened.*

"Biscuit" method: Cut solid shortening into sifted dry ingredients (as for biscuits) till pieces are the size of small peas. Beat egg till thick and foamy; stir in milk and add to flour mixture.

To avoid overstirring, use spoon to push flour lightly from edge of bowl toward center, turning bowl slowly. Go once around the bowl; then chop straight through mixture several times with spoon to combine ingredients further (without stirring). Stir *just enough to dampen all the flour.*

When muffins have to wait after baking, tip them to one side in the pan to prevent steaming crusts; keep warm.

To reheat muffins, wrap in foil and heat in hot oven (400°) for 15 to 20 minutes.

Best-ever Muffins

- 1¾ cups sifted all-purpose flour
- 2 tablespoons sugar
- 2½ teaspoons baking powder
- ¾ teaspoon salt
- 1 well-beaten egg
- ¾ cup milk
- ⅓ cup salad oil or melted shortening

Sift together dry ingredients; make well in center.* Combine egg, milk, and salad oil. Add all at once to dry mixture. Stir quickly only till dry ingredients are moistened. Fill greased muffin pans or paper bake cups ⅔ full. Bake at 400° 25 minutes. Makes 12.

*Or, use "biscuit" method described above.

Best-ever Muffin Variations

Easy ways to dress up Best-ever Muffins—

Blueberry Muffins: Prepare batter, using only ½ cup milk. To 1 cup fresh or *well-drained* frozen blueberries, add 2 tablespoons sugar; toss lightly. Stir gently into batter.

Raisin, Nut, or Date Muffins: Add ½ to ¾ cup seedless raisins, broken nuts, or coarsely cut dates to batter; stir in quickly.

Cranberry-cube Muffins: Prepare batter; fill muffin pans ⅓ full. Cut 1 cup canned jellied cranberry sauce in ½-inch cubes; sprinkle over batter. Spoon in remaining batter.

Jelly Muffins: Top batter in each muffin pan with 1 teaspoon tart jelly before baking.

Cheese-Caraway Muffins: Prepare batter using "biscuit" method. Add 1 cup shredded sharp process cheese and ½ teaspoon caraway seed to flour-shortening mixture.

Sour-milk Muffins: Substitute ¾ cup sour milk or buttermilk for sweet milk. Add ¼ teaspoon soda and reduce baking powder to 1 teaspoon. Sift soda with dry ingredients.

Sugar-crusted Muffins: Bake Best-ever Muffins. While hot, dip tops in ½ cup melted butter; shake in a mixture of ½ cup sugar and 1 teaspoon cinnamon. Serve warm.

Bran Muffins

- 2 tablespoons shortening
- 3 tablespoons sugar
- 1 egg
- ¾ cup milk
- 1 cup bran flakes
- 1 cup sifted all-purpose flour
- 2 teaspoons baking powder
- ½ teaspoon salt

Cream shortening and sugar; add egg and beat well. Stir in milk, then bran flakes. Sift together flour, baking powder, and salt. Stir dry ingredients into bran mixture just till moistened. Fill greased muffin pans ⅔ full. Bake in hot oven (425°) about 20 minutes. Makes 1 dozen muffins.

Tiny Bran Muffins: Bake in greased 2-inch muffin pans in hot oven (425°) for about 12 minutes. Makes 14 tiny muffins.

Muffins as truly good as these rate a revival—try old-fashioned Graham Gems that date back to the days of the player piano and Model-T.

Graham Gems

½ cup sifted all-purpose flour
¼ cup sugar
1 teaspoon salt
4 teaspoons baking powder

• • •

1 cup stirred whole-wheat flour

• • •

1 well-beaten egg
1 cup milk
3 tablespoons butter or margarine, melted

Sift together all-purpose flour, sugar, salt, and baking powder; stir in whole-wheat flour. Combine egg, milk, and butter.

Make a well in dry ingredients and add liquid ingredients all at once. Stir just till flour mixture is moistened. Fill greased muffin pans ⅔ full. Bake in hot oven (425°) for about 15 to 18 minutes or till done. Makes about 10 muffins.

Banana Muffins

These boast two extra-good flavors in one—banana plus bran. They're delicious—just try a batch and see for yourself—

1 cup sifted all-purpose flour
3 tablespoons sugar
2½ teaspoons baking powder
½ teaspoon salt

• • •

1 cup whole bran

• • •

1 beaten egg
1 cup mashed *ripe* banana
¼ cup milk
2 tablespoons salad oil or melted shortening

Sift together flour, sugar, baking powder, and salt. Stir in bran. Combine egg, banana, milk, and salad oil *or* melted shortening.

Add liquid ingredients all at once to dry ingredients, stirring just till flour mixture is moistened. Fill well-greased muffin pans ⅔ full. Bake muffins in hot oven (400°) for about 20 to 25 minutes or till done. Makes about 1 dozen muffins.

Redcap Muffins

Paprika tops give tender, cheesey little breads a gay look. You'll be proud to serve party-pretty muffins like these—

2 cups sifted all-purpose flour
3 teaspoons baking powder
½ teaspoon salt

• • •

¼ cup shortening
1 cup shredded sharp process American cheese
1 teaspoon caraway seed

• • •

1 beaten egg
1 cup milk
Paprika

Sift together sifted flour, baking powder, and salt; cut in shortening till the mixture resembles coarse crumbs. Stir in shredded process cheese and caraway seed. Combine beaten egg and milk.

Add liquid ingredients all at once to dry ingredients. Stir just till flour mixture is moistened. Drop batter from tablespoon into greased muffin pans, filling ⅔ full. Sprinkle paprika over tops. Bake in hot oven (400°) for about 25 minutes or till done. Makes about 1 dozen muffins.

Bacon Cornettes

Double good—corn meal plus bacon bits. Grand partner for breakfast eggs, chef's salad or a cheese casserole—

10 to 12 slices bacon, diced

• • •

1 cup sifted all-purpose flour
¼ cup sugar
4 teaspoons baking powder
¾ teaspoon salt

• • •

1 cup yellow corn meal
2 eggs
1 cup milk
¼ cup salad oil or
soft shortening

Cook bacon till crisp; drain. Sift together flour, sugar, baking powder, and salt; stir in corn meal. Add eggs, milk, and salad oil. With rotary or electric beater, beat till just smooth, about 1 minute (do not overbeat). Stir in cooked bacon.

Fill greased muffin pans or baking cups ⅔ full. If desired, top with a few bits of uncooked bacon. Bake in hot oven (425°) 20 to 25 minutes. Makes about 1 dozen.

Orange-blossom Muffins

These tender muffins get delicate flavor and tempting fragrance from the marmalade—

1 slightly-beaten egg
¼ cup sugar
½ cup orange juice
2 tablespoons salad oil or
melted shortening
2 cups packaged biscuit mix

• • •

½ cup orange marmalade
½ cup chopped pecans

• • •

Spicy Topping

Combine egg, sugar, orange juice, and salad oil. Add the biscuit mix and beat mixture vigorously for 30 seconds. Stir in orange marmalade and chopped pecans.

Grease muffin pans or line with paper bake cups; fill ⅔ full. Sprinkle with Spicy Topping. Bake muffins in hot oven (400°) for about 20 to 25 minutes or till done. Makes 1 dozen muffins.

Spicy Topping: Combine ¼ cup sugar, 1½ tablespoons all-purpose flour, ½ teaspoon cinnamon, and ¼ teaspoon nutmeg; cut in 1 tablespoon butter till crumbly.

Miniature Pumpkin Muffins

Try these delicious dainties teamed with salad lunch or morning coffee—

1½ cups sifted all-purpose flour
2 teaspoons baking powder
¾ teaspoon salt
½ cup sugar
½ teaspoon cinnamon
½ teaspoon nutmeg

• • •

¼ cup shortening
1 beaten egg
½ cup cooked or canned pumpkin
½ cup milk
½ cup seedless raisins

• • •

Sugar

Sift together flour, baking powder, salt, sugar, cinnamon and nutmeg. Cut in shortening until quite fine. Combine egg, pumpkin, and milk; add to flour mixture and mix just until dry ingredients are moistened. Add the seedless raisins.

Fill 1¾-inch or 2½-inch greased muffin pans ⅔ full. Sprinkle sugar over each muffin. Bake in hot oven (400°) 15 to 20 minutes for small size, and about 25 minutes for medium. Serve hot. Makes about 4 dozen small or 1 dozen medium muffins.

Ginger Muffins

½ cup shortening
½ cup sugar
1 egg
1 cup molasses

• • •

3 cups sifted all-purpose flour
1½ teaspoons soda
½ teaspoon salt
1 teaspoon cinnamon
1 teaspoon ginger
½ teaspoon cloves

• • •

1 cup hot water

Cream together shortening and sugar. Beat in the egg, then the molasses. Sift together flour, soda, salt and spices; stir into molasses mixture. Gradually add hot water, beating till smooth. Line muffin pans with paper bake cups; fill ⅔ full. Bake in moderate oven (375°) for about 20 to 25 minutes or till done. Makes 2 dozen.

Note: Leftover muffins will taste fresh-baked if you wrap them in foil and heat in hot oven (400°) for 15 minutes.

Double-apple Fantans

2 cups sifted all-purpose flour
¼ cup sugar
3 teaspoons baking powder
¾ teaspoon salt
½ cup finely chopped pared
tart apple
• • •
1 beaten egg
¾ cup milk
¼ cup salad oil
• • •
3 tablespoons sugar
1 teaspoon cinnamon
½ teaspoon nutmeg
1 cup thinly sliced pared tart apple

Sift flour, ¼ cup sugar, baking powder, and salt; stir in ½ cup finely chopped apple.

Combine beaten egg, milk, and salad oil; add all at once to flour mixture, stirring just till dry ingredients are moistened. Fill greased muffin pans ⅔ full.

Mix 3 tablespoons sugar, cinnamon, and nutmeg. Coat 1 cup thinly sliced apple. Press apple slices into top of batter to make stripes. Bake in hot oven (400°) for 20 to 25 minutes. Makes 12 muffins.

Coffeecake Muffins

Delicate little muffins layered with crunchy-sweet, spiced nuts. They're company-good served with a cup of fresh-brewed coffee—

1½ cups sifted all-purpose flour
½ cup sugar
2 teaspoons baking powder
½ teaspoon salt
• • •
¼ cup shortening
1 beaten egg
½ cup milk
• • •
Spicy Nuts

Sift together dry ingredients; cut in shortening till mixture resembles coarse crumbs. Blend egg and milk; add all at once to flour mixture; stir just till dry ingredients are moistened. Alternate layers of batter and Spicy Nuts in greased muffin pans, (ending with layer of batter), filling ⅔ full.

Bake in moderate oven (375°) for about 20 minutes. Makes 12 muffins.

Spicy Nuts: Combine ½ cup brown sugar, ½ cup chopped walnuts or pecans, 2 tablespoons flour, 2 teaspoons cinnamon, and 2 tablespoons melted butter

Apricot Bran Muffins

⅔ cup finely cut dried apricots
2 tablespoons sugar
• • •
1 cup sifted all-purpose flour
⅓ cup sugar
2½ teaspoons baking powder
¾ teaspoon salt
• • •
1 cup whole bran
¾ cup milk
1 beaten egg
¼ cup salad oil

Pour boiling water over apriocts to cover; let stand 10 minutes. Drain well; mix with 2 tablespoons sugar. Sift together dry ingredients. Mix bran, milk, egg, and oil; add to flour mixture, stirring just till moistened. Gently stir in apricots. Fill greased muffin pans ⅔ full. Sprinkle tops with additional sugar. Bake in hot oven (400°) about 25 minutes or till done. Makes 1 dozen.

Orange Raisin Muffins

Sift together 1¾ cups sifted all-purpose flour, 2½ teaspoons baking powder, ¾ teaspoon salt and ¼ cup sugar.

Combine 1 beaten egg, 1 teaspoon grated orange peel, ¼ cup orange juice, ½ cup milk, and ⅓ cup salad oil; add to dry mixture, stirring just till moistened. Fold in ¾ cup raisins. Fill greased muffin pans ⅔ full. Bake in hot oven (400°) for 20 to 25 minutes. Serve warm. Makes 10.

Peanut Butter Muffins

2 cups sifted all-purpose flour
½ cup sugar
2½ teaspoons baking powder
½ teaspoon salt
½ cup crunch-style peanut butter
2 tablespoons butter
¾ cup milk
2 well-beaten eggs
¼ cup currant jelly, melted
• • •
½ cup finely chopped peanuts

Sift together dry ingredients; cut in peanut butter and butter till mixture resembles coarse crumbs. Add milk and eggs all at once, stirring just till moistened.

Fill 2-inch, greased muffin pans ⅔ full. Bake at 400° for 15 to 17 minutes. Immediately brush tops with melted jelly; dip in peanuts. Serve hot. Makes 22 muffins.

Try Cranberry Muffins

Easy and delicious. Packaged biscuit mix is the time-saver, and pretty cranberry polka-dots add tartness to these tender, tempting muffins. Just the thing to dress up brunch or lunch.

Sesame-Cheese Muffins

1½ cups packaged biscuit mix
¾ cup grated sharp process American cheese

• • •

½ cup chopped onion
1 tablespoon fat
1 beaten egg
½ cup milk

• • •

1 tablespoon toasted sesame seed

Mix together biscuit mix and ½ cup of cheese. Cook onion in fat till tender, but not brown. Combine egg, milk, and onion; add all at once to biscuit-cheese mixture and beat vigorously for 30 seconds. Fill well-greased 2-inch muffin pans ⅔ full. Sprinkle tops with remaining cheese and sesame seed.

Bake muffins in hot oven (400°) for 12 to 15 minutes or till done. Serve warm. Makes about 16 muffins.

Polka-dot Muffins

Cranberry polka-dots add special tart-sweet flavor to these quick goodies—

1 cup fresh cranberries, chopped
½ cup sugar
1 teaspoon grated orange peel

• • •

1 beaten egg
¼ cup sugar
½ cup orange juice
2 tablespoons salad oil

• • •

2 cups packaged biscuit mix

Mix cranberries, ½ cup sugar, and orange peel; set aside. Combine egg, ¼ cup sugar, orange juice, and salad oil; add all at once to biscuit mix; stir just till moistened. Fold in cranberries. Fill greased muffin pans ⅔ full. Bake in hot oven (400°) 25 minutes or till done. Makes 1 dozen muffins.

Oatmeal Muffins

1 cup sifted all-purpose flour
¼ cup sugar
3 teaspoons baking powder
½ teaspoon salt
1 cup quick-cooking rolled oats
• • •
1 slightly-beaten egg
1 cup milk
3 tablespoons salad oil

Sift flour with sugar, baking powder, and salt. Add rolled oats. Combine egg, milk, and salad oil; add all at once to flour mixture, stirring just to moisten. Fill greased muffin pans ⅔ full. Bake in hot oven (425°) about 15 minutes. Makes 12 muffins.

Banana-Bran Muffins

1 cup sifted all-purpose flour
3 tablespoons sugar
2½ teaspoons baking powder
½ teaspoon salt
• • •
1 cup whole bran
1 beaten egg
1 cup mashed *ripe* banana
¼ cup milk
2 tablespoons salad oil

Sift together first 4 ingredients; stir in bran. Mix remaining ingredients; add all at once, stirring just to moisten. Fill well-greased muffin pans ⅔ full. Bake in hot oven (400°) for 20 to 25 minutes. Makes 12.

Date Muffins

Serve them hot for a melt-in-your mouth breakfast treat or a tasty salad go-with—

1¾ cups sifted all-purpose flour
2 tablespoons sugar
2½ teaspoons baking powder
¾ teaspoon salt
⅔ cup coarsely cut pitted dates
• • •
1 well-beaten egg
¾ cup milk
⅓ cup salad oil or melted shortening

Sift dry ingredients into bowl; stir in dates. Make well in center. Combine egg, milk, and salad oil; add all at once to dry ingredients. Stir quickly only till dry ingredients are moistened. Fill greased muffin pans ⅔ full. Bake in hot oven (400°) about 25 minutes. Makes about 1 dozen muffins.

Blueberry Tea Muffins

Sugar-topped, spicy, and filled with berries— see these picture-pretty muffins on page 76—

½ cup butter or margarine
1 cup sugar
2 eggs
• • •
1¾ cups sifted all-purpose flour
1 teaspoon baking powder
¾ teaspoon soda
¼ teaspoon salt
¼ teaspoon nutmeg
Dash cloves
¾ cup buttermilk
¾ cup drained blueberries
• • •
Melted butter
⅓ cup sugar
1 tablespoon grated orange peel

Cream butter and sugar together till light. Add eggs, one at a time, beating well after each addition. Sift together flour, soda, baking powder, nutmeg, cloves, and salt; add to creamed mixture alternately with buttermilk. Beat well. Fold in blueberries.

Fill paper-lined 2-inch muffin pans ⅔ full. Bake in moderate oven (375°) for 20 to 25 minutes, or till done.

Dip tops of muffins in melted butter and then in mixture of ⅓ cup sugar and grated orange peel. Makes 28 muffins.

Golden Corn Stix

No corn-stick pans? Bake them like muffins—

⅓ cup sifted all-purpose flour
1 tablespoon sugar
1 teaspoon baking powder
½ teaspoon soda
½ teaspoon salt
• • •
1⅓ cups yellow corn meal
• • •
1 beaten egg
1 cup sour cream
2 tablespoons salad oil, or
melted shortening

Sift flour, sugar, baking powder, soda, and salt; stir in corn meal. Combine egg, sour cream, and salad oil. Add to dry ingredients and stir till just blended.

Preheat corn-stick pans, then grease generously. Fill pans ⅔ full. Bake corn sticks in hot oven (400°) for about 25 minutes or till done. Makes 10 to 12 sticks.

High, light and puffy— Try them once and these golden brown Popovers will be on your list of favorites. They're crusty on the outside and so light they nearly fly. Serve them hot with lots of butter—delicious!

Popovers

2 eggs
1 cup milk
1 cup sifted all-purpose flour
½ teaspoon salt
1 tablespoon salad oil or
  melted shortening

Place eggs in bowl; add milk, flour, and salt. Beat 1½ minutes with electric or rotary beater. Add salad oil; beat ½ minute. (Do not overbeat.) Fill 6 to 8 *well-greased* custard cups ½ full. Bake at 475° 15 minutes. Reduce heat to 350°; bake 25 to 30 minutes longer, or till browned. A few minutes before removing from oven, prick each with a fork to let steam escape. If you like them dry inside, turn off oven; leave in 30 minutes, door ajar. Serve hot. Makes 6 to 8.

Surprise Popovers

Cut off just the tips of kernels of 2 ears fresh corn, then scrape cobs (reserving liquid), to make ⅓ cup cut corn; add enough milk to liquid to measure 1 cup. Place 2 eggs in bowl; add milk mixture, 1 cup sifted all-purpose flour, and ¾ teaspoon salt. Beat 1½ minutes with electric or rotary beater.

Add 1 tablespoon salad oil or melted shortening; beat ½ minute (don't overbeat). Stir in corn. Fill 6 to 8 well-greased custard cups ½ full. Bake at 475° for 15 minutes. Reduce heat to 350° and continue baking for 25 to 30 minutes, or till browned and firm. A few minutes before removing from oven, prick each popover with a fork to let steam escape. Turn off oven; leave in 15 minutes, door ajar. Makes 6 to 8 popovers.

Loaves and Coffeecakes

Nut Bread Notes

A crack down the center of a nut bread loaf is no mistake—it's typical.

When the bread comes from the oven, turn out of pan and cool on rack.

Most nut breads are better if stored at least a day—the flavors mellow, and the loaf slices more easily. Wrap the thoroughly cooled bread in aluminum foil or saran wrapping or place in an airtight container. Nut breads stay good several days.

The simplest of fillings make delicious nut-bread sandwiches: soft butter or margarine, softened cream cheese, jam or jelly.

Best Nut Loaf

3 cups sifted all-purpose flour
¾ cup sugar
3½ teaspoons baking powder
1½ teaspoons salt
1 beaten egg
1½ cups milk
2 tablespoons salad oil
¾ cup broken California walnuts

Sift dry ingredients together. Combine egg, milk, and salad oil; add to dry ingredients, mixing well. Stir in nuts. Bake in greased 9½x5x3-inch loaf pan at 350° for 1 hour or till done. Remove from pan; cool on rack.

Cranberry-Orange Bread

2 cups sifted all-purpose flour
¾ cup sugar
1½ teaspoons baking powder
1 teaspoon salt
½ teaspoon soda
1 cup coarsely cut cranberrries
½ cup chopped California walnuts
1 teaspoon grated orange peel
1 beaten egg
¾ cup orange juice
2 tablespoons salad oil

Sift dry ingredients together; stir in cranberries, nuts and peel. Combine egg, orange juice and salad oil; add to dry ingredients, stirring just till moistened. Bake in greased 9½x5x3-inch loaf pan at 350° for 50 minutes or till done. Remove from pan and cool.

Glazed Lemon-Nut Bread

¼ cup butter or margarine
¾ cup sugar
2 eggs
2 teaspoons grated lemon peel

• • •

2 cups sifted all-purpose flour
2½ teaspoons baking powder
1 teaspoon salt
¾ cup milk
½ cup chopped California walnuts
2 teaspoons lemon juice
2 tablespoons sugar

Cream together butter and ¾ cup sugar until light and fluffy. Add eggs and lemon peel; beat well. Sift together flour, baking powder, and salt; add to creamed mixture alternately with milk, beating till smooth after each addition. Stir in walnuts. Pour into greased 8½x4½x2½-inch loaf pan. Bake in moderate oven (350°) 50 to 55 minutes or till done. Let cool in pan 10 minutes, then spoon mixture of lemon juice and 2 tablespoons sugar over top. Remove from pan and cool.

Orange Date-Nut Loaf

1 8-ounce package pitted dates, cut up

• • •

2 tablespoons shortening
1 tablespoon shredded orange peel
½ cup fresh orange juice
1 beaten egg

• • •

2 cups sifted all-purpose flour
⅓ cup sugar
1 teaspoon baking powder
1 teaspoon soda
½ teaspoon salt
½ cup chopped walnuts

Pour ½ cup boiling water over dates and shortening; cool to room temperature. Add orange peel and juice; stir in egg. Sift together dry ingredients; add to mixture; stir just till mixed. Stir in nuts.

Grease and flour 8½x4½x2½-inch loaf pan; pour in batter. Bake at 325° for 55 to 60 minutes*. Cool 10 minutes, turn out of pan. For best flavor, store at least a day.

*Or bake in 4½x2¾x2-inch loaf pans at 325° for 40 to 45 minutes or till done.

Good eating any old time with our Best Nut Loaf

Here's that not-too-sweet basic nut bread that serves well in so many ways. Serve it on a snack tray with crisp apple wedges and nut-crusted balls of cream cheese. Another time toast thin slices in the broiler for a breakfast treat—or delight the children by tucking buttered slices in their lunch boxes.

Polka-dot Bread

You use brown sugar for this loaf. Then add plump raisins combined with the gentle hint of orange to give extra-special flavor—

1½ cups seedless raisins
1½ cups water

• • •

1 slightly-beaten egg
1 cup brown sugar
2 tablespoons salad oil or melted shortening
1 tablespoon grated orange peel
2½ cups sifted all-purpose flour
1 teaspoon salt
2 teaspoons baking powder
½ teaspoon soda

Combine raisins and water; bring to boiling. Cool mixture to room temperature.

Combine beaten egg, brown sugar, salad oil, and grated orange peel. Stir in raisin mixture. Sift together the sifted flour, salt, baking powder, and soda; add to raisin mixture, beating well. Pour batter into a greased 8½x4½x2½-inch loaf pan. Bake in a slow oven (325°) for about 60 minutes or till done. Remove from pan and cool on cake rack. Bread is best if stored one day.

Chocolate Date Nut Bread

It's almost like eating chocolate cake—

2 1-ounce squares unsweetened chocolate, melted, cooled

• • •

1 cup boiling water
1 cup chopped dates

• • •

¼ cup shortening
1 cup sugar
1 egg
1 teaspoon vanilla

• • •

2 cups sifted all-purpose flour
½ teaspoon salt
1 teaspoon soda
½ cup chopped California walnuts

Pour boiling water over dates; cool to lukewarm. Cream together the shortening, sugar, egg, and vanilla. Stir in cooled chocolate.

Sift together the sifted flour, salt, and soda; add alternately with dates to the creamed mixture, beating well after each addition. Stir in nuts. Place batter in greased 9x5x3-inch loaf pan. Bake in moderate oven (350°) for about 1 hour and 10 minutes. Cool 10 minutes. Remove from pan.

Honey-Date Bread

½ pound (1½ cups) dates, chopped
1 cup boiling water
2 tablespoons butter
½ cup sugar
½ cup honey
3 cups sifted all-purpose flour
3 teaspoons baking powder
½ teaspoon *each* salt and cinnamon
1 beaten egg
½ cup chopped California walnuts

Combine first 5 ingredients; let cool completely. Sift together dry ingredients. Add egg to cooled date mixture; then stir into dry ingredients. Stir in nuts. Bake in well-greased and floured 9½x5x3-inch loaf pan at 350° for 55 to 65 minutes. Cool.

Butter-Pecan Bread

2¼ cups sifted all-purpose flour
2 teaspoons baking powder
½ teaspoon *each* soda and salt
½ teaspoon cinnamon
¼ teaspoon nutmeg
1 cup brown sugar
1 cup chopped pecans
1 slightly-beaten egg
1 cup buttermilk
2 tablespoons butter, melted

Sift together first 6 ingredients; stir in sugar and nuts. Combine remaining ingredients; add to flour mixture, stirring just till moistened. Bake in a greased 9½x5x3-inch loaf pan at 350° for 45 minutes or till done. Cool slightly before removing from pan.

Pineapple-Date Bread

1 beaten egg
⅓ cup milk
⅓ cup melted shortening or salad oil
1 9-ounce can (1 cup) crushed pineapple
1 cup chopped California walnuts
1 cup chopped dates
3 cups sifted all-purpose flour
¾ cup sugar
3 teaspoons baking powder
¾ teaspoon salt
¼ teaspoon soda

Combine first 6 ingredients. Sift together dry ingredients; add to first mixture and stir just till moistened. Bake in greased 9½x5x3-inch loaf pan in moderate oven (350°) about 55 minutes or till done. Cool.

Marmalade Bread

Orange marmalade both flavors the loaf and makes the pretty glaze. Delicious!—

3 cups sifted all-purpose flour
3 teaspoons baking powder
1 teaspoon salt
¼ teaspoon soda

• • •

1 1-pound jar (1½ cups) orange marmalade
1 beaten egg
¾ cup orange juice
¼ cup salad oil or melted shortening

• • •

1 cup broken California walnuts

Sift together dry ingredients. Reserve ¼ cup of the marmalade. Combine remaining 1¼ cups marmalade, the egg, orange juice, and salad oil; add to flour mixture, stirring till moistened. Stir in nuts. Turn into greased 9½x5x3-inch loaf pan. Bake in moderate oven (350°) about 1 hour or till done. Remove bread from pan and place on baking sheet; spread top with reserved marmalade and return to oven about 1 minute or till glazed. Cool on rack.

Pumpkin-Nut Bread

As spicy and good as pumpkin pie—

1 cup brown sugar
⅓ cup shortening

• • •

2 eggs
1 cup canned pumpkin
¼ cup milk

• • •

2 cups sifted all-purpose flour
2 teaspoons baking powder
½ teaspoon salt
¼ teaspoon soda
½ teaspoon ginger
¼ teaspoon cloves

• • •

½ cup broken California walnuts

Cream together brown sugar and shortening till light and fluffy. Add eggs, one at a time, beating well after each addition. Stir in pumpkin and milk. Sift together dry ingredients; stir into pumpkin mixture. Beat 1 minute with electric or rotary beater. Turn into greased 9½x5x3-inch loaf pan. Bake in moderate oven (350°) about 55 minutes or till done. Remove from pan; cool. Slice and serve with butter or whipped cream cheese.

Midget Date Loaves Shredded sharp cheese bakes right in for a flavorful surprise. Walnuts add crunch. Bake bread in tiny pans for miniature loaves like these or bake it regular size—it tastes wonderful either way!

Midget Date Loaves

Bake petite loaves for dainty tea slices—

¾ cup boiling water
1 8-ounce package (1½ cups) pitted dates, cut up

• • •

1¾ cups sifted all-purpose flour
½ cup sugar
1 teaspoon soda
¼ teaspoon salt

• • •

1 beaten egg
¼ pound sharp process American cheese, shredded (1 cup)
¾ cup broken California walnuts

Pour boiling water over dates and let stand 5 minutes. Sift together the flour, sugar, soda, and salt; add dates, beaten egg, cheese, and walnuts, mixing well.

Turn batter into 4 greased 4½x2¾x2¼-inch loaf pans. *Bake in moderate oven (350°) for about 35 minutes or till done.

*Or, bake in greased 9½x5x3-inch loaf pan for about 55 to 60 minutes or till done.

Apple-Cherry Bread

6 tablespoons butter or margarine
⅔ cup sugar
2 eggs
1 teaspoon grated lemon peel

• • •

1 cup applesauce
2 tablespoons milk

• • •

2 cups sifted all-purpose flour
1 teaspoon baking powder
½ teaspoon soda
½ teaspoon salt
½ cup chopped California walnuts
¼ cup chopped maraschino cherries

Cream butter and sugar till fluffy. Add eggs, one at a time, beating after each addition. Add the grated lemon peel. Combine applesauce and milk.

Sift together flour, baking powder, soda, and salt; add alternately with applesauce mixture to creamed mixture. Stir in walnuts and cherries. Pour into a greased 8½x4½x2¾-inch loaf dish. Bake in moderate oven (350°) for about 55 minutes, or till done. Remove bread from pan. Cool thoroughly.

Whole-Wheat Nut Bread

1 cup sifted all-purpose flour
2 teaspoons baking powder
¼ teaspoon salt
½ teaspoon cinnamon
¼ teaspoon nutmeg
¼ teaspoon allspice
½ cup whole-wheat flour
¼ cup butter or margarine
¾ cup sugar
2 eggs
⅔ cup milk
½ teaspoon vanilla
½ cup chopped California walnuts

Sift together first 6 ingredients. Stir in whole-wheat flour. Cream together butter and sugar. Add eggs one at a time, beating well after each addition.

Add dry ingredients alternately with milk and vanilla to creamed mixture; beat smooth after each addition. Stir in nuts. Turn into greased 8½x4½x2½-inch loaf dish. Bake at 350° for 55 minutes or till done. Cool 10 minutes. Remove from pan.

Tropical Bread

⅓ cup shortening
⅔ cup sugar
2 eggs
1 cup mashed *ripe* bananas
¼ cup buttermilk
1¼ cups sifted all-purpose flour
1 teaspoon baking powder
½ teaspoon salt
½ teaspoon soda

• • •

1 cup whole bran
¾ cup chopped dried apricots
½ cup coarsely chopped walnuts

Cream shortening and sugar; add eggs and beat thoroughly. Combine bananas and buttermilk. Sift together next 4 ingredients; add alternately with banana mixture to creamed mixture. Stir in bran, apricots, and nuts. Pour into greased 9x5x3-inch loaf pan. Bake at 350° for 1 hour, or till done.

Try this combo on a hot day

← Team the grand flavor of tender, moist Whole-Wheat Nut Bread with delectable chunks of fresh fruit. Add tall glasses of iced tea for a cool summer lunch.

Kona Banana Bread

½ cup shortening
1 cup sugar
2 eggs
¾ cup mashed *ripe* banana

• • •

1¼ cups sifted cake flour
¾ teaspoon soda
½ teaspoon salt

Cream shortening and sugar until light. Add eggs, one at a time, beating well after each. Stir in banana. Sift together dry ingredients; add to banana mixture. Mix till well blended. Pour into a greased 9x9x2-inch pan. Bake in moderate oven (350°) 30 to 35 minutes. Cut in squares to serve.

Banana Nut Loaf

⅓ cup shortening
½ cup sugar
2 eggs

• • •

1¾ cups sifted all-purpose flour
2 teaspoons baking powder
½ teaspoon salt
¼ teaspoon soda
1 cup mashed *ripe* banana

• • •

½ cup broken California walnuts

Cream together shortening and sugar; add eggs and beat well. Sift together dry ingredients; add to creamed mixture alternately with banana, beating well after each addition. Stir in walnuts. Pour into a well-greased 8½x4½x2½-inch loaf pan. Bake in moderate oven (350°) about 1 hour or till done. Remove from pan; cool on rack.

Cranberry Honey Bread

½ cup honey
½ cup milk
1 beaten egg

• • •

3 cups biscuit mix
¼ teaspoon salt
1 cup cranberries, coarsely chopped
½ cup chopped nuts

Combine honey, milk, and egg. Add biscuit mix and salt; beat vigorously for 30 seconds. Fold in cranberries and nuts. Spoon into a greased, brown-paper-lined 9x5x3-inch loaf pan. Bake in moderate oven (350°) for about 55 minutes or till done. Cool.

Olive-Nut Bread

Olives add unique flavor note to this nut bread. Good with a Sunday night scrambled-egg supper or a casserole lunch—

2½ cups sifted all-purpose flour
⅓ cup sugar
4 teaspoons baking powder
½ teaspoon salt

• • •

1 beaten egg
1 cup milk

• • •

1 cup sliced stuffed green olives
1 cup broken California walnuts

Sift flour, sugar, baking powder, and salt together in mixing bowl. Combine egg and milk; add flour mixture, stirring just until dry ingredients are moistened. Stir in green olives and walnuts.

Turn batter into a greased 8x1½-inch round baking dish and bake in moderate oven (350°) for about 45 minutes or till done. Remove from pan and cool on rack.

Note: For holiday color, add 1 or 2 tablespoons chopped pimiento to batter.

Poppy-dot Cheese Bread

The choice is yours. Serve this quick and tasty cheese bread two ways—use pretty poppy seeds one time and flavorful caraway the next—

3¾ cups packaged biscuit mix
1¼ cups shredded sharp process American cheese
1 tablespoon poppy seed

• • •

1 beaten egg
1½ cups milk

Combine biscuit mix, cheese, and poppy seed. Add egg and milk; mix just to blend. Beat vigorously 1 minute.

Turn batter into well-greased 9½x5x3-inch loaf pan. Sprinkle top with additional poppy seed. Bake in moderate oven (350°) for about 50 to 60 minutes or until done. Remove bread from pan and cool.

Caraway Cheese Bread: Follow the directions above for Poppy-dot Cheese Bread, but substitute 1½ teaspoons caraway seed for the 1 tablespoon of poppy seed.

Sprinkle loaf with additional caraway seed instead of poppy seed. Bake.

Brown Bread

1 cup sifted all-purpose white flour
1 teaspoon baking powder
1 teaspoon soda
1 teaspoon salt
1 cup corn meal
1 cup stirred graham or whole-wheat flour
¾ cup dark molasses
2 cups buttermilk or sour milk
1 cup seedless raisins

Sift white flour with baking powder, soda, and salt; add corn meal and graham flour. Add remaining ingredients; beat well. Half-fill 5 greased 1-pound baking-powder cans;* cover tightly. Place on rack in deep kettle; pour in boiling water to 1 inch. Cover kettle; steam 3 hours, adding more boiling water if needed. Uncover cans; place in very hot oven (450°) 5 minutes; remove bread from cans. Serve hot.

*Or use 3 greased 1-pound coffee cans.

Perfect Corn Bread

1 cup sifted all-purpose flour
¼ cup sugar
4 teaspoons baking powder
¾ teaspoon salt
1 cup yellow corn meal
2 eggs
1 cup milk
¼ cup soft shortening

Sift first 4 ingredients together; stir in corn meal. Add eggs, milk, and shortening. Beat with rotary or electric beater till just smooth, about 1 minute. (Do not overbeat.) Pour into greased 9x9x2-inch pan. Bake at 425° for 20 to 25 minutes.

Hush Puppies

1½ cups white or yellow corn meal
½ teaspoon salt
¼ teaspoon soda
¼ cup chopped onion
¾ cup buttermilk
⅓ cup water

Combine dry ingredients and onion. Add buttermilk and water; stir just till corn-meal mixture is moistened. Drop rounded teaspoonfuls into deep, hot fat (375°).

Fry till golden brown, turning once, about 2 minutes. Drain on paper towels; serve at once. Makes about 40.

Southern Spoon Bread

Cook and stir 1 cup corn meal and 2 cups milk till consistency of mush. Remove from heat; add 1 teaspoon salt, 1 teaspoon baking powder, 2 tablespoons salad oil *or* melted shortening, and 1 cup milk. Stir in 3 well-beaten egg yolks; fold in 3 stiff-beaten egg whites. Bake in greased 2-quart baking dish at 325° for 1 hour or till done. Spoon into warm dishes; top with butter. Serves 6.

Bacon Spoon Bread

¾ cup corn meal
1½ cups cold water
2 cups shredded sharp Cheddar cheese
¼ cup soft butter or margarine
2 cloves garlic, crushed
½ teaspoon salt
1 cup milk
4 well-beaten egg yolks
½ pound sliced bacon, crisp-cooked, drained, and crumbled
4 stiff-beaten egg whites

Cook and stir corn meal and water till consistency of mush; remove from heat. Add next 4 ingredients; stir to melt cheese. Gradually add milk. Stir in egg yolks; add bacon. Fold in egg whites. Pour into greased 2-quart souffle dish or casserole. Bake at 325° for 65 minutes or till done. Spoon into warm dishes; top with butter. Serves 6.

Dixie Coffee Bread

1½ cups sifted all-purpose flour
¼ cup sugar
4 teaspoons baking powder
½ teaspoon salt
¾ cup corn meal
¾ cup milk
2 slightly-beaten eggs
½ cup melted shortening, cooled
Peanut Topper
½ cup coarsely chopped peanuts

Sift together first 4 ingredients; stir in corn meal. Add milk, eggs, and shortening, stirring just till blended. Pour into greased 9x9x2-inch pan. Bake at 400° for 15 minutes.

Spread Peanut Topper over baked bread; sprinkle with peanuts. Bake 5 minutes longer. Cut in squares. Serve warm.

Peanut Topper: Blend ½ cup *each* brown sugar and peanut butter. Gradually add ⅓ cup milk, beating till fluffy.

Dixie Coffee Bread—delicious peanut-butter topping and crunchy nuts bake atop tender corn bread. Makes a scrumptious after-school snack with milk for hungry scholars.

Banana Ambrosia Ring

Coconut Topper

• • •

2 cups packaged biscuit mix
3 tablespoons sugar
½ cup mashed ripe banana
1 slightly-beaten egg
3 tablespoons melted butter or margarine

• • •

2 tablespoons sugar
1 teaspoon cinnamon
2 tablespoons butter or margarine

Spread Coconut Topper over bottom of 5-cup ring mold. Combine biscuit mix and 3 tablespoons sugar. Stir in banana, egg, and melted butter. Beat vigorously 1 minute. Spoon *half* the batter over coconut in mold. Mix 2 tablespoons sugar with the cinnamon; sprinkle over batter; dot with butter. Cover with remaining batter. Bake in moderate oven (375°) 20 minutes or till done. Invert to unmold. Serve warm.

Coconut Topper: Mix ½ cup flaked coconut with ⅓ cup maple-flavored syrup and 2 tablespoons melted butter or margarine.

Blueberry Buckle

Here's old-fashioned goodness—delicious served warm with cream poured over—

½ cup shortening
½ cup sugar
1 well-beaten egg
2 cups sifted all-purpose flour
2½ teaspoons baking powder
¼ teaspoon salt
½ cup milk

• • •

2 cups fresh blueberries

• • •

½ cup sugar
½ cup sifted all-purpose flour
½ teaspoon cinnamon
¼ cup butter or margarine

Thoroughly cream shortening and ½ cup sugar; add egg and mix well. Sift 2 cups flour, baking powder, and salt; add to creamed mixture alternately with milk. Pour into a well-greased 11½x7½x1½-inch pan; sprinkle blueberries over batter.

Combine ½ cup sugar, ½ cup flour, cinnamon, and butter till crumbly; sprinkle mixture over blueberries.

Bake in moderate oven (350°) 45 to 50 minutes. Cut in squares and serve warm. Pass cream, if desired. Serves 8 to 10.

Honey-top Coffeecake

Triple-topping is honey, fruit and coconut—

1½ cups sifted all-purpose flour
½ cup sugar
2 teaspoons baking powder
¾ teaspoon salt
1 beaten egg
½ cup milk
3 tablespoons melted shortening

• • •

¼ cup butter or margarine
⅓ cup honey
1 9-ounce can (1 cup) crushed pineapple, drained, *or* ¼ cup chopped, cooked and drained dried apricots
¼ cup shredded coconut

Sift dry ingredients together. Combine egg, milk, and melted shortening; add to dry ingredients and mix till just smooth. Pour into greased 8x8x2-inch baking pan. Cream butter and honey. Spread fruit over batter; spoon honey mixture over. Sprinkle with coconut. Bake in hot oven (400°) for about 30 minutes or till done. Serve hot.

Brown Sugar Lemon Coffeecake

4 cups packaged biscuit mix
¼ cup brown sugar
1 teaspoon cinnamon
¼ teaspoon mace *or* nutmeg

• • •

1¼ cups milk
1 beaten egg
¼ cup melted butter

• • •

½ cup brown sugar
1 to 2 teaspoons grated lemon peel
¼ cup chopped California walnuts
2 tablespoons melted butter

Combine biscuit mix, ¼ cup brown sugar, and spices; mix well. Combine milk, egg and ¼ cup melted butter; add to dry ingredients; beat for 30 seconds. For topping, mix together the ½ cup brown sugar, lemon peel, and nuts.

Spread half the batter in the bottom of a greased 9x9-inch baking pan. Drizzle with 1 tablespoon of the melted butter and sprinkle half the topping mixture over. Repeat layers. Bake in moderate oven (350°) for about 35 minutes or till done. Serve warm.

Spicy Raisin Coffeecake

½ cup butter or margarine
1 cup sugar
2 eggs
1 teaspoon vanilla
1 cup dairy sour cream

• • •

2 cups sifted all-purpose flour
1½ teaspoons baking powder
1 teaspoon soda
¼ teaspoon salt

• • •

1 cup broken walnuts
½ cup sugar
1 teaspoon cinnamon
1½ cups seedless raisins, light or dark

Cream together butter and 1 cup sugar till fluffy. Add eggs and vanilla; beat well. Blend in sour cream. Sift together the sifted flour, baking powder, soda, and salt; stir into creamed mixture; mix well. Spread *half* the batter in greased 9x9x2-inch pan. Mix nuts, ½ cup sugar, and cinnamon; sprinkle *half* over batter. Sprinkle raisins over. Spoon on remaining batter; top with remaining nut mixture.

Bake in moderate oven (350°) about 40 minutes. Cut in squares. Serve warm.

Double-deck Orange Coffeecake

2½ cups packaged biscuit mix
3 tablespoons sugar
½ cup milk
1 egg
3 tablespoons melted shortening
   or salad oil

• • •

Orange Filling
Orange Glaze

Mix first 5 ingredients well with fork; beat 15 strokes. Turn out on surface well-dusted with biscuit mix; knead gently 8 to 10 times. Divide dough in 2 almost-equal parts. For lower layer, roll larger part to 8-inch circle; place the circle in greased 9-inch pie plate, patting dough up on sides. Sprinkle dough with Orange Filling.

Roll remaining dough to 7-inch circle; place atop filling. With scissors, snip 1-inch slashes around edge of top layer. Bake at 375° for 20 minutes or till done. Drizzle with Orange Glaze. Top with nuts. Serve hot.

Orange Filling: Mix ⅓ cup brown sugar, ⅓ cup chopped walnuts or almonds, toasted, 2 tablespoons flour, 1 tablespoon grated orange peel, dash salt, and 2 tablespoons melted butter or margarine.

Orange Glaze: Add 1 to 1½ tablespoons orange juice to 1 cup sifted confectioners' sugar. Mix glaze till smooth.

Cowboy Coffeecake

2½ cups sifted all-purpose flour
½ teaspoon salt
2 cups brown sugar
⅔ cup shortening

• • •

2 teaspoons baking powder
½ teaspoon soda
½ teaspoon cinnamon
½ teaspoon nutmeg
1 cup sour milk
2 well-beaten eggs

Combine flour, salt, sugar, and shortening; mix till crumbly. Reserve ½ cup mixture.

To remaining crumbs, add baking powder, soda, and spices; mix thoroughly. Add milk and eggs; mix well. Pour into 2 waxed-paper-lined 8x8x2-inch baking pans; sprinkle with reserved crumbs.

Chopped nuts and cinnamon may be sprinkled over crumbs. Bake in moderate oven (375°) 25 to 30 minutes. Serve warm.

Cocoa Ripple Ring

½ cup shortening
¾ cup sugar
2 eggs

• • •

1½ cups sifted all-purpose flour
¾ teaspoon salt
2 teaspoons baking powder
⅔ cup milk

• • •

⅓ cup instant cocoa (dry)*
⅓ cup broken California walnuts
3 tablespoons butter

Cream together shortening, sugar, and eggs till light and fluffy. Sift together sifted flour, salt, and baking powder; add to creamed mixture alternately with milk, beating well after each addition. Spoon ⅓ of the batter into a well-greased 6½-cup ring mold or 9x9x2-inch pan.

Mix instant cocoa and nuts; sprinkle *half* over batter in pan and dot with *half* the butter. Repeat layers, ending with batter. Bake in moderate oven (350°) 35 minutes or till done. Let stand 5 minutes; turn out of mold. Serve hot. Trim with walnut halves, if desired.

*Or use 2 tablespoons regular cocoa (dry) plus ¼ cup sugar with the nuts.

Spicy Marble Coffeecake

½ cup shortening
¾ cup sugar
1 egg
2 cups sifted all-purpose flour
2 teaspoons baking powder
½ teaspoon salt
¾ cup milk
2 tablespoons light molasses
1 teaspoon cinnamon
¼ teaspoon nutmeg
¼ teaspoon cloves
Spice-Nut Topping

Cream shortening and sugar. Add egg; beat well. Sift together flour, baking powder, and salt; add to creamed mixture alternately with milk, beating after each addition. Divide in 2 parts. To one part, add molasses and spices; mix. Spoon batters alternately into greased 9x9x2-inch pan; zigzag spatula through. Sprinkle with Spice-Nut Topping. Bake at 350° for 30 minutes. Serve warm.

Spice-Nut Topping: Mix ½ cup brown sugar, ½ cup chopped California walnuts, 2 tablespoons all-purpose flour, 1 teaspoon cinnamon, and 2 tablespoons melted butter.

Pancakes and Waffles

Perfect Pancakes

Delicate golden pancakes are a joy to serve, whether as a hearty breakfast, or a luncheon main dish, or a delicious dessert.

To make perfect pancakes every time, it's important *not* to overbeat the batter—stir quickly, only till dry ingredients are just moistened (batter will be lumpy).

Have the griddle at the right temperature. Check it with a griddle thermometer or sprinkle griddle with a few drops of water—they'll dance on the surface when the temperature is just right. For perfect heat control, use an electric skillet or griddle.

If the recipe contains 2 or more tablespoons shortening for each cup of liquid, you won't need to grease the griddle.

To make uniform-size pancakes, dip up batter with a ¼ cup measure—or use a tablespoon for dollar-size cakes.

Turn pancakes when top is bubbly and a few bubbles have broken. Flip once.

Favorite Pancakes

1¼ cups sifted all-purpose flour
3 teaspoons baking powder
1 tablespoon sugar
½ teaspoon salt

• • •

1 beaten egg
1 cup milk
2 tablespoons salad oil or melted shortening or bacon fat

Sift together flour, baking powder, sugar, and salt. Combine egg, milk, and salad oil; add to dry ingredients, stirring just till flour is moistened. (Batter will be lumpy.)

Bake on hot griddle. Makes about 12 dollar-size or eight 4-inch pancakes.

Buttermilk Pancakes: Substitute buttermilk or sour milk for sweet milk in above recipe. Add ½ teaspoon soda and reduce the baking powder to 2 teaspoons.

Feather Pancakes: Reduce the flour to 1 cup. Increase baking powder and sugar to 2 tablespoons each. Add the sifted dry ingredients to the liquid mixture; beat smooth. (For fat cakes, use ¾ cup milk.)

Buckwheat Griddle Cakes

3½ cups stirred buckwheat flour
1 cup sifted all-purpose flour
1 teaspoon salt
1 package active dry yeast
¼ cup warm water
1 teaspoon sugar
3¾ cups lukewarm water or milk

• • •

1 teaspoon salt
2 tablespoons brown sugar
¾ teaspoon soda
1 tablespoon salad oil or melted shortening

Combine flours and salt. Soften yeast in *warm* water. Dissolve sugar in the 3¾ cups lukewarm water or milk; add yeast mixture and stir into dry ingredients. Mix well.

Let stand overnight at room temperature. (Bowl must not be over ½ full.) In the morning, stir batter; add remaining ingredients. Bake on hot lightly greased griddle.

To store leftover batter: Fill glass or plastic container ½ full; store in refrigerator. It will keep several weeks.

To reuse: Add 1 cup lukewarm water for every cup of buckwheat flour you add to starter; stir till smooth; let stand overnight as before. When ready to bake, add 1 teaspoon salt, the brown sugar, soda, and salad oil or melted shortening.

Apple Pancakes

2 cups sifted all-purpose flour
2 tablespoons sugar
4 teaspoons baking powder
1 teaspoon salt

• • •

2 well-beaten egg yolks
2 cups milk
2 tablespoons butter, melted
1 cup finely chopped apple
2 stiff-beaten egg whites

Sift together dry ingredients. Combine egg yolks and milk. Pour into dry ingredients; stir well. Stir in butter and apple. Fold in egg whites. Let batter stand a few minutes.

Bake on hot griddle. Makes seven 8-inch cakes. Dot with butter, sprinkle with confectioners' sugar, roll up. Cut in servings.

Morning brightener— pancakes for breakfast A snap to fix—tender Favorite Pancakes bake atop griddle while bacon sizzles in the broiler. Added treat: Brown-sugar-and-cinnamon-topped grapefruit halves broiled till bubbly.

Easy Sourdough Flapjacks

Here's an updated version of an old-time Alaskan favorite. The modern "starter" is packaged biscuit mix and yeast. Bake big pancakes and pass lots of butter and warm, maple-flavored syrup—

1 package active dry yeast *or*
  1 cake compressed yeast
¼ cup water

• • •

1 egg
2 cups milk
2 cups packaged biscuit mix

Soften dry yeast in *warm* water or compressed yeast in *lukewarm* water. Beat egg; add milk and biscuit mix. Beat with rotary beater until blended. Stir in softened yeast.

Allow batter to stand at room temperature for 1 to 1½ hours. *Do not stir.*

Bake on a hot, lightly greased griddle or in a skillet. (For uniform pancakes, pour from a ¼-cup measure.) Turn pancakes when top side is bubbly and a few bubbles have broken. Flip only once. Makes about 2 dozen 4-inch pancakes.

Iowa Corn Pancakes

Come and get 'em! Old West flapjacks flavored with the gentle crunch of meal.

1½ cups sifted all-purpose flour
2 tablespoons sugar
1 teaspoon soda
1 teaspoon salt
½ cup yellow corn meal

• • •

2 slightly-beaten eggs
2 cups buttermilk
2 tablespoons butter or
  bacon fat, melted

Sift flour, sugar, soda, and salt into mixing bowl; stir in corn meal. Add eggs, buttermilk, and melted butter, stirring until flour is barely moistened. Drop batter from ¼ cup measure onto hot, lightly buttered griddle, or electric skillet heated to 375°. Turn pancake when the top side is bubbly and a few bubbles have broken. Flip only once. Makes about 1½ dozen 4-inch pancakes. Makes a hearty breakfast for would-be cowboys. Serve with butter and syrup, tart jelly, or honey.

Onion Pancakes

⅓ cup finely chopped onion
1 tablespoon salad oil

• • •

1¼ cups sifted all-purpose flour
3 teaspoons baking powder
1 tablespoon sugar
½ teaspoon salt

• • •

1 beaten egg
1 cup milk
1 tablespoon salad oil

Cook onion in 1 tablespoon salad oil till tender but not brown. Meanwhile, sift together dry ingredients. Combine remaining ingredients; add to dry mixture, stirring just till flour is moistened. (Batter will be lumpy.) Add onions to batter. Bake on hot griddle. Makes about eight 4-inch pancakes. Serve with creamed ham, or tuna.

Western Flapjacks

1 egg
1¼ cups buttermilk
1¼ cups sifted all-purpose flour
1 teaspoon sugar
1 teaspoon baking powder
½ teaspoon soda
½ teaspoon salt
1 tablespoon *soft* shortening

Break egg into mixing bowl. Add remaining ingredients.* With rotary beater, beat *just* till smooth. Bake on a hot, lightly greased griddle. Flip when few bubbles break on top and the underneath is brown.

Serve at once with warm maple syrup. Makes 12 four-inch flapjacks.

*For variation, add ½ cup canned or frozen blueberries (well drained), or a *thinly* sliced apple—good with melted butter and a dusting of cinnamon and sugar.

Oven Pancakes

To 3 slightly-beaten eggs, slowly add ½ cup flour, beating constantly. Stir in ¼ teaspoon salt, ½ cup milk, and 2 tablespoons butter, melted. Grease a 10-inch skillet (handle must be removable or heatproof); pour batter into the cold pan; bake in oven pre-heated to 450° for 18 minutes; reduce heat to 350°, bake 10 minutes longer. Serve pancakes with melted butter, powdered sugar, and a lemon wedge, if desired.

Swedish Dessert Pancakes

3 eggs
1¼ cups milk
¾ cup sifted all-purpose flour
1 tablespoon sugar
½ teaspoon salt

• • •

Lingonberry Sauce

Beat the eggs till thick and lemon-colored. Stir in milk. Sift together dry ingredients; add to egg mixture, mixing until smooth. Drop small amount of batter (1 tablespoon for 3-inch cakes) onto moderately hot, buttered griddle (or bake on special Swedish griddle). Spread batter evenly to make thin cakes. Turn when underside is delicately browned. (To keep first pancakes warm, place them on towel-covered baking sheet in very slow oven.) To serve; spoon melted butter over cakes; sprinkle with sugar. Pass Lingonberry Sauce. Makes 3½ dozen.

Lingonberry Sauce: Drain 4 cups lingonberries; wash and pick out leaves. Place in saucepan. Add ½ cup water; bring to boiling. Add 1 cup sugar; stir to dissolve. Simmer 10 minutes. Remove from heat; place saucepan in cold water; stir sauce a minute or two. Serve warm with pancakes. Makes about 3 cups sauce.

Blintz Pancakes

Like blintzes without the filling—the cottage cheese and sour cream are built right into the batter. Light and fluffy—

1 cup sifted all-purpose flour
1 tablespoon sugar
½ teaspoon salt

• • •

1 cup dairy sour cream
1 cup small-curd cream-style cottage cheese
4 well-beaten eggs

Sift dry ingredients into bowl. Add sour cream, cottage cheese, and beaten eggs; fold only till flour is barely moistened. Bake on a hot, lightly greased griddle or in skillet. (For uniform pancakes, use a ¼-cup measure.) Turn cakes when bubbles on surface break. Stack pancakes and serve with warm maple-flavored syrup or *Blueberry Sauce:* Combine one 1-pound can (2 cups) blueberries and 2 teaspoons cornstarch. Cook and stir till thick and clear. Add 1 teaspoon lemon juice. Makes about 16 4-inch pancakes.

Peaches 'n Crepes

½ cup sifted all-purpose flour
2 eggs
1½ tablespoons sugar
¾ cup milk
Dash salt
3 drops vanilla
Crepe Sauce

Combine ingredients; beat with rotary beater till smooth. Refrigerate the batter several hours to let it thicken a little.

Heat a heavy 6-inch skillet till a drop of water will dance on it. Then grease lightly and pour in 2 tablespoons batter. Lift skillet off heat and tilt from side to side till batter covers bottom evenly. Now cook till underside of crepe is lightly browned; the cooking should take only *seconds.* Roll-up crepes; place in chafing dish or skillet with peach slices. To serve, pour Crepe Sauce over all; heat through. *Keep warm till ready to serve.* Makes about 10 crepes (5 servings).

Crepe Sauce: Mix ⅓ cup sugar, 1 tablespoon cornstarch, dash salt. Blend in ¼ cup orange juice. Heat 1¼ cups orange juice to boiling; stir in sugar mixture; cook and stir till clear. Remove from heat; add butter and ½ to 1 teaspoon orange peel; stir till butter melts. Serve over crepes.

Pecan Pancakes with Peach Sauce

2 cups milk
1 slightly-beaten egg
2 tablespoons shortening, melted
½ cup finely chopped pecans
2 cups pancake mix

• • •

¼ cup sugar
1 tablespoon cornstarch
¼ cup water
1 12-ounce package frozen peaches, chopped (reserve syrup)
2 teaspoons lemon juice

Combine milk, egg, and shortening. Stir into pancake mix. Pour ¼ cup batter for each pancake onto hot, lightly greased griddle. Sprinkle each with about ½ tablespoon pecans. Bake till golden brown on each side; flip only once. Serve with Peach Sauce.

Peach Sauce: Blend sugar, and cornstarch. Stir in water, peaches, and peach syrup. Cook and stir till mixture boils; boil 1 minute. Stir in lemon juice. Makes 1½ cups.

Sunshine Roll-ups

⅔ cup milk
1½ tablespoons butter
⅓ cup pancake mix
1 well-beaten egg

Heat milk with butter till butter melts. Cool to lukewarm. Blend milk mixture and pancake mix into the beaten egg.

Lightly grease small skillet; heat. Pour in 2 tablespoons batter; lift pan from heat and tip from side to side so batter covers pan. Return to heat; cook till underside is lightly browned. Remove. Fry remaining pancakes; stack till ready to fill.

To serve, spoon 2 tablespoons Cheese Filling across center of each pancake; roll up. Place folded side down in skillet (You may fill pancakes ahead; chill till needed.)

Just before serving, pour Orange Sauce over filled pancakes; heat till sauce bubbles: Serve warm. Makes 8 servings.

Cheese Filling: Soften two 3-ounce packages cream cheese. Blend in 2 tablespoons sugar, 2¼ teaspoons grated orange peel, 1½ tablespoons orange juice, and 2 tablespoons chopped pecans. (Add ¼ cup chopped dates, if desired.) Whip till fluffy.

Orange Sauce: Mix ½ cup sugar, 1½ tablespoons cornstarch, and dash salt; blend in ¼ cup orange juice. Heat 1¼ cups orange juice to a boil; stir in sugar mixture, and cook and stir till thick and clear. Remove from heat. Add ¼ cup broken pecans and 2 tablespoons butter. Stir till butter melts.

Orange Pancake Delight

Wonderful flavor! Easy dessert starts with pancake mix and frozen juice—

1 beaten egg
1 cup light cream
1 6-ounce can frozen orange juice concentrate
1 cup pancake mix
Orange Syrup

Combine egg, cream, and ¼ cup of the orange-juice concentrate (reserve remainder). Add pancake mix, stirring to remove most of lumps. Bake on hot greased griddle, turning once. Serve with warm Orange Syrup. Makes about 18 pancakes.

Orange Syrup: Combine ½ cup butter or margarine, 1 cup sugar, and reserved orange-juice concentrate. Heat just to boiling, stirring occasionally. Makes 1½ cups.

Swedish Pancakes

2 eggs
1 cup light cream*
½ cup sifted all-purpose flour
1½ teaspoons sugar
¼ teaspoon salt

Beat eggs just enough to blend yolks and whites; add light cream. Sift flour, sugar, and salt into liquid ingredients; beat until smooth with rotary beater. Let mixture stand at least 2 hours, so batter thickens and cakes will hold shape on griddle.

Heat electric griddle or skillet to 375° or until drop of water will dance on surface. Butter lightly. Beat batter up again and pour from drip-cut pitcher or use 2 tablespoons batter for each pancake. Brown cakes on both sides. (If you find it difficult to turn pancakes without breaking at first, loosen edge with spatula and lift pancake with fingers, peeling it off the griddle.)

Roll or fold pancakes and place on oven-proof platter; cover. Keep warm in slow oven (300°). To serve, unroll and fill with strawberries or your favorite filling; then reroll. Pass Lingonberry Butter. Makes 1 dozen 5-inch pancakes.

*Or use ½ cup whipping cream plus ½ cup water instead of 1 cup light cream.

Lingonberry Butter

Fold ½ cup drained canned lingonberries (or ½ cup drained whole cranberry sauce) into one recipe Whipped Butter.

Super Strawberry Pancakes

These would be perfect for brunch or dessert—

Thaw two 10-ounce packages frozen strawberries; drain. Fill each Swedish Pancake with spoonful of strawberries and roll up. Arrange 3 pancakes on a plate for a serving. Sift confectioners' sugar over the top, if desired. Center with a dollop of whipped cream and a whole strawberry.

Manhattan Pancakes

Place a heaping tablespoon of dairy sour cream in center of each Swedish Pancake and roll up. Place 3 pancakes on each plate; sift confectioners' sugar over and top with generous dollop of sour cream.

Spicy Apple Pancakes

Prepare and bake Swedish Pancakes. Keep warm in oven till all are baked. Serve pancakes flat with several spoonfuls of Cinnamon Apple Slices in center.

Sift confectioners' sugar over top. Offer Whipped Orange Butter and pass the syrup from Cinnamon Apple Slices.

Cinnamon Apple Slices: Simmer 1 cup sugar, 1 cup water, and 1 teaspoon cinnamon in skillet till syrup is thick (takes about 5 minutes). Add 1 No. 2 can (2½ cups) sliced pie apples and simmer 5 to 10 minutes. Makes about 2¾ cups.

Super Strawberry Pancakes—
just one of the delectable ways you
can serve delicate, tender,
and lacy-edged Swedish Pancakes

Best Buttermilk Pancakes

Serve these plain, or try one of the variations below. Either way they're great—

2 cups sifted all-purpose flour
1 teaspoon soda
1 teaspoon salt
2 tablespoons sugar

• • •

2 slightly-beaten eggs
2 cups buttermilk
2 tablespoons melted butter
  or bacon fat

Sift flour, soda, salt, and sugar into bowl. Add eggs, buttermilk, and melted butter, stirring only until flour is barely moistened. (There will be a few lumps.)

Bake on hot, lightly greased griddle or electric skillet heated to 375°. For uniform pancakes, use a ¼-cup measure—or use a drip-cut pitcher and count 1-2-3 as you pour. Turn cakes when center springs back to touch, or when bubbles on surface break. Flip cakes only once. Serve with Whipped Orange Butter and syrup or sauce. Makes about 1½ dozen 4-inch cakes.

Blueberry Pancakes

Best Buttermilk pancakes dressed up (inside and outside) with tasty berries—

Drain one 1-pound can blueberries. Add ⅔ cup drained berries to Best Buttermilk Pancake batter. Bake. To serve, arrange hot cakes in circle on plates. Sift confectioners' sugar over. Center with Whipped Orange Butter; sprinkle with remaining blueberries.

Hawaiian Pancakes

Drain one 9-ounce can (1 cup) crushed pineapple. Fold drained pineapple into Buttermilk Pancake batter. Bake cakes according to directions for Buttermilk Pancakes. To serve, sift confectioners' sugar over top and offer Whipped Orange Butter.

African Banana Pancakes

Add ½ cup diced banana to Buttermilk Pancake batter. Garnish the hot cakes with banana slices and confectioners' sugar. Sprinkle with chopped pecans; serve with Whipped Butter and warm syrup.

Coconut Hot Cakes with Kauaiian Sausage

2 cups sifted all-purpose flour
4 teaspoons baking powder
Dash salt
2 beaten eggs
2 cups milk
¼ cup butter, melted
Fresh grated or flaked coconut
10 cooked smoked sausage links

Sift together dry ingredients. Combine eggs, milk, and melted butter; add to dry ingredients, stirring just till flour is moistened. (Batter will be lumpy.) Bake on hot griddle, turning only once. Spread warm cakes with honey or coconut syrup; roll up each. Place 3 cakes on a mound of flaked coconut for a serving; drizzle with melted butter. Top with butter pats and sizzling sausage. Offer guava jelly, papaya jam, poha jelly, and warm maple syrup. Makes 5 servings.

Orange Pancakes

½ cup orange juice
½ cup milk
1 egg
2 tablespoons salad oil
1 teaspoon grated orange peel
1 cup pancake mix

Combine orange juice, milk, egg, salad oil, and orange peel. Add pancake mix, stirring to remove most of the lumps. Bake on greased hot griddle. Turn when bubbles on surface break; flip only once. Makes 12 to 14 4-inch pancakes. Serve with Whipped Orange Butter or warm maple syrup.

Whipped Butter

Let ¼ pound (1 stick or ½ cup) butter stand at room temperature for 1 hour. Place in mixing bowl and run mixer at lowest speed until large chunks smooth out. Gradually increase mixer speed to fastest position and whip until butter is fluffy (takes about 8 minutes). Cover butter until ready to use. (If made ahead and refrigerated, remove from refrigerator an hour before using.) Makes about 1½ cups spread.

Whipped Orange Butter

Dice small orange; *do not remove peel;* grind. Fold into 1 recipe Whipped Butter.

Wonderful Waffles

Waffles are a breakfast byword—and they're just as delicious for lunch or supper. They dress up, too, for extra-special desserts.

Waffles will be tender if you are careful to stir the batter just enough to mix (it will look pebbly). The stiffer the batter, the shorter the mixing period should be. If you use melted shortening, cool it slightly first.

To prevent sticking, follow manufacturer's directions for care and preheating of waffle baker. Be sure it's hot enough before you add batter. If baker has no preheat indicator, sprinkle a few drops of water on grid; when they dance, the griddle's ready.

For even baking, close lid quickly, and *don't* peek! If you open the lid too soon, the waffle may fall, or stick and pull apart. Wait for signal light, or till steam stops.

For crisp waffles, let waffle remain on grid a few seconds after opening lid. Or, as you take up waffle, hold it on fork for a moment. For extra-crisp waffles, bake longer.

Leftover batter can be refrigerated and used the next day.

Everyday Waffles

1¾ cups sifted all-purpose flour
or 2 cups sifted cake flour
3 teaspoons baking powder
½ teaspoon salt

• • •

2 beaten egg yolks
1¼ cups milk
½ cup salad oil *or* melted shortening

• • •

2 stiff-beaten egg whites

Sift together dry ingredients. Combine egg yolks and milk; stir into dry ingredients. Stir in oil. Fold in egg whites, leaving a few little fluffs—don't overmix. Bake in preheated waffle baker. Makes about 8 waffles.

Everyday Waffle Variations

Buttermilk Waffles: Substitute buttermilk for sweet milk. Add ½ teaspoon soda and cut baking powder to 2 teaspoons.

Ham Waffles: Sprinkle 2 tablespoons finely diced cooked ham over, before closing baker.

Cheese Waffles: Cut shortening to 2 tablespoons; add ½ cup shredded process cheese.

Corn Waffles

1¾ cups sifted all-purpose flour
or 2 cups sifted cake flour
1 to 2 tablespoons sugar
3 teaspoons baking powder
½ teaspoon salt
2 beaten egg yolks
1 cup milk
2 cups canned cream-style corn
½ cup salad oil *or* melted shortening
2 stiff-beaten egg whites

Sift together dry ingredients. Combine next 4 ingredients; stir into dry mixture. Fold in egg whites; leave a few little fluffs—don't overmix. Bake. Makes about 9 waffles.

"Oh Boy" Waffles

2¼ cups sifted all-purpose flour
4 teaspoons baking powder
¾ teaspoon salt
1½ tablespoons sugar
2 beaten eggs
2¼ cups milk
¼ cup salad oil

Sift together dry ingredients. Combine eggs, milk and oil; add just before baking, beating only till moistened. (Batter is thin.) Bake in preheated baker. Makes 10 to 12.

Crisp Corn-meal Waffles

1 cup sifted all-purpose flour
2 teaspoons baking powder
1 teaspoon soda
1 teaspoon sugar
½ teaspoon salt

• • •

1 cup yellow corn meal
2 beaten eggs
2 cups buttermilk
¼ cup salad oil

Sift first 5 ingredients; stir in corn meal. Combine remaining ingredients; add, mixing just till moistened. Bake. Makes 8 to 10.

Date Dessert Waffles

Sift together 2 cups sifted all-purpose flour, 3 teaspoons baking powder, 1 teaspoon salt; stir in ¼ cup brown sugar. Combine 1¾ cups milk, ½ cup salad oil, and 2 slightly-beaten egg yolks. Add to dry mixture; blend well. Fold in 2 stiff-beaten egg whites. Finely chop enough dates to make 1 cup. Pour batter into preheated waffle baker; sprinkle with ⅓ cup of the dates; bake. Serve with Lemon Topping. Makes 3.

Dessert Waffles

1¼ cups sifted cake flour
½ teaspoon salt
3 teaspoons baking powder
• • •
2 well-beaten whole eggs
1 cup light cream
¼ cup butter, melted
2 stiff-beaten egg whites

Sift dry ingredients. Blend whole eggs and cream; stir in. Add butter. Fold in egg whites. Bake. Makes three 10-inch waffles. Serve a la mode or with sweetened fresh fruit.

Chocolate Waffles: Add 6 tablespoons cocoa (dry) and ½ cup sugar with dry ingredients. Decrease cream to ¾ cup. Add ¼ teaspoon vanilla. Mix and bake as above.

Polka-dot Waffles: Sprinkle semisweet chocolate pieces over batter in baker.

Orange Waffles: Add 1 tablespoon grated orange peel. Pass *Orange Butter:* Whip ½ cup soft butter; add 1 tablespoon confectioners' sugar and ¼ teaspoon grated orange peel.

Spicy Party Waffles

Each spicy-crisp waffle gets a fluff of whipped cream flavored with ginger—

½ cup shortening
1 cup brown sugar
2 eggs
• • •
1½ cups sifted all-purpose flour
2 teaspoons baking powder
½ teaspoon salt
1 teaspoon cinnamon
1 teaspoon allspice
½ teaspoon cloves
½ cup milk
½ cup broken California walnuts
• • •
2 to 3 tablespoons chopped candied ginger
1 cup whipping cream, whipped

Cream together shortening and sugar. Add eggs, one at a time, beating well after each.

Sift together flour, baking powder, salt, and spices; add to creamed mixture alternately with milk. Stir in walnuts. Bake in preheated waffle baker. Fold candied ginger into whipped cream, serve atop waffles. Makes 2 to 3 large waffles.

Sour-cream Waffles

1 cup sifted all-purpose flour
½ tablespoon sugar
1 teaspoon baking powder
¼ teaspoon soda
¼ teaspoon salt
1 well-beaten egg yolk
1 cup dairy sour cream
¼ cup milk
3 tablespoons butter, melted
1 stiff-beaten egg white

Sift together dry ingredients. Combine egg yolk, sour cream, milk and butter; add to flour mixture and beat smooth. Fold in beaten egg white. Bake. Makes 4.

Maple Waffles

1¾ cups sifted all-purpose flour
3 teaspoons baking powder
½ teaspoon salt
2 beaten egg yolks
1 cup milk
½ cup maple-flavored syrup
½ teaspoon maple flavoring
¼ cup salad oil
2 stiff-beaten egg whites

Sift together dry ingredients. Combine next 5 ingredients; stir into dry mixture. Stir in oil. Fold in egg whites; do not overmix. Bake. Serve with butter and confectioners' sugar sprinkled over. Makes 4 to 6 waffles.

Toppers for Pancakes, Waffles

Maple Syrup: Combine 1 cup light corn syrup, ½ cup brown sugar, ½ cup water; cook and stir till sugar dissolves. Add few drops maple flavoring, 1 tablespoon butter.

Lemon Topping: Combine 1 cup sour cream, ¼ cup sugar, 2 tablespoons lemon juice, ½ teaspoon grated lemon peel. Makes 1 cup.

Cranberry-Orange Butter: Put 1 small unpeeled orange (diced), ¼ cup raw cranberries, and ¼ cup sugar in electric blender. Blend 40 seconds; fold into Whipped Butter.

Blueberry Sauce: Cook and stir one 1-pound can blueberries and 2 teaspoons cornstarch till thick. Add 1 teaspoon lemon juice.

Orange Sauce: Combine ½ cup butter, 1 cup sugar, ½ cup frozen orange-juice concentrate. Bring just to boil; stir occasionally.

Calico Cuts—a tasty, pizza-like snack. Quick-and-easy crust is from a mix.

Speedy, delicious Walnut Coffeecake Sticks start from ready-made bread.

Crunch Sticks—ready in minutes—just call on refrigerator biscuits.

Short-cut Breads

Packaged foods save you time and work!

Flip the pages to find exciting ways to use quick mixes, ready-made breads, and jiffy foods. There are easy-to-make dinner breads, coffeetime treats, snacks for the kids, plus many more grand ideas.

Start with a mix

Cinnamon Pan Rolls

1 package hot-roll mix
2 tablespoons butter or margarine, melted
½ cup sugar
2 teaspoons cinnamon
¾ cup seedless raisins
Confectioners' Icing

Prepare hot-roll mix and let rise following package directions. On lightly floured surface roll to 20x12-inches. Brush with butter.

Combine sugar, cinnamon, and raisins; sprinkle over dough. Roll as for jelly roll, beginning with long side. Seal edge. Cut in 1-inch slices; place cut side down in 2 greased 8x1½-inch round pans. Cover. Let rolls rise according to the package directions. Bake at 400° for about 15 minutes or till done. Let stand 2 to 3 minutes; turn out of pan and then invert on serving plate. Drizzle tops with Confectioners' Icing.

Confectioners' Icing: Mix ½ cup sifted confectioners' sugar and 1½ teaspoons milk.

Quick Hot Cross Buns

1 package hot-roll mix
2 tablespoons butter or margarine, melted
2 tablespoons golden seedless raisins
2 tablespoons chopped candied fruits and peels
⅓ cup sugar
1 teaspoon cinnamon
½ teaspoon nutmeg

Prepare hot-roll mix according to package directions, adding butter, raisins, fruits and peels, sugar and spices to flour mixture; mix well. Cover with damp cloth and let rise in warm place till double (about 1 hour). Turn out on lightly floured surface and knead until smooth. Shape in 12 buns. Place on lightly greased baking sheet. Cover and let rise until almost double (about 45 minutes). Using sharp scissors (or knife), snip top of buns to form shallow cross. If a glaze is desired, brush with 1 slightly beaten egg mixed with 1 tablespoon water. Bake at 375° about 15 minutes or till done. Cool slightly; fill crosses with Confectioners' Icing. Makes 12.

Onion Buns

Burgers taste wonderful in these good buns—

1 cup chopped onion
2 tablespoons butter or margarine

• • •

1 package hot-roll mix

Cook onion in butter till tender but not brown. Cool. Prepare dough as directed on hot-roll-mix package, adding onion to the dry mix. Cover and let rise in a warm place until double (30 to 60 minutes).

Shape in 12 round buns. Place on greased baking sheet and flatten slightly. Cover and let rise until almost double (30 to 60 minutes). Bake in moderate oven (375°) for about 20 to 25 minutes. Makes 1 dozen.

Calico Cuts

1 package hot-roll mix

• • •

2 eggs
⅔ cup evaporated milk or light cream
1 teaspoon salt
1 teaspoon celery seed
¼ cup chopped pimiento
4 cups (1 pound) shredded sharp process American cheese

• • •

¼ teaspoon coarse black pepper

Prepare dough from hot-roll mix and let rise according to package directions. Meanwhile, combine eggs and evaporated milk, beating just to blend; add salt, celery seed, pimiento, and shredded cheese.

Divide dough into two parts. On lightly floured surface roll to a little less than ¼ inch. Pat out each piece very thin in a well-greased 15½x10½x1-inch jelly-roll pan. (Or use one jelly-roll pan and three 9-inch pie plates.) Let rise until light (about 30 to 60 minutes).

Spread topping *evenly* on dough, almost to edge. Sprinkle with pepper. Bake in hot oven (425°) about 12 minutes. Lift out onto cake racks and snip in 4x2-inch rectangles. Serve hot. Makes about 32 pieces.

Note: Don't use baking sheets without sides; the cheese mixture will run over.

Airy Hot Cross Buns They're plump, full of currants, and light as can be—a true traditional favorite. We give the quick-to-make version here, but the crisscross and spicy-good flavor remain the same.

Dixie Puffs

Crisp, crusty, golden "pillows," hollow on the inside—that's how these puffs come from your deep-fat fryer. They taste almost like doughnuts—wonderful with coffee!—

1 package hot-roll mix
½ teaspoon salt

• • •

Sifted confectioners' sugar

• • •

Jelly, jam or marmalade

Prepare dough from hot-roll mix, adding salt, and letting rise according to package directions. Divide dough in half.

Turn dough out on a lightly floured surface and roll each piece to a 10-inch square, ¼-inch thick. Cut square with pastry wheel or sharp knife in strips 2 inches wide; then cut diagonally to make diamonds.

Fry in deep, hot fat (375°) until golden brown (about 2 to 3 minutes), turning once. Drain on paper towels.

Sprinkle puffs with sifted confectioners' sugar. Serve hot with jelly, jam, or marmalade. Makes about 2½ dozen.

Mexican Swirls

Light rolls swirled with yummy cheese filling. Add pepper to suit your family's taste—

1 package hot-roll mix

• • •

1 slightly beaten egg
½ teaspoon salt
½ teaspoon celery seed
2 tablespoons chopped pimiento
2 cups shredded sharp process American cheese
Dash coarse black pepper

Prepare mix and let rise following label directions. Meanwhile, combine remaining ingredients. Divide dough into two parts. On lightly floured surface, roll each to a 12x9-inch rectangle. Spread with filling.

Starting at long side, roll each rectangle up as for jelly roll. Seal edges. Cut in 1-inch slices. Place cut side down in well-greased muffin cups (about 2¾-inch diameter). Cover; let rise till almost double (30 to 40 minutes). Bake at 400° for 15 minutes or till done. Makes about 2 dozen rolls.

Butterscotch Pecan Rolls—they're gloriously good!

Here are terrific treats in the sweet-tooth department! These rolls are just wonderful with a syrup of brown sugar and butter that bubbles in the bottom of the pan and up the sides to give each roll a glossy, rich coat. They're spicy with cinnamon rolled inside, crunchy with nuts. And there's an added bonus for Mom—these rolls get going fast with a package of hot-roll mix! Make plenty and serve them oven-hot with a big stick of butter—no dainty little butter pats this time, please!

Butterscotch Pecan Rolls

1 package hot-roll mix
¼ cup butter or margarine
1 cup brown sugar
½ cup dark corn syrup
⅔ cup pecans

Prepare hot-roll mix and let rise as directed on package. Melt butter; add brown sugar and corn syrup; heat and stir till blended. Pour into two 9½x5x3-inch loaf pans. Sprinkle ⅓ cup pecans in each pan.

On lightly floured surface, roll dough to a 24x12-inch rectangle. Spread with 2 tablespoons soft butter or margarine. Sprinkle with mixture of ½ cup granulated sugar and 1½ teaspoons cinnamon. Beginning at long side, roll as for jelly roll. Cut in 20 slices; place cut side down in prepared pans. Let rise till light, about 40 minutes. Bake at 375° about 25 minutes. Cool 5 minutes; invert on rack; remove pans. Makes 20 rolls.

Note: Or cut roll of dough in 24 slices and bake in two 8x1½-inch round pans.

Baba Buns

1 package hot-roll mix
2 tablespoons butter or margarine, melted
⅓ cup light seedless raisins
⅓ cup currants
1 12-ounce can (1½ cups) apricot nectar
¾ cup sugar
1 tablespoon lemon juice
1 teaspoon rum extract (optional)

Prepare dough from hot-roll mix according to package directions, adding melted butter with yeast and egg. Cover; let rise till double (30 to 40 minutes.) Add raisins and currants; beat well. Spoon into well-greased muffin cups, filling half full.* Cover; let rise till almost double (30 to 60 minutes). Bake at 375° for 20 to 25 minutes or till done.

Meanwhile, combine apricot nectar and sugar in saucepan. Bring to boiling, reduce heat and simmer 10 minutes. Remove from heat and add lemon juice and extract. Remove hot rolls from pans. Place rolls in shallow baking dish; pour hot syrup over; let stand few minutes. If desired, dip tops of buns in Confectioners' Icing. Serve warm. Makes about 1½ dozen.

*Batter may be baked in 2 well-greased 5-cup ring molds instead of muffin cups.

Cinnamon Coffee Crescent

1 package hot-roll mix
3 well-beaten eggs
½ cup soft butter or margarine

• • •

1 slightly-beaten egg
2 cups seedless raisins
1 cup chopped California walnuts
1 cup sugar
2 tablespoons cinnamon

Soften yeast in large bowl as directed on hot-roll-mix package. Add beaten eggs, the mix, and butter. Blend thoroughly. Cover; let rise in warm place till double (45 to 60 minutes). Sprinkle about ½ cup sifted all-purpose flour on board; knead in so that dough is still very soft but not sticky.

Divide dough in half. On lightly floured surface, roll each piece in 15x12-inch rectangle, ⅛ inch thick. Brush with beaten egg. Combine remaining ingredients and sprinkle half over each piece of dough.

Roll each as for jelly roll, starting with long edge. Place sealed side down on greased baking sheet, curving to form crescent and pinching ends to seal. Cover and let rise till light (about 30 minutes). Bake in moderate oven (375°) for about 20 to 25 minutes or till done. Frost, if desired, with Confectioners' Icing; trim with walnut halves. Makes 2.

Apple-Nut Ring

1 package hot-roll mix
1 cup brown sugar
1 cup chopped pared tart apples
¼ cup soft butter or margarine
2 teaspoons cinnamon

• • •

¼ cup butter or margarine, melted
½ cup chopped California walnuts
¼ cup honey

Prepare dough and let rise as directed on package. Mix brown sugar, apples, soft butter, and cinnamon; spread on bottom of 10-inch tube pan. On lightly floured surface, knead dough till smooth and satiny.

Shape in 1-inch balls. Dip in melted butter; roll in nuts. Place layer of balls in prepared pan. Drizzle half of honey over. Add second layer, staggering balls; drizzle remaining honey over. Cover and let rise in warm place till nearly double (40 to 45 minutes). Bake at 350° about 40 minutes or till done. Cool in pan 10 minutes. Invert on rack; invert again onto plate and serve warm.

Sage

Quick Raisin Loaf

1 package hot-roll mix
½ cup seedless raisins
• • •
Confectioners' Icing

Prepare hot-roll mix according to package directions; add raisins along with the egg. Cover and let rise in warm place till double (about 45 minutes). Shape in loaf and place in greased 8½x4½x2½-inch loaf pan. Cover and let rise till dough is almost double (about 45 minutes). Bake in moderate oven (375°) 45 to 50 minutes or till done. Let cool 10 minutes; remove from pan. Cool; frost with Confectioners' Icing.

Confectioners' Icing: Combine 1 cup confectioners' sugar, 1 to 1½ tablespoons milk, and ¼ teaspoon vanilla; mix smooth.

Christmas Bread Ring

1 package hot-roll mix
½ cup candied fruits and peels
½ cup broken California walnuts
¼ cup seedless raisins
• • •
Confectioners' Icing

Prepare hot-roll mix according to package directions; add the candied fruits and peels, walnuts and seedless raisins.

When dough has doubled, (about 1 hour), divide in half. Roll each half into a rope about 24 inches long. On a greased baking sheet, twist the two ropes together to form a ring. Cover and let rise till almost double (about 40 minutes). Bake in moderate oven (375°) about 20 to 25 minutes, or till done. When bread is cool, brush with Confectioners' Icing; trim with additional candied fruits and peels.

Confectioners' Icing: Combine 1 cup confectioners' sugar, 1 to 1½ tablespoons milk and ¼ teaspoon vanilla; mix smooth.

It's easy—start with a mix

← Here's old-fashioned baking with a modern flair—Enjoy delicious Quick Raisin Loaf, or the pleasing flavor of Old-time Herb Loaf, often, and with so little work! (See index listing for Cloverleaf Rolls and Butterhorn Rolls pictured in basket.)

Old-time Herb Loaf

Beautiful round loaf has subtle herb flavor. Delicious for sandwiches or just plain eating—

1 package hot-roll mix
1 teaspoon sage
½ teaspoon basil, crushed

Reserve ¼ cup of hot-roll mix. Prepare remaining hot-roll mix according to package directions; add sage and basil to dry mix. Turn out on surface sprinkled with reserved roll mix. Knead dough till smooth and mix is worked in (about 2 to 3 minutes).

Place dough in a greased bowl, turning once to grease top. Cover and let rise in warm place until double (about 1 hour). Punch down. Shape dough into a ball; let rise on greased baking sheet or in a greased 9-inch pie plate, (sides will be higher), about 40 minutes. Bake in moderate oven (375°) for about 35 to 40 minutes or till done.

Remove loaf from pan; brush with butter, if desired. To serve, cut loaf in quarters, then slice the quarters at right angles to each other (see picture at left).

Cardamom Braid

So quick and simple—cardamom and plump raisins add special goodness to a mix. This sugary-crusted braid is tops served hot—

1 package hot-roll mix
2 tablespoons butter or margarine, melted and cooled
1½ to 2 teaspoons ground cardamom or 1 teaspoon crushed cardamom
½ cup golden seedless raisins

Prepare hot-roll mix according to package directions; add butter, cardamom, and raisins; mix well. Cover; let rise in warm place till double (about 1 hour).

On lightly floured surface, knead dough about 1 minute; divide in thirds. Roll each third under hands to form a strand 10 inches long, tapering ends. Place strands, 1 inch apart, on greased baking sheet.

Beginning in middle, braid the 3 strands *loosely*, working toward either end. Pinch ends together. Cover and let rise till almost double (about 40 minutes). Brush braid with milk and sprinkle with sugar. Bake bread in moderate oven (375°) for about 25 minutes or till done. Serve hot.

Little Orange Loaves

Orange-muffin mix turns into nut bread—

1 package orange-muffin mix
¾ cup canned whole cranberry sauce
1 cup chopped California walnuts

Prepare batter from muffin mix according to package directions. Stir in cranberry sauce and walnuts. Spoon into 6 greased 6-ounce frozen-juice-concentrate cans. Bake in moderate oven (375°) about 30 to 35 minutes or till done. Cool 5 minutes; ease out of cans with spatula (cut end out of can). Bread slices best the second day.

Blueberry Supper Bread

1 package blueberry-muffin mix

• • •

½ cup sugar
¼ cup all-purpose flour
2 tablespoons butter or margarine

Prepare batter from muffin mix according to package directions for coffeecake or loaf cake. Pour into a greased 8½-inch round baking dish. Sprinkle with Crumb Top; bake in hot oven (400°) 30 minutes or till done. Cut in wedges to serve. Serve warm with plenty of butter. Makes 6 to 8 servings.

Crumb Top: Combine sugar, and flour; cut in butter till crumbly.

Call on muffin mix to whip up this surprise in a hurry. Tempting Blueberry Supper Bread boasts golden crumb topping. Serve it warm.

Muffin-mix Coffeecake

½ package (1 packet) orange-muffin mix
2 tablespoons pineapple-apricot preserves

• • •

3 tablespoons sugar
3 tablespoons all-purpose flour
2 tablespoons butter or margarine
3 tablespoons chopped California walnuts

Prepare muffin mix according to package directions. Pour into greased 8x1½-inch round pan. Dot preserves (cut any large pieces) evenly over batter. Combine sugar and flour; cut in butter till crumbly and stir in nuts; sprinkle over batter. Bake in hot oven (400°) for about 18 to 20 minutes or till done. Serve warm.

Orange-Date Nut Bread

½ of 14-ounce package (about 1½ cups) orange-muffin mix
½ of 14-ounce package (about 1½ cups) date-muffin mix

• • •

2 eggs
½ cup water
1 cup chopped California walnuts

Combine dry mixes. Blend eggs and water; stir into dry mixes till completely moistened. Fold in walnuts. Pour into a greased 8½x4½x2½-inch loaf pan. Bake in moderate oven (350°) for about 45 to 50 minutes or until done. Remove from pan; cool.

Easy Date Nut Bread

½ cup hot water
1 14-ounce package date-bar mix

• • •

3 slightly-beaten eggs
¼ cup sifted all-purpose flour
1 teaspoon baking powder
1 cup mashed banana

• • •

¾ cup chopped California walnuts

Stir hot water into date filling portion of the mix. Add crumbly portion of mix, eggs, flour, baking powder, and banana. Beat vigorously 2 minutes. Stir in walnuts. Pour into greased 9½x5x3-inch loaf pan. Bake in moderate oven (350°) for 50 to 55 minutes or till done. Remove from pan; cool.

Banana-Date Loaf

¾ cup mashed fully ripe, flecked-with-brown banana
⅓ cup water
• • •
1 package date-muffin mix

Combine banana and water. Prepare batter from muffin mix according to package directions, *using banana mixture in place of the water.* Pour into greased 8½x4½x2½-inch loaf pan. Bake in moderate oven (350°) 45 to 55 minutes or till done. Remove from pan and cool. Loaf will slice better on second day.

Double Corn Muffins

It's a delicious combo—corn plus ham—

1 package corn-muffin mix
1 1-pound can (2 cups) whole kernel corn, drained
• • •
1 2¼-ounce can deviled ham

Prepare muffin mix according to package directions; stir in the whole kernel corn. Spoon batter into greased muffin pans, filling ⅔ full. Drop a spoonful of deviled ham on the center of each muffin. Bake in moderate oven (375°) for about 20 minutes or till done. Makes 1 dozen muffins.

Bread Sticks

Hot-roll mix makes these a snap—

1 package hot-roll mix
1 cup warm water
• • •
1 slightly-beaten egg white
1 tablespoon water

Prepare hot-roll mix according to package directions *but using 1 cup warm water and omitting the egg.* When time to shape, place dough on lightly floured surface.

Turn several times. Cut off pieces slightly smaller than golf balls. Roll each with your hands on surface to get 10- to 12-inch stick, pencil thin. If ends of stick look knobby, cut off to make smooth stick.

Place on a greased baking sheet. Brush with a mixture of 1 slightly-beaten egg white and 1 tablespoon water. Let rise uncovered about 20 minutes. Brush rolls again with egg-white mixture. Sprinkle with coarse salt. Bake in very hot oven (450°) about 12 minutes. Makes 2½ dozen.

Cheese Bread Sticks

1 package hot-roll mix
1 cup shredded sharp process American cheese
1 tablespoon poppy seed
¼ cup butter or margarine, melted

Prepare hot-roll dough according to package directions; add cheese and poppy seed. After dough has risen, divide in half. On lightly floured surface, roll each half to a 10x6-inch rectangle, about ½ inch thick. Cut in twenty 6-inch-long sticks. (For a smoother shape, roll sticks under hand pencil fashion.) Place on greased baking sheet. Brush with melted butter. Let rise till double (30 to 45 minutes). Bake in hot oven (400°) 10 minutes or till done. Makes 40.

Onion Supper Bread

½ cup chopped onion
2 tablespoons butter or margarine
1 package corn-muffin or corn-bread mix
½ cup dairy sour cream
½ cup shredded sharp process American cheese

Cook onion in butter till tender but not brown. Prepare mix according to package directions. Pour into greased 8x8x2-inch pan. Sprinkle with cooked onion. Mix sour cream and cheese; spoon over the top. Bake in hot oven (400°) 25 minutes or till done. Let stand a few minutes; cut in 9 squares.

Quick Cheesed Corn Muffins

These golden beauties rate praises galore. They're moist and tender—corn kernels and tangy cheese make scrumptious flavor combo—

1 8-ounce package corn-muffin mix*
1 beaten egg
1 8-ounce can (1 cup) cream-style corn
½ cup shredded sharp process American cheese
⅛ teaspoon bottled hot pepper sauce

Combine corn muffin mix and remaining ingredients; mix well. Pour into well-greased 2½-inch muffin pans ⅔ full. Bake in hot oven (425°) for 15 to 20 minutes or till done. Makes about 12 muffins.

*Or, use one 14-ounce package corn muffin mix; follow above recipe *adding* ½ cup milk with remaining ingredients. Makes 16.

Topper Corn Bread has a rich baked-on "crust" of onion bits, celery seed, and sharp cheese; the corn-bread layer is speedy with a mix!

Topper Corn Bread

¼ cup chopped onion
1 tablespoon butter or margarine
1 package corn-muffin mix or corn-bread mix
1 cup shredded sharp process American cheese
1 teaspoon celery seed

Cook onion in butter just till tender but not brown. Prepare the mix according to package directions; spread batter in greased 10x 6x1½-inch baking dish. Sprinkle cheese evenly over batter; dot onion-butter mixture over all; sprinkle with celery seed. Bake at 375° about 20 minutes. Serve at once.

Corn Crackle

1 8-ounce package corn-muffin mix
1 cup coarsely chopped salted peanuts
½ cup grated Parmesan cheese
1 teaspoon garlic salt
3 tablespoons butter or margarine, melted

Prepare the mix according to package directions; spread evenly in well-greased 15½x 10½x1-inch jelly-roll pan. Sprinkle with peanuts, cheese, and garlic salt; drizzle butter over top. Bake at 375° about 25 minutes or till crisp and lightly browned. Immediately cut into squares; cool slightly, remove from pan. Serve warm.

Green-chile Corn Bread

⅓ cup drained canned green chiles

• • •

1 package corn-muffin mix or corn-bread mix
1 9-ounce can (1 cup) cream-style corn
2 tablespoons bacon drippings or butter, melted

• • •

1 cup shredded sharp process American cheese

Rinse and seed chiles; cut in strips and drain on paper towels. Prepare the mix according to package directions; stir in corn and the bacon drippings. Spoon *half* the batter into a greased 9x9x2-inch pan. Lay chiles over batter; sprinkle with *half* the cheese. Top with remaining batter, then remaining cheese. Bake according to package directions. Serve hot.

Quick Pizza Crust

Prepare 1 package hot-roll mix, following package directions, but *using 1 cup warm water* and *omitting egg. Do not let rise.* Divide dough in half. On greased baking sheets, pat or roll each piece of dough into a 13-inch circle. Build up edge slightly.

Top with your favorite filling. Bake in hot oven (425°) about 18 to 20 minutes or till crust is done. Makes crusts for 2 pizzas.

Double-corn Cakes

Creamed corn and corn meal make hearty flavor all the way through these pancakes—

1 cup packaged pancake mix
1 cup corn meal
1 teaspoon baking powder
2 slightly-beaten eggs
1 1-pound can (2 cups) cream-style corn
1 cup milk
2 tablespoons salad oil

Stir together dry ingredients. Combine eggs, corn, milk, and oil; add to dry ingredients, stirring just till all is moistened. Drop batter from ¼-cup measure onto hot, lightly greased griddle or skillet. Turn once. Makes about sixteen 4-inch pancakes.

Fast Flapjacks

Nothing beats breakfast outdoors, especially when it's hot cakes!—

Prepare batter from your favorite pancake mix according to package directions.

Season griddle with salt: Tie salt in a piece of cloth; rub vigorously over griddle heated on grill top. Or sprinkle salt directly on griddle and rub in with paper towels. Then rub off. Repeat the salt after each batch of pancakes.

Test griddle by sprinkling on a few drops water. If water dances, griddle is ready. Dip batter with ¼-cup measure; pour on griddle. Pancakes are ready to turn when edges look cooked and top is covered with tiny bubbles. Turn once.

Golden Apricot Roll-ups

1 cup packaged pancake mix
½ cup apricot jam
2 slightly-beaten eggs
½ cup corn-flake crumbs
2 tablespoons butter or margarine

Prepare pancake mix according to package directions, but using 1 *cup milk*, 1 egg, and 1 tablespoon salad oil or melted shortening. Bake on griddle as directed.

Spread about a tablespoon jam over each hot cake. Roll up. Dip rolls in egg, then in corn-flake crumbs. Place, seam side down, in skillet. Brown on all sides in butter over low heat. Serve hot. Pass melted butter, if desired. Makes 8 roll-ups.

Dessert Pancake Roll-ups

Each pancake gets a luscious filling of fluffy orange-flavored butter—

Prepare 1 cup packaged pancake mix following package directions, *but using 1¼ cups milk*, 1 egg, and 1 tablespoon salad oil or melted shortening. Bake on griddle as directed on package. Keep pancakes warm.

Just before serving, spread each pancake with Whipped Orange Butter; roll up. Place in chafing dish to serve; drizzle cakes with a little orange juice and sprinkle with sugar for a sparkling finish. Offer Cinnamon Honey, warm maple-flavored syrup, marmalade, and additional Orange Butter. Makes about ten 5-inch pancakes.

Whipped Orange Butter: Let ¼ pound (1 stick or ½ cup) butter stand at room temperature for 1 hour.

With electric mixer at lowest speed, mix till large chunks smooth out. Gradually increase mixer speed to high, and whip until butter is fluffy (8 to 10 minutes).

Stir 1 tablespoon grated orange peel and 2 tablespoons orange juice into the whipped butter. Cover until ready to use. (If made ahead and refrigerated, remove from refrigerator an hour before using.) Makes about ¾ cup whipped butter.

Cinnamon Honey: Thoroughly mix 1 cup honey with ½ teaspoon cinnamon and dash nutmeg; heat through. Serve warm. Pass with filled roll-ups.

Peanut-butter Waffles

Peanut butter does good things for waffles —you'll like the new flavor. They're perfect for brunch or Sunday-night supper—

1 cup packaged pancake mix
2 tablespoons sugar
⅓ cup chunk-style peanut butter
1 egg
1 cup milk
2 tablespoons salad oil or melted shortening

Combine all ingredients. Beat with rotary or electric beater just till almost smooth. (There will be a few lumps).

Bake in pre-heated waffle baker. Makes eight 4-inch waffles. Pass butter, jelly, or maple-flavored syrup.

Tricks with a loaf of bread!

Toasted Cheese "Rolls"

1 unsliced sandwich loaf, about 11 inches long
½ cup soft butter or margarine
2 5-ounce jars sharp spreading cheese
Poppy seed

Cut crusts from top and sides of unsliced loaf. Make 8 slices crosswise, cutting to, *but not through*, bottom crust; make one cut lengthwise down the center of the loaf. Place on baking sheet.

Blend butter and cheese. Spread between slices, over top and sides. Sprinkle lightly with poppy seed or celery seed. Tie string around loaf to hold together. Bake in hot oven (400°) until cheese is melted and bread is crusty, about 15 minutes. Serve hot like pan rolls. Makes 16 rolls.

Accordion Cheese Loaf

Easy on the hostess—everyone breaks off a delicious slice—

1 unsliced sandwich loaf, about 11 inches long

• • •

¼ cup soft butter or margarine
2 teaspoons prepared mustard
1 cup shredded sharp process American cheese
¼ cup chopped stuffed green olives
Melted butter or margarine

Cut loaf in half lengthwise. At 1-inch intervals, slice each half-loaf crosswise on the bias, cutting *almost through to bottom crust.* Combine soft butter, mustard, cheese, and olives; spread between slices of bread. Brush tops with melted butter.

Place on baking sheet; toast in hot oven (400°) about 12 minutes or till crusty. Makes about 11 servings of 2 pieces each.

Crusty Cheese Sticks

Cut unsliced sandwich bread into long, thin strips; toast. Brush with melted butter or margarine, then sprinkle generously with grated Parmesan cheese. Serve warm with spaghetti and meat balls.

Cheese Toast Cups

These cheese-lined holders for creamed dishes are extra special. They make a ladies luncheon a real event—they're that good!

1 1-pound 4-ounce unsliced sandwich loaf

• • •

⅓ cup butter, melted

• • •

1 beaten egg
½ cup light cream
2 cups (½ pound) shredded sharp process American cheese

Freeze bread for easy handling. Trim crusts from unsliced loaf; cut in 6 jumbo slices, each 1¾ inches wide.

For square cups: Cut a long slit ½ inch from bottom of each slice, extending to within ½ inch of the corners and other sides. Leaving ½ inch around all sides, cut a square straight down from the top all the way to the slit. Lift out inner square.

For triangular cups: Cut each big slice diagonally in half. On the long side of each triangle, cut a slit ¼ inch from the bottom, extending to within ¼ inch of the corners and other sides—careful, don't cut through. Leaving ¼ inch around all sides, cut a triangle straight down from the top all the way to the slit. Now lift out inner triangle.

For cheese-custard lining: Place bread cups on ungreased baking sheet: brush with melted butter, inside and out. Combine egg, cream, and cheese; fill cups ½ full. Bake in moderate oven (350°) for about 15 to 20 minutes or till golden brown and custard is set. Fill the toast cups with creamed chicken or sea food. Makes 6 square cups or 12 triangular cups.

Easy Toasted Cheese "Rolls"

A loaf of sandwich bread becomes a pan of "rolls!" Each roll boasts a toasty cheese jacket, but inside is moist and pillow-soft. Poppy seed gives a flavorful accent. →

Parmesan Toast Strips

Crisp toast fingers take on a zesty topping of corn chips and Parmesan cheese—

4 slices bread, toasted
¼ cup butter or margarine, melted
½ teaspoon onion salt
1 cup corn chips, finely crushed
¼ cup grated Parmesan cheese

Remove crusts from toast; cut each slice in 5 strips. Combine butter and onion salt; roll strips in mixture. Combine corn chips and Parmesan; dip one side of strips in mixture. Bake, cheese side up, on baking sheet at 400° 5 to 8 minutes or till crisp. Makes 20.

Caraway Coney Fingers

Dandy idea for leftover coneys—

6 coney rolls
¼ cup garlic spread, melted
¼ cup butter or margarine, melted
¼ cup grated Parmesan cheese
Caraway seed

Cut rolls in fourths lengthwise to make "fingers." Combine garlic spread and butter; brush on cut sides of rolls. Sprinkle with cheese, then caraway seed. Bake on baking sheet in very hot oven (450°) 5 to 8 minutes or till toasty. Serve hot.

Miniature Garlic Rounds

Cut *hard rolls* crosswise in ½-inch slices. In oven, melt enough butter or margarine in baking dish to cover bottom generously.

Remove from oven. Add 1 or 2 cloves garlic, minced. Arrange roll slices in baking dish; turn once to butter both sides. Let stand 10 minutes; heat at 400° 10 minutes.

Easy Cheese Slices

Each slice is covered with Parmesan cheese and poppy seed, then toasted till crusty—

¼ cup butter or margarine, melted
½ cup grated Parmesan cheese
6 1-inch slices French bread
1 tablespoon poppy seed

Mix butter and cheese; spread on both sides of bread slices. Sprinkle slices on both sides with poppy seed. Place on baking sheet and toast in moderate oven (350°) about 12 minutes, turning once.

Onion Slices

Loaf is cut in half lengthwise—gives twice as many flavorful pieces—

1 loaf French bread, about 18 inches long
½ cup chopped green onions and tops
½ cup soft butter or margarine

Cut bread in half horizontally. Combine onions and butter; spread on cut sides of bread. Then slash each half loaf on the bias in 1½- to 2-inch slices, *but don't cut quite through bottom crust.* Place slices on baking sheet and heat in hot oven (400°) for about 10 minutes or till toasty.

Speedy Onion Bread

Fresh onion flavor that's great with salads—

2 teaspoons instant onion
1 tablespoon water
½ cup soft butter or margarine
2 tablespoons snipped parsley
1 loaf French bread, about 18 inches long

Let instant onion stand in water 5 minutes, then combine with butter and parsley, mixing well. Slash bread on the bias in 1-inch slices, cutting to, *but not through* bottom crust. Spread onion butter generously on one side of each slice. Wrap loaf in foil. Heat on grill 20 to 30 minutes or till hot, turning occasionally. Or heat in moderate oven (350°) about 25 minutes.

Parsleyed French Slices

Unique and delicious flavor with just a few simple ingredients—

½ to ⅔ cup soft butter or margarine
2 tablespoons chopped onion
1 tablespoon chopped parsley
1 tablespoon whole basil
1 teaspoon lemon juice
1 loaf French bread, about 15 inches long

Combine all the ingredients except bread. Cut loaf in ¾-inch slices, *almost to bottom crust.* Spread each slice with mixture. Place loaf on baking sheet or foil and heat uncovered in very slow oven (250°) about 25 minutes. To serve, separate slices and keep toasty on electric warming tray or in bun warmer. Makes about 17 slices.

Zippy Barbecue Bread

Perfect complement for a patio supper—

½ cup (1 stick) soft butter
1 tablespoon prepared mustard
½ cup shredded Parmesan cheese
¼ cup snipped parsley
• • •
1 loaf French bread, about 18 inches long

Combine first 4 ingredients. Slash bread on the bias in 1-inch slices, cutting to, *but not through*, bottom crust. Spread butter mixture generously on one side of each slice. Wrap in foil. Heat in moderate oven (350°) 25 to 30 minutes or till hot through.

Sesame Garlic Logs

You start with an unsliced sandwich loaf for this style of garlic bread—

1 unsliced sandwich loaf, about 11 inches long
• • •
½ cup butter or margarine, melted
2 cloves garlic, minced
¼ cup sesame seed, toasted

Trim all crusts from bread. Cut loaf in half crosswise, then in half lengthwise. Cut each piece crosswise in 4 logs about 1¼ inches thick. Combine butter and garlic; brush on all sides of logs and sprinkle with sesame seed. Arrange in 13x9x2-inch baking dish—don't let logs touch each other. Toast in hot oven (400°) about 10 minutes. Makes 16.

Melba Rye Chips

They're crispy-good and cheese flavored—

1 "icebox" rye loaf (tiny size)
½ cup butter or margarine, melted
Grated Parmesan cheese

With a very sharp knife or slicer, cut rye loaf in paper-thin slices. Place slices in single layer on trays; allow to dry in the air until crisp and the edges curl.

Spread half the melted butter over bottom of large baking pan at least 2 inches deep. Scatter slices over butter. Drizzle remaining butter over top. Broil about 4 inches from the heat until delicately browned. Stir chips so bottom pieces can brown. Don't let chips get too dark. Sprinkle with grated Parmesan cheese while hot.

Hot Garlic Loaf

1 loaf French or Vienna bread
½ cup soft butter or margarine
1 or 2 cloves garlic, crushed

Slice bread on the bias, cutting to, *but not through*, bottom crust. Mix butter or margarine and crushed garlic; spread on one side of each slice. Wrap loaf in foil. Heat at 350° for 25 to 30 minutes or till hot through.

Baby Pizzas

Serve everybody a whole one for a luncheon main dish—or cut them in wedges for tasty appetizers. Easy to make and good!—

4 large or 6 small English muffins
½ cup chili sauce
• • •
1 teaspoon salt
¼ teaspoon pepper
½ teaspoon ground oregano
• • •
½-pound package brown-and-serve sausage
¾ cup grated process American cheese

Split muffins and toast the cut side. Spread with chili sauce; combine salt, pepper, and oregano and sprinkle over. Cut each sausage link in fourths and place polka-dot fashion over muffins. Top with cheese. Broil 4 inches from heat until hot through, about 2 to 3 minutes. Makes 4 to 6 servings.

Pizza Sardine Snacks

A delicious Italian touch for your appetizer tray. Speedy to prepare, too—

4 large English muffins
Tomato paste
Monosodium glutamate
Crushed oregano
Sardines
½ cup grated sharp process American cheese

Split English muffins in half. Toast cut side in broiler. Spread each round with 1 tablespoon tomato paste; sprinkle with monosodium glutamate and oregano. Place 3 or 4 sardines on each; sprinkle each with 2 tablespoons grated cheese. Place on greased baking sheet. Broil about 3 inches from heat till cheese melts and buns are warm through. Cut in wedges; serve hot.

Toasty Rye Curls

Appetizer crisps to dip in garlic butter—

With very sharp knife or slicer, cut "ice-box" rye loaf (tiny size) in paper-thin slices. Place in single layer on baking sheet. Dry in slow oven (300°) until crisp and the edges curl, about 30 minutes.

Garlic Croutons

These will add a chef's touch to your favorite tossed green salad—

2 cups ½-inch bread cubes

• • •

¼ cup butter or margarine
1 clove garlic

Toast bread cubes in slow oven (325°), stirring frequently, till dry and golden brown. Croutons should be so dry they'd float on water! Then they'll stay crunchy when tossed with the dressing and greens.

Melt butter in skillet; add garlic and croutons. Toss lightly till croutons are well coated with butter.

Note: These are handy to have on hand. Store in covered jar in refrigerator to keep crispness. Heat in oven before using.

Cheese Puffs

12 2-inch bread rounds

• • •

¼ cup mayonnaise
½ package (1 packet) onion dip mix
2 tablespoons grated Parmesan cheese

• • •

1 stiff-beaten egg white

Toast bread rounds on one side in broiler. Combine mayonnaise, dip mix, and cheese. Fold stiff-beaten egg white into mayonnaise mixture. Spoon onto untoasted side of bread rounds. Bake in very hot oven (450°) about 10 minutes or until golden. Serve hot.

Outdoor Hard Rolls

Here's an outdoors way for "stuffing" to go with rotisserie chicken—

Split hard rolls lengthwise. Blend soft butter or margarine with a good dash of poultry seasoning (or with small dash each of thyme and marjoram). Spread rolls with the seasoned butter, then wrap in foil. Heat rolls on grill while you carve the chicken.

Marmalade Slices

1 loaf French bread, 12 inches long
⅓ to ½ cup soft butter or margarine
½ cup orange marmalade
Cinnamon

Cut bread in 1- to 1½-inch diagonal slices. Spread with butter, then with marmalade (don't skimp!). Sprinkle cinnamon generously over top. Place slices marmalade side up on broiler rack and broil 5 to 6 inches from heat 6 to 7 minutes. Topping will be *extra hot*, so let cool a few minutes before serving. Makes 8 to 10 slices.

Coconut Squares

1 1-pound unsliced sandwich loaf
¾ cup brown sugar
⅓ cup soft butter or margarine
¼ cup flaked or shredded coconut
3 tablespoons honey
¼ to ½ teaspoon cinnamon

Cut crusts from top and sides of loaf. Place loaf on greased baking sheet. Make one cut lengthwise down center of loaf, *almost to bottom crust*. Now slice crosswise, at about 1½-inch intervals, cutting *almost to bottom crust*.

Combine brown sugar, butter, coconut, honey, and cinnamon; spread between bread squares and over top of loaf. Sprinkle additional coconut over top. Tie string around loaf to hold together. Heat in hot oven (400°) about 10 minutes. Remove string. Serve "rolls" while warm. Makes about 12.

Walnut Coffeecake Sticks

¾ cup butter or margarine, softened
¾ cup brown sugar
1 tablespoon milk or light cream
1 teaspoon cinnamon
1 unsliced sandwich loaf, about 11 inches long
1 to 1½ cups chopped California walnuts

Cream together butter, sugar, milk, and cinnamon till light and fluffy.

Trim all crusts from bread; then cut loaf crosswise in 3 equal, large cubes. Cut each cube in thirds, then in thirds again in the opposite direction, making 9 sticks per cube. Spread butter mixture on all surfaces except bottom. Roll in nuts. Bake on baking sheet in moderate oven (375°) for about 15 minutes or till crispy. Makes 27 sticks.

Toasted Coconut Bars

1 cup shredded coconut
1 cup Grape-Nuts
• • •
4 slices day-old bread
⅔ cup sweetened condensed milk

Mix coconut and Grape-Nuts. Remove crusts from bread. Cut bread in 1-inch strips; dip in condensed milk till well coated; roll in coconut mixture. Place on greased baking sheet. Bake in moderate oven (350°) about 10 minutes. Makes 15.

Shaggy Mochas

Doughnuts get a coffee-coconut topping—

2 teaspoons instant coffee
2 tablespoons water
½ cup flaked coconut
• • •
1 cup sifted confectioners' sugar
2 tablespoons light cream or milk
12 plain doughnuts

In pint jar, dissolve coffee in water; add coconut. Cover and shake until coconut is coffee color. Spread coconut on ungreased baking sheet; dry in slow oven (300°) for about 25 minutes, stirring occasionally.

Meanwhile combine confectioners' sugar and cream to make icing. Frost tops of doughnuts. While icing is soft, sprinkle with the coffee-flavored coconut.

Rocky-Road Rings. Simply melt ½ cup semi-sweet chocolate pieces in double boiler. Dip tops of 8 doughnuts in melted chocolate, then in coarsely broken California walnuts.

Apricot Split-ups. Halve doughnuts. Broil cut side down 3 to 4 inches from heat ½ to 1 minute. Spread cut surface with apricot jam; sprinkle with broken nuts; broil till jam is bubbly.

Frosted Doughnuts

12 plain doughnuts
• • •
1 cup sifted confectioners' sugar
½ teaspoon orange peel
2 tablespoons orange juice

Heat doughnuts in moderate oven (375°) 5 minutes or till very hot. Meanwhile combine the confectioners' sugar, orange peel, and juice. Dip one side of doughnut in glaze.

For heavier glaze, double the confectioners' sugar, orange peel, and juice and dunk each doughnut twice. (Use tongs for easy dipping.) Place doughnuts, glaze side up, on rack to drip and set.

Cinnamon Doughnuts

12 plain doughnuts
½ cup sugar
1 to 2 teaspoons cinnamon

Heat doughnuts on baking sheet in moderate oven (375°) 5 minutes or till very hot. Remove from oven and shake in paper or plastic sack containing mixture of sugar and cinnamon. Serve warm.

Dress-ups for jiffy breads

Spicy Coffee Ring

Perfect California walnut halves

• • •

1 package refrigerated biscuits
Melted butter or margarine
⅓ cup brown sugar
1 teaspoon cinnamon
2 tablespoons seedless raisins

Place ring of walnut halves in greased 5½-cup ring mold. Dip biscuits in melted butter, then in mixture of brown sugar and cinnamon. Place in mold, overlapping slightly. Tuck raisins between biscuits. Bake in hot oven (425°) for about 13 to 15 minutes.

Honey Roll-ups

¼ cup honey
¼ teaspoon cinnamon
1 package refrigerated biscuits
¼ cup seedless raisins
¼ cup finely chopped nuts
Melted butter or margarine

Combine honey and cinnamon. Roll each biscuit to a 4-inch circle. Spread with honey mixture. Sprinkle chopped nuts or raisins over. Fold biscuit into shape of a cornucopia, pinching the pointed end to seal. Arrange in a circle in 8x1½-inch round pan with pointed ends toward center. Brush with melted butter and bake in moderate oven (375°) 15 to 20 minutes. Remove from pan. Sprinkle with confectioners' sugar.

Caramel Buns

You make the sauce right in the baking pan—

2 tablespoons butter or margarine
½ cup brown sugar
¼ cup light or dark corn syrup
¼ cup pecan halves
2 packages refrigerated biscuits

Melt butter in bottom of 9x1½-inch pan. Add brown sugar and corn syrup; heat in oven to dissolve sugar. Arrange pecans to form design. Place biscuits atop in single layer. Bake in hot oven (425°) 15 minutes or till biscuits are done. Let stand 4 minutes. Invert on serving plate. Serve warm.

Speedy Orange Coffeecake

1 package refrigerated biscuits
2 tablespoons butter or
margarine, melted
¼ cup sugar
2 tablespoons finely chopped walnuts
2 teaspoons grated orange peel

Dip biscuits in butter, then in mixture of sugar, walnuts, and peel. Overlap biscuits in circle in 9-inch pie plate.* Bake at 400° for 15 minutes or till done. Serve hot.

*Or to match picture on opposite page, bake double recipe in 11-inch pie plate.

Orange Ring-around: Double recipe for Speedy Orange Coffeecake. Dip biscuits in butter, then in sugar mixture as directed. Overlap biscuits in circle in greased 9-inch ring mold. Bake in hot oven (400°) about 20 minutes. Invert on plate. Serve at once.

Quickie Stickies

⅓ cup honey
3 tablespoons butter or
margarine, melted
¼ cup broken California walnuts
1 package refrigerated biscuits
Melted butter or margarine
Cinnamon

Blend honey and melted butter; divide mixture among 7 muffin cups. Sprinkle a few walnuts into each cup. Brush one side of each biscuit with melted butter; sprinkle with cinnamon. Cut biscuits in half.

Place 3 halves, cut side down (curved side will be top) and buttered sides touching, in each muffin cup, (One muffin cup will have only 2 halves). Bake biscuits in moderate oven (350°) 15 minutes or till done. Remove immediately. Makes 7.

All from packaged biscuits

Looking for easy treats? These two fairly → jump from a tube of biscuits! Speedy Orange Coffeecake and Quickie Stickies are perfect for impromptu snacking.

Jiffy Doughnuts

Just deep-fat fry refrigerated biscuits—

Stretch and flatten slightly each biscuit from a refrigerated package. With finger, punch hole in center and shape in doughnut. Fry in deep hot fat (375°) about 2 minutes, turning once. Drain on paper towels. Roll in cinnamon-sugar mixture. Serve warm. Makes 10 doughnuts.

Campfire Doughnut Holes

If you're looking for a spectacular on a small scale, this is it—

Cut refrigerated biscuits (from a tube) in thirds, and roll each piece into a ball. String on skewers, leaving about ½ inch between balls. "Bake" over *hot* coals, *turning constantly* until browned and completely done, about 7 minutes. At once, push off skewers into melted butter; roll in cinnamon-sugar mixture. Eat right away! One tube of refrigerated biscuits makes 30.

Quick Bismarcks

Luscious jelly-filled treats for breakfast or dessert. Coffee is a must—

1 package refrigerated biscuits
Jam or jelly

Flatten each biscuit to ¼ inch. Place 1 teaspoon jam or jelly on *half* the biscuits; cover with remaining biscuits; seal edges well. Fry in deep hot fat (375°) for 3 minutes on each side. Drain on paper towels. Dust each with confectioners' sugar, if you like. Serve warm. Makes 5 bismarcks.

Cinnamon Twists

1 package refrigerated biscuits
• • •
2 tablespoons melted butter
¼ cup sugar
1 teaspoon cinnamon
• • •
2 tablespoons chopped pecans

Roll each biscuit to 7-inch stick; dip in melted butter, then in sugar-cinnamon mixture. Fold each stick in half. Seal ends; twist. Place on greased baking sheet; sprinkle with nuts. Bake in hot oven (425°) for 10 minutes. Makes 10.

Pineapple Turnover Biscuits

½ cup crushed pineapple
¼ cup brown sugar
2 tablespoons butter or
  margarine melted
½ teaspoon cinnamon
• • •
10 California walnut halves
1 package refrigerated biscuits

Drain pineapple, reserving syrup. Combine pineapple, brown sugar, butter, and cinnamon; divide in 10 muffin cups and center each with walnut half. Add 1 teaspoon pineapple syrup to each cup and top with a refrigerated biscuit. Bake in hot oven (425°) 12 to 15 minutes. Invert pan immediately on serving plate. Cool 1 minute before removing pan. Makes 10 biscuits.

Crunch Sticks

Perfect partner for soup or salad—

1 package refrigerated biscuits
Milk
• • •
1½ cups crisp rice cereal,
  coarsely crushed
2 tablespoons caraway seed,
  celery seed, or dill seed
2 teaspoons salt

Cut biscuits in half; roll each part into pencil-thin stick (about 4 inches long). Brush with milk. Mix cereal crumbs, seed, and salt in shallow pan (be sure salt is well distributed); roll sticks in mixture.

Place on greased baking sheet. Bake in very hot oven (450°) 10 minutes or till lightly browned. Makes 20.

Jam Brown-and-Serves

Quick sweet rolls for breakfast—

1 teaspoon butter or
  margarine, melted
6 brown-and-serve dinner rolls
• • •
6 teaspoons apricot preserves
  or marmalade

Brush butter over tops of rolls. Make a lengthwise cut in the top of each. Insert 1 teaspoon preserves in each cut. Bake rolls in greased shallow pan in hot oven (400°) for about 10 to 12 minutes or till browned. Serve warm. Makes 6 rolls.

Blue-cheese Biscuits

1 package refrigerated biscuits
¼ cup butter or margarine
3 tablespoons blue cheese, crumbled

Cut biscuits in quarters. Arrange in two 8-inch round baking dishes. Melt together butter and cheese; pour over biscuit pieces, being sure to coat them all. Bake at 400° about 15 minutes or till golden brown. Serve hot as appetizers. Makes 40.

Parsley Fantans

2 tablespoons butter, melted
1 teaspoon lemon juice
6 brown-and-serve butterflake rolls
2 tablespoons chopped parsley
2 teaspoons chopped chives

Combine butter and lemon juice. Partially separate sections of rolls. Brush between sections with part of the lemon butter; sprinkle with most of the parsley and chives. Place rolls in muffin cups. Brush tops with remaining lemon butter; sprinkle with parsley and chives. Brown at 400° about 6 minutes.

Parmesan Biscuits

1 clove garlic, minced
¼ cup butter or margarine, melted
2 packages refrigerated biscuits
¼ cup shredded Parmesan cheese

Add garlic to butter; dip biscuits in mixture. Overlap 13 biscuits around outer edge of 9x1½-inch round metal cake pan. Overlap remaining biscuits in center. Drizzle remaining butter over top; sprinkle with cheese. Bake at 425° for 15 to 20 minutes. Makes 20.

Quick Onion Biscuits

2 tablespoons instant minced onion
2 tablespoons butter, melted
• • •
1 package refrigerated biscuits

Add onion to butter. Place biscuits on ungreased baking sheet. Pressing with bottom of small glass dipped in flour, make a hollow in center of each biscuit. Fill with onion-butter mixture. Bake in very hot oven (450°) about 8 to 10 minutes or till biscuits are done. Makes 10 biscuits.

Parsley Fantans are a snap to fix—you dress up brown-and-serve butterflake rolls. They make a bright accent for fruit salad.

A tray of treats! Left to right: Corned-beef Fold-overs, Ham-Cheese Toasties, Tricorn Snacks, Pigs in Blankets, Onion Rounds.

Corned-beef Fold-overs

1 package refrigerated biscuits
1 cup corned-beef hash
1 tablespoon chili sauce
1 small onion, chopped

Roll biscuits to 4-inch circles. Mix the hash, chili sauce, and onion. Place a tablespoon of mixture on half of each circle. Fold in half and seal edges with tines of fork. Prick top in a design. Bake in hot oven (425°) about 12 to 15 minutes. Makes 10.

Pigs in Blankets

Pat refrigerated biscuits out lengthwise until you can wrap each around a Vienna sausage. Fasten biscuits around sausages with toothpicks or seal edges with fingers. Bake in hot oven (425°) 12 to 15 minutes or till done. Serve piping hot.

Tricorn Snacks

1 package refrigerated biscuits
• • •
¼ pound liver sausage
¼ cup chili sauce
⅓ cup pickle relish

Roll biscuits to 4-inch circles. Mix liver sausage, chili sauce, and relish. Place spoonful of mixture in center of each biscuit circle. Fold up 3 sides and seal edges; prick sides in a design. Brush with melted butter. Bake in hot oven (425°) about 10 minutes or till done. Serve immediately.

Ham-Cheese Toasties

Tasty little open-facers, with olive trim—

1 package refrigerated biscuits
• • •
1 2¼-ounce can deviled ham
1 tablespoon mayonnaise
1 teaspoon salt
5 slices sharp process American cheese
Stuffed green olives, sliced

Bake the biscuits as directed on package. Split. Combine deviled ham, mayonnaise, and salt. Spread on biscuit halves. Cut cheese in quarters and place a square atop each biscuit. Decorate with a slice of olive. Broil 5 or 6 inches from heat till cheese melts, about 4 minutes. Serve hot. Makes 20.

Onion-Cheese Rounds

As good as they are speedy—

1 package refrigerated biscuits
• • •
3 tablespoons butter or margarine, melted
5 slices process American cheese, cut in quarters
Thin onion slices

Bake the biscuits as directed on package. Split. Brush with butter. Place a cheese square on each biscuit half and top with onion slice. Brush onion with butter. Broil 5 or 6 inches from heat till cheese melts, about 4 minutes. Serve hot. Makes 20.

In-a-skillet Biscuits

Preheat electric skillet to about 380° and grease lightly with butter or margarine. Place biscuits from refrigerated package in skillet—don't let them touch each other. Cover and bake 3 minutes. Turn biscuits; cover and bake about 3 minutes more.

Hibachi Cheese Biscuits

Cut refrigerated biscuits (from a tube) in thirds; roll each piece into a ball. Dip in melted butter or margarine, then in grated Parmesan cheese. String on skewers, leaving about ½ inch between balls.

"Bake" over *hot* coals, *turning constantly*, till browned and completely done, about 7 minutes. Eat right now! One tube of refrigerated biscuits makes 30 appetizer biscuits.

Midget Pizzas

½ pound Italian sausage
1 tablespoon crushed oregano
1 clove garlic, minced
1 package refrigerated biscuits
Tomato paste
1 cup shredded sharp process
American cheese
¼ cup grated Parmesan cheese

Brown sausage; drain. Add oregano and garlic. On a greased baking sheet, flatten refrigerated biscuits to 4-inch circles with floured custard cup; leave rim. Fill with tomato paste and sausage. Sprinkle with American cheese and Parmesan cheese. Bake in hot oven (425°) about 10 minutes.

Broiled Olive Snacks

1 package refrigerated biscuits
3 tablespoons butter or
margarine, melted
1 cup shredded sharp process
American cheese
½ cup chopped stuffed green olives
2 stiff-beaten egg whites
3 or 4 slices bacon, finely diced

Bake biscuits as directed on package. Split. Brush cut side with butter.

Fold cheese and olives into egg whites; spoon on buttered side of biscuits. Sprinkle with bacon. Top each with an olive slice. Broil 4 to 5 inches from heat 5 to 8 minutes or till bacon browns and cheese melts.

Toasty Cheese Canapes

1 package refrigerated biscuits
3 tablespoons butter or
margarine, melted
2 stiff-beaten egg whites
1¼ cups coarsely grated Swiss cheese
⅔ cup finely chopped green pepper
1 teaspoon chopped parsley
½ teaspoon salt
Dash pepper
3 to 4 slices bacon, finely diced

Bake biscuits as directed on package. Split. Brush with butter.

Into egg whites fold the cheese, green pepper, parsley, salt, and pepper; spoon on buttered side of biscuit. Sprinkle bacon over top of each. Place on broiler pan; broil 4 to 5 inches from heat 5 to 8 minutes or till bacon browns and cheese melts. Makes 20.

Brown-and-serve Rolls on a Spit

A slick trick! Rolls get crusty on all sides, stay soft in center—

Shortly before you give the come-and-get-it call, thread brown-and-serve rolls on a spit. Brush rolls with melted butter. Let rotate over coals about 10 to 15 minutes.

Parsley-Lemon Loaves

Each little loaf will serve 2 to 3 people—

2 large brown-and-serve French
rolls, each about 8 inches long

• • •

¼ cup soft butter or margarine
¼ cup snipped parsley
2 teaspoons lemon juice
Long skewers

Slice rolls diagonally in 1-inch slices. Combine butter and parsley; blend in lemon juice. Spread one side of each slice with parsley butter. Reassemble each roll on a long skewer, inserting skewer through center of slices. Broil 3 to 4 inches from heat 5 to 6 minutes, turning to brown evenly. (Or brown over very hot coals.)

Note: A small wire whip is good tool for blending butter and lemon juice.

Parsley-Lemon Loaves look like big kabobs. Pass the butter-y slices right on the skewers—let folks "unthread" to help themselves.

Sand-wiches

When it comes to sandwiches, the sky's the limit! You'll find here spectacular sandwiches—hearty supper stack-ups, dainty teatime bites, show-off sandwiches for company. Each one is easy to make, and delicious!

Five ways to serve a sandwich

← Down front are Hot-dog Burgers—two favorites in one bun! Next up the stairsteps, you see Ten-in-one Sandwich Loaf—pull off your own serving of salami-and-cheese-on-white. Above are Shrimp Boat (sea-food salad via a Vienna-loaf bowl) and Seven-league Pizzaburger (Italian-style ground beef on French bread). Up high is Big Top Sandwich with fillings of egg salad, tomatoes, and deviled ham.

Hearty Sandwiches

Sandwiches fill the bill in a variety of ways. So easy to make and eat, they are just the thing for packing in lunch boxes or picnic baskets. Ideal for summer; no cooking is necessary. And for long cold months, there are scores of hot grilled sandwiches to serve.

We show party sandwich ideas, too. Choose from an array of open-faced dainties and pretty frosted loaves for party snacks and gay entertaining.

Big Top Sandwich

A summer sandwich loaf in the round—

Deviled Ham Filling:

1 4½-ounce can deviled ham
¼ cup shredded sharp Cheddar cheese
¼ cup finely chopped celery
2 tablespoons finely chopped green pepper

Egg Filling:

3 hard-cooked eggs, finely chopped
¼ cup finely chopped dill pickle
3 tablespoons sliced green onions
3 tablespoons mayonnaise or salad dressing
¼ teaspoon salt
Dash bottled hot pepper sauce

Tomato Filling:

Leaf lettuce
2 medium tomatoes, thinly sliced
2 tablespoons clear French or Italian dressing

• • •

1 round loaf rye bread (8 or 9 inches in diameter)
Soft butter or margarine

Prepare the first two fillings by mixing ingredients listed under each; chill. Chill lettuce and tomatoes for the third filling. Cut loaf crosswise into 4 round slices; butter slices. Spread bottom slice with Ham Filling. Add next bread round; cover with leaf lettuce (first pat dry on paper towels). Slice tomatoes; place in a layer over lettuce and drizzle with dressing. Add third slice of bread; spread with Egg Filling. Top with last slice. Insert skewers or picks down through loaf—1 in each serving—to secure layers while cutting. Cut loaf in wedges. Sandwich makes 6 to 8 servings.

Seven-league Pizzaburger

French bread is the easy pizza crust—

1 loaf French bread, about 18 inches long
1 pound ground beef
⅓ cup grated Parmesan cheese
¼ cup finely chopped onion
¼ cup chopped pitted ripe olives
1 teaspoon salt
½ to 1 teaspoon crushed oregano
Dash pepper
1 6-ounce can (⅔ cup) tomato paste
3 tomatoes, peeled and sliced
6 slices sharp process American *or* Mozzarella cheese, halved diagonally

Cut loaf lengthwise in half. Combine meat with next 7 ingredients. Spread evenly on each half loaf. Broil 5 inches from heat 12 minutes or till done. Alternate tomato and cheese slices across top. Broil 1 to 2 minutes more or just till cheese begins to melt. Cut each half in 4 or 5 slices.

Ten-in-one Sandwich Loaf

2 cups shredded process American cheese *or* 2 5-ounce jars spreading cheese
¼ cup mayonnaise or salad dressing
1 teaspoon prepared mustard
1 teaspoon grated onion
⅔ cup chopped ripe olives

• • •

1 unsliced sandwich loaf, about 11 inches long
20 thin slices large salami (about ½ pound)
Melted butter or margarine

Blend cheese, mayonnaise, mustard, and onion; stir in olives. Cut crusts from *top* and both sides of loaf. Make ½-inch slices, cutting to, *but not through*, bottom crust. Spread facing sides of first cut with cheese filling. Repeat with *every other* cut.

Insert 2 salami slices in each "cheese sandwich." Spread remaining cheese over top. To hold shape, tie string around loaf 1 inch from top. Brush sides with butter. Toast on baking sheet in 350° oven 25 to 30 minutes. To serve, snip string and cut through bottom crust in unfilled sections.

Take-two Sandwich

1 loaf French bread, about 18 inches long
Soft butter or margarine
Leaf lettuce
• • •
5 thin slices boiled ham
5 thin slices large salami
Large dill pickles, sliced thin lengthwise
• • •
5 slices Swiss cheese
5 thin slices tomato

Cut French loaf in 3/4-inch slices, *almost to, but not through*, bottom crust, making 19 cuts in all. Butter facing sides of first cut and line with lettuce. Repeat with every other cut —this will leave unfilled cuts in between, where sandwiches can be broken off at serving time. In first lettuce-lined cut, insert a folded slice each of ham and salami with a slice of pickle in the middle. In second lettuce-lined cut, insert a cheese slice folded in half around a tomato slice. Alternate these fillings in remaining lettuce-lined cuts. Pass bowls of mayonnaise, prepared mustard, and olives. Makes 10 sandwiches or 5 double-sandwich servings.

All-in-a-Roll Supper

3/4 pound ground beef
1/4 cup chopped onion
• • •
2 large brown-and-serve French rolls, each about 8 inches long
1 beaten egg
3 tablespoons snipped parsley
1 to 2 tablespoons prepared mustard
2 tablespoons water
3/4 teaspoon salt
1/4 teaspoon oregano
Dash pepper
2 tablespoons butter or margarine, melted
1 clove garlic, minced

Brown ground beef. Add onion; cook till tender but not brown. Drain off excess fat. Cut off one end of each roll; reserve. With a fork, hollow out roll centers and pull apart enough bread to make 1 cup crumbs. Mix crumbs with meat and next 7 ingredients. Fill rolls, replacing ends; tack with toothpicks. Mix butter and garlic; brush over rolls. Heat on baking sheet in moderate oven (375°) for about 20 minutes or till hot. Cut in 4 or 6 servings.

Lobster Fantans

1 5- or 6½-ounce can lobster*, drained
½ cup cubed Swiss cheese
3 tablespoons chopped green pepper
2 tablespoons minced onion
½ teaspoon salt
¼ cup mayonnaise or salad dressing
1 teaspoon lemon juice
4 or 5 oblong soft rolls, about 4x3 inches
Soft butter or margarine

Break lobster in chunks; toss with cheese, green pepper, onion, and salt. Blend mayonnaise and lemon juice; add to lobster mixture; toss lightly. Cut rolls crosswise in 4 slices, *not quite through bottom crust.* Spread cut sides with butter; fill in between with lobster mixture. Wrap in aluminum foil and place on baking sheet. Heat in moderate oven (350°) 20 minutes or till hot. This sandwich is a fork food. Makes 4 to 5 servings.

*Or use one 6½- or 7-ounce can tuna, drained, instead of the lobster.

Shrimp Boat

3 cups cooked or canned cleaned shrimp
1 cup diced celery
4 hard-cooked eggs, chopped
⅓ cup sliced green onions
¼ cup chopped dill pickle
2 tablespoons drained capers (optional)
• • •
1 cup mayonnaise or salad dressing
2 tablespoons chili sauce
2 teaspoons prepared horseradish
1 teaspoon salt
• • •
1 loaf Vienna bread, about 11x5 inches
Melted butter or margarine

Reserve a few large shrimp for garnish; cut up remainder. Combine first 6 ingredients. Blend mayonnaise and seasonings; add to shrimp mixture and toss lightly. Chill.

Meanwhile, cut a large deep wedge out of Vienna loaf to make "boat." Brush the cut surfaces with melted butter. Place loaf on ungreased baking sheet and toast in moderate oven (350°) for 15 minutes or till lightly browned. Cool before filling.

Line bread "boat" with lettuce; mound with shrimp salad. Trim with whole shrimp and "sails" of lemon slices flagged with water cress, if desired. Pass lemon wedges. Cut "boat" in 6 to 8 slices.

Serve sandwich sizzlers—Spring Sandwich Puff, Grilled Corned Beef 'n Rye, Burgers in Bologna Boats, Ho

Hot-dog Burgers

1 pound ground beef
1 teaspoon salt
Dash pepper
⅓ cup evaporated milk
3 frankfurters, halved lengthwise
6 Coney buns, split, toasted, buttered

Combine first 4 ingredients; shape into 6 flat rectangles (coney-bun size). Press half a frank into each burger. Broil 3 inches from heat, turning once, 8 to 10 minutes. Serve in buns. Makes 6 servings.

Grilled Corned Beef 'n Rye

Spread 6 slices of pumpernickel bread with Thousand Island dressing (takes about ½ cup). Top each with 1 slice Swiss cheese, 1 tablespoon drained sauerkraut, very thin slices of cooked or canned corned beef (takes ¼ to ½ pound), and another slice of bread.

Butter top and bottom of each sandwich. Grill on both sides on griddle or sandwich grill till toasty and hot through and cheese is melty. Anchor with toothpick topped by stuffed green olive. Makes 6.

'izza Sandwiches, and Gourmet Steak on Toast. Butter-brown some canned peaches for a fruit go-with.

Burgers in Bologna Boats

Shape 1 pound ground beef in 4 patties (same size around as Bologna slices). Grill, turning once; sprinkle with salt and pepper. Slip each patty onto a thin slice of large Bologna. Grill till Bologna is lightly browned and edges cup around patty. Cut 2 to 4 slices sharp process American cheese into strips; form lattice on top of patties. Split and toast 4 hamburger buns; spread bottom halves with prepared mustard; top with patties and bun tops. Makes 4 servings.

Hot Pizza Sandwiches

Spread canned pizza sauce on one side of 8 slices of bread (takes 2/3 cup). Top 4 slices with 1 large or 2 small salami slices, then with 1 slice sharp process American cheese; sprinkle with garlic salt. Add remaining bread slices, sauce side down. Generously butter top and bottom of sandwiches. Grill both sides on griddle or sandwich grill till sandwiches are toasted and cheese melts. Pass pickles, olives, crisp radishes, green onion. Makes 4 sandwiches.

Spring Oven Sandwich

6 slices bread
6 slices process American cheese
Hot cooked asparagus

• • •

3 egg yolks
¼ cup salad dressing
¼ teaspoon salt
Dash pepper
3 stiff-beaten egg whites

In broiler, toast bread slices on one side. Place a slice of cheese on each untoasted side; broil to partially melt cheese. Remove from heat, and place 3 or 4 spears of hot cooked asparagus on top of each cheese slice. Beat egg yolks till thick and lemon-colored, stir in salad dressing, salt, and pepper; fold in stiff-beaten egg whites. Pile mixture on top of asparagus. Bake in moderate oven (350°) for about 13 minutes or till egg mixture is set. Makes 6 servings.

Gourmet Steak on Toast

½ cup canned condensed beef broth*
½ cup cooking claret
1 or 2 green onions, finely sliced
Dash pepper
Dash marjoram and thyme
1 small bay leaf

• • •

¼ teaspoon lemon juice
1 teaspoon snipped parsley
2 teaspoons butter or margarine

• • •

4 cube steaks, ¼ inch thick
8 tomato wedges
4 ½-inch-wide green-pepper strips
4 bias-cut, ½-inch slices French bread, toasted

For Chef's Sauce, combine broth, cooking claret, green onions, and seasonings; cook fast to reduce the volume by ½. Remove bay leaf; add lemon juice, parsley, and butter. (Set sauce aside but keep hot.)

Grill cube steaks 1 to 2 minutes per side on lightly greased griddle. Meanwhile grill green pepper and tomatoes alongside. Sprinkle all with salt and freshly ground pepper. To serve, dip a slice of toast quickly in Chef's Sauce; place a steak atop and arrange a green-pepper strip and 2 tomato wedges on steak. Spoon any remaining sauce over sandwiches. Makes 4 servings.

*Or dissolve ½ beef bouillon cube in ½ cup hot water.

Dad's Denvers

6 hamburger buns, split and toasted
1 4½-ounce can deviled ham

• • •

4 eggs
¼ cup milk
¼ teaspoon salt
Dash pepper

• • •

¼ cup chopped green onions
2 tablespoons butter, margarine, or bacon drippings

• • •

6 thin tomato slices
6 slices sharp process American cheese

Spread lower half of buns with deviled ham. Combine eggs, milk, salt, and pepper. Beat slightly for gold-and-white effect, thoroughly for all-yellow. Add chopped onions. Heat butter in skillet till just hot enough to make a drop of water sizzle. Pour in egg mixture. Reduce heat and cook, lifting and folding occasionally, till eggs are set, but still moist. Pile eggs atop deviled ham and add tomato slices and cheese slices.

Place sandwiches on baking sheet; broil about 4 inches from heat just till cheese melts. Cover hot sandwiches with bun tops. Makes 6 servings.

Deviled-ham Rollwiches

A knife-and-fork broiler special—

4 brown-and-serve hard rolls

• • •

Softened butter or margarine
Prepared mustard
1 4½-ounce can deviled ham
8 thin slices peeled tomato, cut in half
1 medium green pepper, cut in strips
1 small onion, cut in thin slices and separated in rings

• • •

8 narrow strips process American cheese

Split rolls in half lengthwise. Broil, cut side down, till nicely browned. Spread cut side of each half roll with butter, mustard, and ham. Top each with 2 pieces tomato, green-pepper strips, and onion rings.

Broil 3 to 4 inches from heat 4 to 5 minutes or till hot. Place cheese strip diagonally across tops. Broil just till cheese starts to melt. Makes 4 servings.

Delicious Dad's Denvers This one will be a family favorite. Onion-spiked scrambled eggs team up with deviled ham, tomatoes, and cheese—all broiled till hot and melty. Good served with a crisp salad.

Grilled Crab Sandwiches

1 6½- or 7½-ounce can (about 1 cup) crab meat, drained and flaked
½ cup shredded sharp process American cheese
¼ cup chopped celery
2 tablespoons drained sweet-pickle relish
2 tablespoons chopped green onions and tops
1 hard-cooked egg, chopped
3 tablespoons salad dressing or mayonnaise
½ teaspoon lemon juice
½ teaspoon prepared horseradish
10 slices bread, buttered generously
5 tomato slices

Combine first 9 ingredients; spread on unbuttered side of 5 bread slices. Add tomato slices; season with salt and pepper. Top with bread slices, buttered side up. Grill on griddle, sandwich grill, or in skillet till sandwiches are golden brown and hot through. Makes 5 grilled sandwiches.

Sausage French Toasties

Here's a dandy way to say "good morning!" French bread is flavored with orange and topped with hot sizzling sausages—

Brown-and-serve sausage links

• • •

2 slightly-beaten eggs
1 tablespoon sugar
1½ teaspoons grated orange peel
½ cup orange juice

• • •

4 slices bread

Brown sausage three minutes according to package directions.

Blend slightly-beaten eggs, sugar, grated orange peel, and orange juice. Remove crusts from bread. Dip bread slices in egg and orange mixture. Fry in small amount of melted butter or margarine until golden brown on each side. Top each piece of toast with a few hot sausage links. Serve piping hot. Makes 4 servings. Offer warm maple syrup, jelly, and Whipped Butter.

Corned-beef Stag Sandwiches

1 cup packaged biscuit mix
1 12-ounce can corned beef, chilled
1 tablespoon mayonnaise or salad dressing
1 tablespoon prepared mustard
½ cup pitted ripe olives, sliced
1 large tomato, thinly sliced
4 slices sharp process American cheese

Prepare biscuit mix according to package directions for rolled biscuits. Roll to a 12x7-inch rectangle, about ⅜ inch thick. Place on ungreased baking sheet. Cut corned beef in 10 slices; arrange over dough. Mix mayonnaise and mustard; spread over meat. Sprinkle with olives. Bake at 425° 10 minutes. Top with tomato slices, dash with pepper. Halve cheese slices diagonally; arrange over tomatoes. Return to oven till cheese melts, about 5 minutes. Cut in 6 squares.

Hot Curried Chicken Sandwiches

4 slices buttered toast
4 large slices cooked chicken or 1½ cups cubed
½ cup salad dressing
⅓ cup finely chopped celery
¼ cup sliced green onions and tops
½ cup coarsely shredded pared tart apple
¾ teaspoon curry powder
½ teaspoon salt
Dash pepper

Arrange toast on baking sheet. Cover with chicken; dash with salt and pepper. Mix remaining ingredients; spread over chicken. Broil 7 or 8 inches from heat 5 to 8 minutes or till hot. Makes 4 servings.

Hot Ham Buns

¼ cup soft butter or margarine
2 tablespoons prepared horseradish-mustard
2 teaspoons poppy seed
2 tablespoons finely chopped onion
4 hamburger buns, split
4 thin slices boiled ham
4 slices process Swiss cheese

Mix butter, mustard, poppy seed, and onion; spread on cut surfaces of buns. Tuck a slice of ham and cheese in each bun. Arrange on baking sheet. Bake in moderate oven (350°) for about 20 minutes or till hot through. Makes 4 servings.

Grilled Pizza Sandwiches

A grilled quickie sure to please those pizza fans in your family—

⅔ cup canned pizza sauce
8 slices bread
• • •
4 large or 8 small slices salami
4 slices sharp process American cheese
Garlic salt or salt
• • •
Soft butter or margarine

Spread pizza sauce on one side of each bread slice. Top 4 with salami slices, then with cheese; sprinkle with garlic salt. Add remaining bread slices, sauce side down.

Generously butter top and bottom of sandwiches. Grill both sides on griddle, sandwich grill, or in a skillet until sandwiches are toasted and cheese melts. Makes 4.

Inside-out Pizza

Spread inner surfaces of sandwich with spaghetti or pizza sauce; sprinkle one side of them with basil. Add several slices of Provolone cheese to make a generous filling. Brush the outer surfaces of the sandwich with soft butter or margarine.

Grill slowly on ungreased griddle, sandwich grill, or in skillet.

Piquant options: Sprinkle 2 or 3 drops of bottled hot pepper sauce inside each sandwich. Or shake grated Parmesan or Romano cheese on one inner surface.

Peanut-'n-Apple Sandwiches

Chopped apple adds crunch and fresh flavor—

½ cup peanut butter
2 tablespoons mayonnaise or salad dressing
2 teaspoons lemon juice
• • •
½ cup finely diced pared tart apple
6 slices bacon, crisp-cooked and crumbled
• • •
Buttered bread slices

Blend peanut butter, mayonnaise, and lemon juice. Stir in apple and bacon. Use as a filling between buttered slices of bread. Add lettuce, if desired. Makes 1 cup filling—enough for 4 or 5 sandwiches.

Chicken Skillet Sandwiches

4 slices sandwich bread

• • •

1 can condensed cream of chicken soup
½ cup light cream
6 slices canned or cooked chicken
⅔ cup grated sharp process American cheese
Catsup

Toast the bread lightly; remove crusts; cut slices in triangles. Place one triangle in bottom of each of 2 individual skillets or shallow casseroles. Blend chicken soup and cream; add chicken and heat to boiling. Pour over toast in skillets. Sprinkle with cheese. Broil till cheese is bubbly and golden brown, about 5 minutes. Add 3 more toast triangles around edge of each casserole; center with a teaspoon of catsup. Serves 2.

Ripe-olive Susans

1½ cups shredded process American cheese
½ cup mayonnaise or salad dressing
1 cup ripe-olive slices
½ cup thinly sliced green onions
½ teaspoon curry powder (optional)

• • •

6 slices enriched sandwich bread, toasted

Combine cheese, mayonnaise, olive slices, onions, and curry; spread on toast. Broil 4 to 6 inches from heat 2 minutes or till topping bubbles. Cut sandwiches diagonally in half. Makes 6 servings.

Jumbo Burgers

1 loaf Vienna bread, about 12x5 inches
Soft butter or margarine

• • •

1½ pounds ground beef
½ cup chopped onion
2 tablespoons Worcestershire sauce
1¼ teaspoons salt

Cut loaf in half lengthwise; spread with butter. Combine remaining ingredients; spread about ½ inch thick on each half loaf, building edges up slightly. Broil about 6 inches from heat 15 minutes, or till meat is done the way you like. Top with a pat or two of butter if desired; garnish with onion rings. To serve, cut each half-loaf in husky crosswise slices. Makes 8 servings.

Blue-cheese Puff-ups

1 3-ounce package cream cheese
2 ounces blue cheese, crumbled (⅓ to ½ cup)

• • •

1 tablespoon light cream
1 tablespoon chopped parsley
¼ teaspoon onion juice
¼ teaspoon Worcestershire sauce
Dash monosodium glutamate

• • •

6 slices bread
3 small tomatoes, peeled and thinly sliced
6 slices bacon, cut in half

Soften cheeses at room temperature; blend well. Beat in cream; add parsley, onion, and seasonings. Toast bread on one side. Butter untoasted side. Place tomato slices on bread and spread with cheese mixture. Top each slice with bacon. Broil sandwiches slowly until bacon is crisp. Serve at once. Makes 6 open-face sandwiches.

Corned-beef Toastwiches

Toast 3 bread slices on one side in broiler. Butter untoasted side and cover with slices of corned beef. Place two ½-inch strips of process American cheese on each of 3 more bread slices. Broil all six slices slowly, 3 inches from heat about 3 minutes, or till cheese melts slightly. Make sandwiches with the cheese toast atop the corned beef, and dill-pickle slice between. Makes 3.

Ham 'n Rye

1 cup ground baked or canned ham
¼ cup diced celery
¼ cup pickle relish
¼ cup mayonnaise or salad dressing
1 teaspoon horseradish

• • •

10 slices buttered rye bread
5 slices Swiss cheese
10 slices tomato
Salt

Combine ham, celery, pickle relish, mayonnaise, and horseradish; chill. Spread 5 slices bread with ham mixture. Top each with cheese slice, then 2 tomato slices; sprinkle with salt. Cut remaining bread in half and place on top with slices "ajar" for peekaboo effect. Toothpick pickle slice and stuffed green olive atop for garnish. Makes 5.

Grilled Cheese Italiano These savory hot sandwiches will please Italian-food lovers. Salami and Mozzarella cheese slices are flavored gently with oregano, then grilled to a toasty golden brown. Delicious!

Grilled Cheese Italiano

For each sandwich, top slice of Italian bread with a slice of Mozzarella and a slice or two of salami. Dash on oregano and top with second bread slice.

Generously butter top and bottom of sandwich. Grill on both sides till sandwich is toasty and golden brown. Anchor with cherry pepper speared on toothpick, as shown in picture above. Pass olives, relishes.

Meat-Cheese Open Facers

Combine 1 cup shredded sharp process cheese, 3 tablespoons mayonnaise, 2 tablespoons chopped green onion.

Slice one 12-ounce can luncheon meat in 12 thin slices. Lightly spread 6 slices toasted bread with prepared mustard; top each with 2 slices of luncheon meat. Spread meat with cheese mixture. Broil 4 inches from heat 3 minutes or till cheese melts. Makes 6.

Bean-salad Coneys

Easy sandwiches to make a splash with all your little swimmers—

1 1-pound can (2 cups) kidney beans, drained
2 hard-cooked eggs, chopped
½ cup cubed process American cheese
½ cup chopped celery
¼ cup pickle relish
2 tablespoons chopped green onion
¼ cup mayonnaise or salad dressing
1 tablespoon prepared mustard
½ teaspoon salt
Dash pepper

• • •

8 coney buns, split, toasted, and buttered

Combine all ingredients except the buns; mix well. Fill the toasted, buttered buns generously with the bean mixture. Makes 8 servings. Pass pickles and relishes.

Tuna-Olive Towers

Here are skyscraper "clubs" you can serve for special luncheons—

1 6½- or 7-ounce can (1 cup) tuna, flaked
2 hard-cooked eggs, chopped
½ cup chopped cucumber
½ cup chopped celery
¼ cup pickle relish
¼ cup mayonnaise
1 tablespoon lemon juice
¼ teaspoon salt
Dash pepper

• • •

16 slices white bread

• • •

8 slices whole-wheat bread, buttered
1 cup chopped stuffed green olives
8 leaves lettuce

Combine the tuna, eggs, cucumber, celery, and pickle relish with mayonnaise, lemon juice, and seasonings.

Butter 8 slices of the white bread and spread with tuna mixture. Add whole-wheat slices, buttered side up, and spread with chopped olives. Top olives with lettuce, then with remaining white bread slices.

Cut sandwiches in half on the bias. Garnish each with tomato slice and stuffed green olives on toothpicks. Makes 8.

Ham-'n'-eggwiches

A hearty version of ham and eggs—

1 4½-ounce can (½ cup) deviled ham
¼ cup finely chopped celery
¼ cup pickle relish
1 tablespoon mayonnaise

• • •

3 hard-cooked eggs, chopped
3 tablespoons chopped stuffed green olives
3 tablespoons minced parsley
1 tablespoon finely chopped onion
1 tablespoon prepared mustard
1 tablespoon mayonnaise

• • •

4 hamburger buns, split and buttered
4 leaves lettuce

For Ham Filling: Combine first 4 ingredients; chill. *For the Egg Salad Filling:* Combine next 6 ingredients; chill. Spread the bun halves with Ham Filling. Then, spread Egg Salad over the ham on bun bottoms; add lettuce, then bun tops. Makes 4.

Ham Salad on Rye

1 cup ground cooked ham
¼ cup diced celery
¼ cup pickle relish
¼ cup mayonnaise
1 teaspoon horseradish

• • •

10 slices buttered rye bread
5 slices Swiss cheese
5 slices tomato
Salt

Combine first 5 ingredients; chill. Spread 5 slices bread with ham mixture; top with slice of cheese, then tomato; sprinkle with salt. Top with remaining bread. Makes 5.

Chef's Salad in a Roll

Brown big brown-and-serve French rolls (about 8 inches long) according to package directions. Split rolls in half, but not quite through. (If you like, scoop out some of centers to make room for filling.) For each supersize sandwich, line bottom half of roll with romaine lettuce; drizzle with 1 teaspoon French dressing. Pile on slices of chicken; dash with salt, pepper. Add 1 or 2 slices boiled ham and Swiss cheese, halved to fit roll. Top with hard-cooked egg slices; salt. Cover with romaine and tomato slices; season. Drizzle with 2 teaspoons more dressing. Add roll tops, anchor with picks.

Chicken Cheese Puff

1½ cups chopped cooked chicken
1 hard-cooked egg, chopped
¾ cup finely chopped celery
¼ cup pickle relish
¼ cup mayonnaise
Salt to taste
½ pound sharp process American cheese, softened at room temperature
1 well-beaten egg
2 tablespoons mayonnaise
1 tablespoon prepared mustard
12 slices buttered white bread

Combine first 6 ingredients. Combine cheese and egg; blend with rotary beater or electric mixer; add mayonnaise and mustard; blend. Spread chicken mixture on 6 slices of bread. Top with remaining bread. Toast in broiler till golden on one side; turn and pile cheese mixture on each. Broil 3 to 4 inches from heat 2 to 3 minutes, or till cheese is slightly browned and puffy. Makes 6 sandwiches.

Offer folks a Dutch-lunch There's dried beef and corned beef both in these Double-beef Sandwiches. Add a stack-up of cheese, lettuce, dill pickles, onions, and zingy horseradish—it's a man-talk special.

Double-beef Sandwiches

12 slices rye bread, buttered
2 tablespoons prepared mustard
Leaf lettuce
4 ounces dried beef, pulled apart
4 ounces sliced Muenster or brick cheese
4 ounces cooked or canned corned beef, sliced very thin*
2 large dill pickles, thinly sliced
1 onion, thinly sliced
1 tablespoon prepared horseradish
Ripe olives

Spread half the bread slices with mustard and add layers of lettuce, dried beef, cheese, corned beef, pickle, and onion. Top each stack-up with more lettuce. Spread remaining bread slices with horseradish, and complete sandwiches. Anchor each with toothpick topped with a ripe olive. Makes 6.

*For easy slicing, have corned beef chilled.

Egg Salad Sandwiches

6 hard-cooked eggs, finely chopped
½ cup finely chopped celery
⅓ cup drained sweet-pickle relish
½ cup salad dressing
¾ teaspoon salt
Dash pepper

Combine ingredients. Chill mixture thoroughly. To serve, spread generously between buttered bread slices. Makes 2 cups.

Grilled Turkey Hamwich

On one slice of bread, stack thin slices of roast turkey, canned jellied cranberry sauce, and boiled ham. Top with a second slice of bread. Generously butter top and bottom of sandwiches. Grill on both sides on griddle, sandwich grill, or in a skillet till bread is toasted to a golden brown.

Deviled-ham Bunwiches

Tasty sandwich combo of deviled ham and egg—served warm and toasty—

1 4½-ounce can deviled ham
2 to 3 tablespoons chopped sweet pickles
2 hard-cooked eggs (chopped)
1 tablespoon catsup
1 tablespoon prepared mustard

• • •

4 coney buns, split and buttered

Combine all ingredients; spread in the buttered coney buns. Wrap each sandwich in foil, sealing securely.

Place on baking sheet. Heat sandwiches in slow oven (300°) for about 15 minutes or till hot through. Makes 4 servings.

Tugboat Supper

Choose a long loaf of French or Italian bread and allow one-fourth to one-third loaf per person. (Or buy little individual brown-and-serve loaves.) Split loaf in half, but don't cut quite through. If you like, scoop out some of the center of the loaf to make room for plenty of filling.

Spread generously with mustard, garlic butter, and/or mayonnaise with curry powder. Or sprinkle bread with clear French dressing. Line bottom half of loaf with leaf lettuce. Pile on slices of corned beef, boiled ham, Bologna, salami, pickled tongue, chicken, herring—your choice of several or all. Add slices of American and Swiss cheese; onion slices, sweet pickles—you name it. Cut loaf on diagonal—suit lengths to appetite.

Peanut-butter Specials

These are tops for packing in lunch boxes—

• Spread slices of rye bread with softened butter or margarine; then spread generously with peanut butter. Top the peanut butter with a layer of thin radish slices; top with additional buttered bread slice.

• Spread slices of white bread with softened butter or margarine; then spread with peanut butter and top with tart jelly.

• Blend together peanut butter and mayonnaise; spread on whole-wheat bread. Top with finely grated raw carrot.

Meat, Sea-food Sandwiches

• Ground cooked meat combined with pickle relish or pickled onion, mayonnaise, and prepared mustard or horseradish.

• Crumbled crisp-cooked bacon, peanut butter, and mayonnaise or salad dressing.

• Liverwurst, chopped stuffed green olives, salad dressing, and lettuce on rye bread.

• Diced cooked chicken, finely diced celery, chopped sweet pickle, and mayonnaise.

• Two parts each of chopped cooked chicken and broken California walnuts, with one part drained crushed pineapple, moistened with salad dressing or mayonnaise.

• Liverwurst, lettuce, and sliced tomato on whole-wheat bread slices.

• Sardines and chopped hard-cooked egg, moistened with lemon juice.

• One part flaked tuna, crab meat, or lobster with one part finely cut celery, moistened with mayonnaise.

Cheese and Egg Sandwiches

• Eggs scrambled with minced onion and green pepper, and finely chopped ham.

• Cottage cheese, minced green pepper and onion, salt, paprika on whole-wheat bread.

• Cream cheese combined with orange marmalade, cranberry jelly, or crushed pineapple—serve open-face or between whole-wheat or rye bread slices.

• Cream cheese with ¼ as much crumbled blue cheese and a dash Worcestershire sauce.

• Chopped hard-cooked eggs, chopped stuffed green olives, and salad dressing, on leaf lettuce and rye bread.

• Grilled cheese on toast with crisp bacon slices, and sliced tomato.

• One 3-ounce package cream cheese, 3 finely cut uncooked prunes, 1 tablespoon finely chopped nuts, ½ teaspoon sugar, and ¼ teaspoon cinnamon mixed together.

Party Sandwiches

Party-sandwich tips

- For neat sandwiches, freeze bread first. Cut and spread while frozen.
- Spread bread to edges with soft butter or margarine before spreading filling. This prevents sogginess.
- If you make sandwiches a day ahead, wrap in foil and seal well; or, wrap in waxed paper, then in damp towel; refrigerate.
- Freezer tip: Make fancy sandwiches up to two weeks ahead and store in freezer at 0°. Wrap in foil or tuck in plastic box. Freeze immediately. Allow about 3 hours for thawing before serving.
- Best fillings to freeze: Peanut butter, American cheese, sliced or ground meat, fish, chicken, turkey. Skip mayonnaise, lettuce, tomatoes, celery, carrots, egg salad.

Poinsettia Sandwich "Cake"

Ham Filling: Combine two 4½-ounce cans (1 cup) deviled ham, ⅓ cup pickle relish, and ¼ cup finely chopped celery.

Egg Filling: Combine 5 hard-cooked eggs, chopped, ⅓ cup chopped stuffed olives, ⅓ cup mayonnaise or salad dressing, 1½ teaspoons prepared mustard, and 1 teaspoon grated onion. Salt and pepper to taste.

To fix loaf: Trim off all crusts (top, bottom, sides) from 1 round white loaf, about 8 inches in diameter. Slice loaf crosswise in 3 circles 1 inch thick; spread each with soft butter or margarine. Spread bottom slice with Ham Filling. Add second slice; spread with Egg Filling. Top with third slice, buttered side down. Wrap loaf tightly in aluminum foil, saran wrapping, or waxed paper with moist towel as outer wrap. Chill several hours before serving.

To trim: Beat two 8-ounce packages cream cheese till smooth; gradually add ⅓ cup light cream and beat till fluffy. Spread sides and top of loaf with cheese mixture. Trim top with a poinsettia cut from pimiento and centered with sieved hard-cooked egg yolk. Decorate sides with holly leaves cut from green pepper. Serves 10.

Frosted Ribbon Loaf

Ham Filling:

1 cup ground cooked ham
⅓ cup finely chopped celery
2 tablespoons drained pickle relish
½ teaspoon horseradish
¼ cup mayonnaise

Egg Filling:

4 hard-cooked eggs, chopped
⅓ cup chopped stuffed green olives
2 tablespoons finely chopped green onion
2 teaspoons prepared mustard
¼ cup mayonnaise
Unsliced sandwich loaf
4 3-ounce packages cream cheese, softened
⅓ cup milk

Ham Filling: Combine ham, celery, pickle relish, horseradish, ¼ cup mayonnaise.

Egg Filling: Combine eggs, olives, onion, mustard, and ¼ cup mayonnaise. Trim crusts from loaf. Slice bread lengthwise in 3 equal layers; butter slices. Spread first slice, buttered side up, with ham filling, second slice with egg filling; end with third slice. Wrap in foil and chill.

At serving time*, beat cream cheese with milk till fluffy. Frost top and sides of loaf. Sprinkle generously with snipped parsley. Makes 10 slices.

*Or, frost early, cover loosely, and store in refrigerator till serving time.

Diploma Sandwiches

Unsliced sandwich loaf
Pickle relish
Deviled ham

Trim crusts from all sides of an *unsliced* sandwich loaf. Slice *very thin**, immediately placing each slice between dampened towels to keep soft enough for rolling up when filled. Add a little pickle relish to canned deviled ham, and spread on slices, lightly rolling up each one as you go. Place the diplomas seam side down until time to tie in center with baby ribbon. Keep fresh by covering with saran wrapping or aluminum foil.

*Easier to do if you freeze bread, then slice while partially frozen.

Frosted Ribbon Loaf

This loaf is all dressed up for the holidays with a luscious parsley-flecked cream-cheese frosting and tomato-rose trim. The pretty layers of egg and ham filling are truly delicious.

Date-roll Ginger Snips

Cream cheese sandwiches with a new twist—ginger's been added—

1 3-ounce package cream cheese
1 tablespoon milk
2 tablespoons very finely chopped candied ginger

• • •

1 can date-nut roll

Soften cream cheese; stir in milk. Add candied ginger. Slice date-nut roll about 3/8 inch thick. Spread half the slices with cream-cheese mixture. Top with remaining slices. Cut a crescent from one side of each sandwich. Part remaining will be petal-shaped.

For easier spreading and cutting, partially freeze the date-nut roll.

Pepper Pinwheels

They're decorated with green pepper strips—

Unsliced enriched sandwich loaf

• • •

1 5-ounce jar pimiento-cheese spread
1 medium green pepper, sliced in 1/8-inch strips

Trim crusts from bread. Cut bread in lengthwise slices 1/4 inch thick. Spread each long slice with the cheese; place green-pepper slices across bread at 1-inch intervals. Roll as for jellyroll, beginning at narrow end. Wrap the rolls in aluminum foil and chill. For pinwheels, cut in 3/8-inch slices.

If you want to save last minute time, make sandwiches ahead and freeze for a few days. Let thaw before serving.

One sandwich serves everyone

Frosted Sandwich Loaf is ideal for your summer patio luncheons. Delicious with a chilled fresh fruit plate and iced tea.

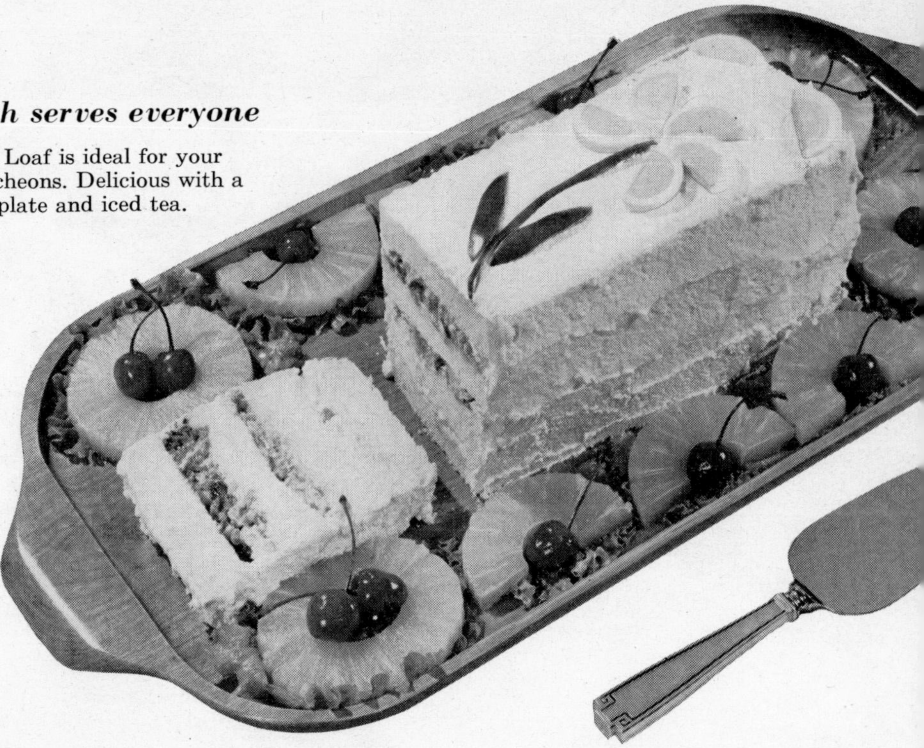

Frosted Sandwich Loaf

Egg-salad Filling:
4 hard-cooked eggs, chopped
3 tablespoons mayonnaise
2 teaspoons prepared mustard
1 teaspoon grated onion
½ teaspoon salt

Ham Filling:
1 cup ground cooked ham
⅓ cup mayonnaise
1 teaspoon prepared horseradish

Chicken Filling:
1 5-ounce can boned chicken, chopped
¼ cup finely chopped celery
¼ cup mayonnaise
2 tablespoons pickle relish

• • •

1 unsliced sandwich loaf

Combine ingredients for each filling. Trim crusts from loaf. Slice bread lengthwise in 4 equal layers. Butter slices.

Spread first slice, butter side up, with Egg-salad Filling; second slice with Ham Filling; third slice with Chicken Filling. End with fourth slice. Wrap loaf in foil; chill. Beat three 3-ounce packages softened cream cheese with 5 tablespoons light cream till fluffy; frost loaf. Trim. Makes 10 slices.

Note: In a hurry? Try quick version—Sandwich Loaf, Sliced-bread style.

Sandwich Loaf, Sliced-bread Style

Egg Filling:
3 hard-cooked eggs, chopped
3 tablespoons finely chopped onion
2 tablespoons chopped stuffed olives
2 tablespoons mayonnaise
1 teaspoon prepared mustard
¼ teaspoon salt

Ham Filling:
1 2¼-ounce can deviled ham
2 tablespoons finely chopped celery
1 tablespoon finely chopped green pepper
1 teaspoon prepared horseradish

• • •

8 slices regular bread
Soft butter or margarine

Egg Filling: Combine first 6 ingredients. ***Ham Filling:*** Combine next 4 ingredients. Trim crusts from bread; butter. Arrange 2 slices, butter side up, with narrow ends *touching*. Spread with *half* the Egg Filling. Top with 2 slices bread. Spread with Ham Filling. Top with 2 more bread slices; spread with remaining Egg Filling. Top with last 2 bread slices, butter side down. Wrap; chill. Blend two 3-ounce packages softened cream cheese with 1½ tablespoons mayonnaise. Frost loaf; chill. Trim with stuffed-olive slices. Cut in 6 or 7 1-inch slices.

Party Sandwich Filling

1 8-ounce package cream cheese, softened
¾ cup chopped California walnuts
¼ cup chopped green pepper
¼ cup chopped onion
3 tablespoons chopped pimiento
1 tablespoon catsup
3 hard-cooked eggs, finely chopped
¾ teaspoon salt
Dash pepper

Combine all ingredients. Use as filling between lightly buttered slices of sandwich bread. Trim crusts. Cut each sandwich diagonally in 4 triangles. Makes 2⅓ cups.

Swiss Sandwich Puffs

Hot canapes boast onion-spiked filling—

Toast 16 slices tiny "icebox" rye bread on both sides. Combine ½ cup mayonnaise or salad dressing, ¼ cup finely chopped onion, and 2 tablespoons snipped parsley; spread on toast. Cut out rounds of process Swiss cheese, (takes 8 slices), to fit toast; place a cheese round atop each slice, covering mayonnaise mixture. Broil 3 to 4 inches from heat till cheese is puffy and golden, about 2 to 3 minutes. Trim tops with sliced ripe olive, if desired. Serve hot. Makes 16.

Carrot-Olive Bars

1 cup finely grated carrots
¼ cup minced celery
½ cup chopped ripe olives
1½ tablespoons minced onion
¼ teaspoon salt
¼ cup mayonnaise or salad dressing

• • •

5 sliced enriched sandwich bread
5 slices whole-wheat sandwich bread

For filling, combine first 6 ingredients and chill. Spread on white bread; top with whole-wheat slices. Trim off crusts. Cut sandwiches lengthwise in thirds. Trim with fans of ripe-olive strips. Makes 15 bars.

Cheese-Bacon Bars: Soften one 3-ounce package cream cheese. Blend in 1 tablespoon milk, 4 slices crisp-cooked bacon, crumbled, 1 teaspoon horseradish, and ½ teaspoon Worcestershire sauce. Substitute this filling for filling in above recipe, using 6 slices of each kind of bread. Makes 18 bars.

Lobster Canapes

2½ dozen 2-inch bread rounds, cut from thinly sliced bread
Salad oil
1 5-ounce can (1 cup) lobster, shredded
½ cup canned condensed cream of mushroom soup
2 tablespoons cooking sherry
1 tablespoon chopped pimiento
¼ teaspoon salt
Few drops bottled hot pepper sauce
¼ cup buttered fine dry bread crumbs

Brush bread rounds lightly with oil; put on cooky sheet. Heat in extremely slow oven (225°) 1¼ to 1½ hours or till dry and crisp. Combine remaining ingredients except bread crumbs. Spread mixture on the toasted bread rounds. Sprinkle with buttered bread crumbs. Broil 2 to 3 minutes or till crumbs are browned. Makes 2½ dozen.

Onion Sandwiches

Cut thin slices of white bread into small circles with biscuit cutter, and spread with mayonnaise. Sandwich a thin slice of onion (season with salt and pepper) between two of the bread circles. Spread edges of sandwiches with mayonnaise, and roll in very finely chopped parsley.

Shrimp Luncheon Sandwiches

1 3-ounce package cream cheese, softened
2 tablespoons mayonnaise or salad dressing
1 tablespoon catsup
1 teaspoon prepared mustard
Dash garlic powder

• • •

1 cup chopped canned or cooked cleaned shrimp
¼ cup finely chopped celery
1 teaspoon finely chopped onion
10 slices lightly buttered sandwich bread

Blend cheese with mayonnaise; mix in catsup, mustard, and garlic powder. Stir in shrimp, celery, and onion. Use as a filling between slices of sandwich bread. Trim crusts, if desired. Cut each sandwich diagonally in 4 triangles. Makes 1 cup filling—enough for about 20 tea sandwiches.

Flowerpots

Unsliced enriched bread
1 6½-ounce can (1 cup) crab meat, flaked
½ cup finely chopped celery
¼ cup finely chopped green pepper
¼ teaspoon salt
Dash pepper
1 tablespoon lemon juice
⅓ cup mayonnaise or salad dressing

Cut bread in 1-inch slices; freeze. Cut circles from frozen slices with round cutter (about 1 inch in diameter). Hollow out centers with scissors or paring knife, leaving bottom and sides about ¼ inch thick. Combine next 5 ingredients. Add lemon juice and mayonnaise; mix. Chill. Heap filling in "flowerpots." Garnish with parsley.

Little Ribbon Triangles

1 cup ground cooked ham
⅓ cup finely chopped celery
2 tablespoons pickle relish
½ teaspoon horseradish
3 tablespoons mayonnaise
3 hard-cooked eggs, chopped
3 tablespoons chopped stuffed green olives
3 tablespoons minced parsley
1 tablespoon finely chopped green onions
1 teaspoon prepared mustard
¼ cup mayonnaise
6 slices whole-wheat bread
6 slices enriched bread
Soft butter or margarine
⅓ cup cream cheese with chives
1 8-ounce package cream cheese
¼ cup milk

Ham Filling: Combine first 5 ingredients.

Egg Filling: Combine next 6 ingredients. Trim crusts from breads. Butter one side of each slice. Spread 3 slices white bread with Ham Filling. Top each with slice of whole-wheat, buttered side down. Spread with softened chive cheese; top with white bread, and spread with Egg Filling. Top with whole-wheat, buttered side down. Wrap the 3 sandwiches tightly in foil; chill several hours. To softened cream cheese, gradually add milk and beat fluffy. Cut sandwiches diagonally and spread tops and sides (except diagonal) with cream-cheese mixture. Garnish with sliced stuffed green olives and green onion. Makes 6 sandwiches.

Jigsaw Sandwiches

1 3-ounce package cream cheese
1 tablespoon milk
1 teaspoon Worcestershire sauce
4 to 5 slices crisp-cooked bacon, crumbled
Sliced enriched sandwich loaf
Sliced whole-wheat sandwich loaf

Soften cream cheese; blend in milk and Worcestershire. Add bacon. Cut breads in 2-inch rounds with cooky cutter. Spread *half* of rounds (equal number of whole-wheat and white with cheese mixture). Top each with *Double Rounds* or *Stripes:* Divide the remaining rounds in two groups, each with an equal number of light and dark rounds. Use one group each for Double Rounds, Stripes. *Double Rounds:* With hole of doughnut cutter, cut tiny circles from center of rounds. Fit the tiny whole-wheat circles in the holes of large white ones and vice versa. *Stripes:* Cut rounds in three strips, making center strip widest. Fit large white strip between two smaller whole-wheat strips and vice versa, holding the stripes together with a bit of cheese.

Sandwich Bars

Combine 1 cup finely grated carrots, ¼ cup minced celery, ½ cup chopped ripe olives, 1½ tablespoons minced onion, ¼ teaspoon salt, ¼ cup mayonnaise or salad dressing; chill. Spread filling on 5 slices enriched sandwich bread; top with 5 slices whole-wheat sandwich bread; trim off crusts; cut each sandwich lengthwise in thirds. Garnish with olive fans.

Date-roll Sandwiches

Soften one 3-ounce package cream cheese. Stir in 1 tablespoon milk, 2 tablespoons very finely chopped candied ginger. Slice canned date-nut roll ⅜ inch thick. Spread half the slices with cheese mixture. Top cheese with remaining slices. Cut a crescent from one side of each sandwich. Center piece makes a petal-shaped sandwich.

Cornucopias

Trim crusts from bread slices. Top with softened pineapple-cheese spread. Roll in cornucopias (cone-shaped, as in picture on opposite page). Trim with ripe-olive petals. Chill seam side down.

Make party-pretty sandwiches—

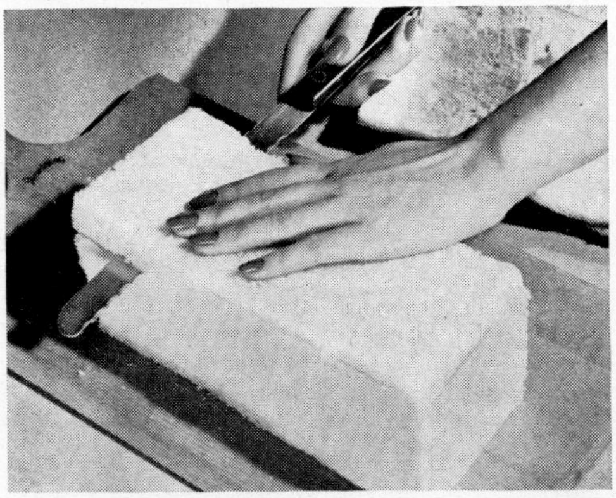

1 For Checkerboards or Ribbon Sandwiches, from each of 2 loaves (1 white, 1 whole-wheat) cut 6 lengthwise slices ½ inch thick.

2 *Ribbon Sandwiches:* Alternate 2 long slices whole-wheat and 2 white to make a Ribbon Loaf. Slice crosswise for "ribbons."

3 *Checkerboards:* Make Ribbon loaves. Cut in 6 *lengthwise* slices; put 4 slices together alternating colors. Chill; slice crosswise.

Guests will want to sample each kind, so make plenty of these sandwiches. Between the rows of Checkerboards are Fold-ups, Diamonds, Cornucopias, and Date-roll Sandwiches.

Ribbons and Checkerboards

Remove crusts from 2 unsliced sandwich loaves—1 white and 1 whole-wheat. From each loaf, cut 6 lengthwise slices ½ inch thick. (Or have bread sliced at the bakery.) This will make 3 Ribbon Loaves.

Ribbon Sandwiches: Make Ribbon Loaf: Use Cheese Butter to put 4 long slices of bread together, alternating 2 whole-wheat and 2 white. Wrap; chill. Slice crosswise to make thin "ribbons."

Checkerboards: Make 2 Ribbon Loaves. Cut each in 6 *lengthwise* slices. Put 4 slices together, alternating colors (makes 3 checkerboards). Wrap and chill. Slice *crosswise.*

Cheese Butter: Mix one 5-ounce jar sharp spreading cheese, ½ cup soft butter.

Seafood Diamonds

Combine flaked tuna, crab meat, *or* lobster with an equal part finely chopped celery. Moisten with mayonnaise, adding lemon juice to taste. Spread on diamonds of whole-wheat bread. Trim with pimiento.

Orange-Date Fold-ups

Trim crusts from sliced white bread. Spread the squares with Orange-Date Filling: Mix ½ cup finely chopped dates, ½ cup finely chopped California walnuts, and ⅓ cup orange juice. Bring 2 opposite corners of each square together at center and hold with toothpick and sprig of water cress.

Bread Mates

Here are all the extras that make a neighborhood coffee a compliment or an elegant tea truly memorable. We give all the directions for perfect tea and coffee, plus a score of variations. You'll also find fancy butters to dress up whatever bread you're serving.

Frankly fancy coffees—internationally good!

← Here's what's brewing, left to right. Cafe au Lait is French breakfast coffee—part coffee, part milk; pass with Brioche, the airy topknot rolls. Next to the tarts is Caffe espresso. It's nice to have a real espresso machine to brew dark-roast coffee by steam pressure. But you can spoon instant espresso out of a jar—what could be easier!

Beverages

A perfect cup of coffee

You can make good coffee every time! Just follow these golden rules which connoisseurs and manufacturers have established as essential for making good coffee.

- Always start with thoroughly clean coffee maker. After each use, clean with sudsy hot water and a stiff brush to get rid of the fats and oils that form on the sides of the coffee maker. Rinse thoroughly; dry.
- Just before using, scald coffee maker with boiling water to remove stale odors.
- Use fresh, cold water for making coffee.
- The fresher the better—that's how coffee should be. Store it in an airtight container in a cool place.
- Get the right grind of coffee for your coffee maker—saves you money and gives you the best flavor.
- Measure coffee accurately. Allow 2 level measuring tablespoons of coffee (or 1 coffee measure) for each ¾ cup standard measuring cup of water. These proportions may vary with individual taste, brand of coffee, and coffee maker. Find the amount that suits you best, then measure both coffee and water each time for uniform strength.
- The water should come to a full rolling boil before you let it come in contact with the ground coffee.
- Never boil coffee. If you do, you lose the good flavor of the brew.
- Accurate timing is important. Find the best timing, then stick to it.

Automatic Coffee: Coffee makers are so foolproof that all you need to do is live up to the golden rules above and set the controls. Be sure to follow manufacturer's directions.

Percolator Coffee has full body and rich flavor that make it the favorite of many.

Measure cold water into the percolator; place over heat. When the water boils briskly, take it off the heat and measure the coffee into the basket; cover and place over heat again. Let the coffee perk ever so *gently* about 6 to 8 minutes. Remove basket, and keep coffee hot till served over *very low heat* or handy table warmer.

Vacuum Coffee is characterized by its clearness and lack of bitterness.

Measure fresh cold water into the lower bowl; place over heat. Insert the filter in the upper bowl and add the correct measure of finely ground coffee. When water boils, insert upper bowl into lower bowl.

When water rises to top bowl, stir mixture. Reduce heat. Wait 2 or 3 minutes, then remove coffee from heat. Let coffee return to lower bowl before removing upper one.

Drip Coffee is an aromatic infusion, deep amber in color, and without bitterness.

After the water comes to a rolling boil, measure the coffee into the coffee basket. Then measure the exact amount of water (¾ standard measuring cup for each 2 level tablespoons of coffee); pour into top water container; let drip through coffee. Remove the basket and water container, and then stir the brew briskly.

Coffee—instantly. For each cup needed, place 1 rounded teaspoon instant coffee and ¾ measuring cup boiling water in coffeepot. Heat over *low* heat 5 minutes. For just a few, fix coffee right in the cups.

Iced Coffee

Make coffee double-strength, using 4 level tablespoons for each measuring cup water. Pour hot into ice-filled glasses.

Or use instant coffee: Use double the amount you would use for a cup. Dissolve in ½ glass cold water, fill with ice; stir.

Swedish Egg Coffee

For 40 servings: Mix 1 or 2 slightly-beaten eggs with 1 pound coffee—any grind. Place in a wet muslin bag large enough to hold twice that amount; tie. (First boil muslin in clear water, then rinse.) Bring 2 gallons (8 quarts) fresh cold water to a rolling boil, then reduce heat below boiling point. Add dash salt. Add bag of coffee, being sure to submerge it. Cover, brew over low heat (don't boil) at least 30 minutes. Push coffee bag down several times while brewing. Remove bag and keep coffee hot.

Enhance the wonderful flavor of fresh-baked breads with a steaming cup of tea, or try a dark-roast, foreign coffee for special goodness.

Demitasse

Use 3 to 4 tablespoons coffee to 1 measuring cup water. Use any desired method. Serve hot in small cups, usually black. Pass sugar.

To make six ⅓-cup servings instantly, measure 3 tablespoons instant coffee (more or less to suit your taste) into your coffee server. Stir in 2 cups boiling water.

Viennese Spiced Coffee

⅓ cup instant coffee
3 tablespoons sugar
8 whole cloves
3 inches stick cinnamon
3 cups water
• • •
Whipped cream
Ground cinnamon

Combine coffee, sugar, spices, and water. Cover, bring to boiling. Remove from heat and let stand, covered, about 5 minutes to steep. Strain. Pour into cups; top each with a spoonful of whipped cream; dash lightly with cinnamon. Serve with cinnamon sticks as muddlers. Makes 4 to 6 servings.

Caffe espresso

This Italian coffee (pronounced "kah-fay' es-press'-so") is a popular demitasse. Wonderfully strong and dark, true espresso is made only in an espresso machine—an electric model is pictured on page 151. The brew is expressed by steam pressure and rapid filtration. Good Italian coffee may also be made in a macchinetta (say "mah-key-net'-tah"). The word means "little machine," and is the Italian-style drip pot (not shown) that is flipped upside down for brewing.

Special pulverized coffee, an Italian or French roast, is used in either the espresso maker or the macchinetta. It is pungent, and black as midnight. If you prefer, you can use a drip grind of any coffee.

The simple way to come by Italian coffee is to get a jar of instant espresso or instant dark-roast coffee. Serve in demitasse cups—let guests sweeten their own coffee, if they wish, and add a twist of lemon peel. Traditionally, cream is not passed.

For Italian coffee with cream, see recipe for Caffe di Cioccolata.

Cafe au Lait

Half strong coffee, half rich milk—mild and soothing. An aside to calorie-counters: Omit cream in favor of all milk—

1 cup milk
1 cup light cream
3 tablespoons instant coffee
2 cups boiling water

Over low heat or in double boiler, heat milk and cream till hot. Meanwhile, dissolve coffee in boiling water.

Before serving, beat milk mixture with rotary beater till foamy. Pour milk mixture into one warmed pitcher or server, and coffee into another.

To serve: Fill cups from both pitchers at the same time, making the streams meet en route. Makes 6 servings.

Caffe di Cioccolata

Italian version of a mocha drink—

¼ cup instant espresso or instant dark-roast coffee
¼ cup instant cocoa
2 cups boiling water
Whipped cream
Finely shredded orange peel or ground cinnamon

Combine coffee and cocoa. Add boiling water and stir to dissolve. Pour into demitasse cups. Top each serving with whipped cream and a sprinkle of shredded orange peel. Makes 6 or 7 small servings.

Cappuccino

The color is like the brown robes of Capuchin monks, hence its name—

¼ cup instant espresso or instant dark-roast coffee
2 cups boiling water

• • •

½ cup whipping cream, whipped
Cinnamon, nutmeg, or finely grated orange peel

Dissolve coffee in boiling water. Pour into small cups (tall ones, like chocolate cups, if you have them), filling only about half full. Offer sugar to those who wish it.

Now pass whipped cream—everyone adds a big spoonful, dashes it lightly with cinnamon, nutmeg, or a few flecks of orange peel, then folds in the whipped cream till frothy. Makes 6 or 7 small servings.

West Indies Coffee

The brown sugar adds mellow sweetness. Stir with cinnamon sticks—

3½ cups milk
¼ cup instant coffee
¼ cup brown sugar
Dash salt

Bring milk just to boiling. Pour over coffee, brown sugar, and salt, stirring to dissolve. Serve in mugs. Makes 4 to 6 servings.

Cardamom Coffee

Spicy aroma makes it doubly good!—

Place two crushed cardamom seeds in each demitasse cup. Fill cups with hot double-strength coffee (3 tablespoons instant coffee in 2 cups boiling water serves 6).

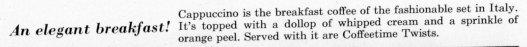

An elegant breakfast! Cappuccino is the breakfast coffee of the fashionable set in Italy. It's topped with a dollop of whipped cream and a sprinkle of orange peel. Served with it are Coffeetime Twists.

Gold Coast Coffee

Ready in the time it takes to boil water—

1 cup instant-cocoa mix
⅓ cup instant coffee
4 cups boiling water

Combine cocoa mix and instant coffee. Gradually add boiling water, stirring constantly. Pour into cups, then top with dollops of whipped cream or pass pitcher of cream. Makes 6 servings.

Chocolate Coffee

From Brazil come both coffee and chocolate—and also this recipe for combining them in one fabulous mocha drink—

2 tablespoons instant coffee
¼ cup sugar
Dash salt
2 1-ounce squares unsweetened chocolate
1 cup water

• • •

3 cups milk
Whipped cream

In saucepan combine coffee, sugar, salt, chocolate, and water; stir over low heat until chocolate has melted. Simmer 4 minutes, stirring constantly. Gradually add milk, stirring constantly until heated.

When piping hot, remove from heat and beat with rotary beater until frothy. Pour mixture into cups and sail a dollop of whipped cream on each. Makes 6 servings.

Brazilian Chocolate

It's almost a milk shake. The flavor is mocha. If you prefer a fancy iced coffee, make this drink with water—

3 tablespoons instant coffee
¼ cup sugar
2 cups milk or water

• • •

1 pint chocolate ice cream
½ cup whipping cream, whipped and sweetened

Combine coffee, sugar, and milk; stir to dissolve. Add ice cream; stir until almost smooth. Place an ice cube in each of 4 tall glasses. Pour in chocolate mixture. Top with fluffs of whipped cream and shaved unsweetened chocolate, if desired.

French Chocolate

2½ 1-ounce squares unsweetened chocolate
½ cup water
⅔ cup sugar
½ teaspoon salt
½ cup whipping cream, whipped

• • •

Hot milk

Heat chocolate and water over very low heat, stirring till chocolate melts. Add sugar and salt. Bring to boiling, reduce heat; simmer 4 minutes. Cool to room temperature. Fold in whipped cream. Store in refrigerator till ready to use.

To serve, place 1 heaping tablespoon in each cup and fill with hot milk; stir well. Makes 8 to 10 teacup servings.

Perfect Hot Tea

Black tea, green tea, oolong, and exotic perfumed teas differ only in processing. They may come from the same tea plant and are brewed in the same way.

Use 1 teaspoon tea or 1 tea bag for each cup. Place tea in teapot heated by rinsing with boiling water. Bring freshly drawn cold water to a bubbling boil; immediately pour over tea. Steep tea 5 minutes. Give tea a stir and serve at once. If you like a weak brew, dilute by adding a little hot water to the cup.

Quick Hot Tea: Just measure instant tea into each cup, following directions on label. Fill cup with boiling water; stir.

Perfect Iced Tea

To make 4 glasses of iced tea, measure 2 tablespoons tea or 6 tea bags into teapot. Pour 2 cups fresh, vigorously boiling water over the leaves. Cover and let tea stand 5 minutes; stir. Then pour brew through a tea strainer into a pitcher. Immediately add 2 cups cold water and let tea cool at room temperature till serving time.

Pour tea into tall ice-filled glasses. Offer juicy lemon wedges and sugar.

Note: To make cloudy tea sparkle again, pour tea into pan and reheat (don't boil) till clear. Remove from heat at once; add ½ cup *boiling* water for each quart tea.

Instant Iced Tea: Couldn't be easier—follow the speedy directions on the label.

Fancy ways with butter

Whipped Butter

So creamy and light—this butter makes an elegant topper for pancakes or steaks—

Let ¼ pound (1 stick or ½ cup) butter stand at room temperature for 1 hour.

Place in mixing bowl and run electric mixer at lowest speed until large chunks smooth out. Gradually increase mixer speed to fastest position, and whip until butter is fluffy (takes about 8 minutes). Cover until ready to use. (If made ahead and chilled, remove from refrigerator an hour before using.) Makes about ¾ cup.

Mustard Butter: Blend ¼ cup prepared mustard into Whipped Butter. Grand spread for ham or cheese sandwiches.

Herb Butter: Blend 1 tablespoon minced parsley, 1 teaspoon lemon juice, ½ teaspoon savory, and ¼ teaspoon salt into Whipped Butter. Delicious on potatoes.

Blue-cheese Butter: Beat ¼ to ½ cup crumbled blue cheese into Whipped Butter. A gourmet touch for hamburger steak.

Garlic Butter: Blend 1 clove garlic, minced, into Whipped Butter. Zesty bonus for French bread or roast beef.

Horseradish Butter

A dollop of this adds zest to baked potatoes, corned beef, roast beef or veal—

Cream 1 cup softened butter until light and fluffy. Blend in ¼ cup horseradish and 2 tablespoons finely chopped parsley. Makes about 1¼ cups.

Lobster or Crab Butter

You'll like this for canapes, topped with a dab of mayonnaise—

Cream ½ cup butter until light. Add ½ cup cooked or canned lobster or crab meat, mashed to a fine paste, and a dash of bottled hot pepper sauce. Beat until well blended. Makes about ¾ cup.

Golden Butter

Nice on toasted rounds of salty rye bread or crisp crackers—

Cream 1 cup butter until light and fluffy. Blend in 4 hard-cooked egg yolks, mashed, 1 teaspoon prepared mustard, and dash pepper. Makes about 1½ cups.

Ham 'n Egg Butter

A flavorful sandwich or canape spread in itself—go-withs not needed—

Cream 1 cup butter until light and fluffy. Blend in ½ cup finely ground cooked ham, 2 hard-cooked egg yolks, mashed, 1 teaspoon prepared mustard, and dash pepper. Makes about 1½ cups spread.

Bacon Butter

Try this combination on hot vegetables—it perks up the flavor. Good on cheese or tomato sandwiches, too—

Cream ½ cup butter until light and fluffy. Blend in ¾ teaspoon prepared mustard, and 4 slices crisp bacon, crumbled. Makes about ½ to ⅔ cup spread.

Creole Butter

Tasty and colorful on sea food, broiled meat, and frankfurters—with cheese—on green beans or asparagus—

Cream ½ cup butter until light. Sieve ⅓ cup pimientos; add to butter with 2 tablespoons finely chopped green pepper, 2 tablespoons chopped sweet pickle, and ½ teaspoon salt. Mix well. Makes ¾ to 1 cup.

Cinnamon Butter

Rich, spicy flavor that's so good on hot toast, waffles, French toast—

Let ¼ pound (1 stick or ½ cup) butter stand at room temperature for 1 hour.

Cream the softened butter until light and fluffy (about 8 minutes). Gradually beat in 1 cup medium-brown sugar and 2 teaspoons cinnamon. Makes about 1 cup spread.

Parsley Butter

Delectable on hot rolls, baked potatoes, and on broiled or roasted meat or fish—

½ cup butter
• • •
1 tablespoon finely chopped parsley
1 teaspoon lemon juice
½ teaspoon savory
¼ teaspoon salt
Dash pepper

Cream butter till light. Blend in remaining ingredients. Makes ½ cup.

Date Butter

If you like it sweet, try this spread on hot breads, nut and cereal loaves—

1 cup pitted dates
1 cup water
• • •
½ cup butter
½ teaspoon grated lemon peel

Combine dates and water; bring to a boil, drain, mash to a paste, and cool. Cream butter till light; blend in dates and peel. Makes about 1¼ cups.

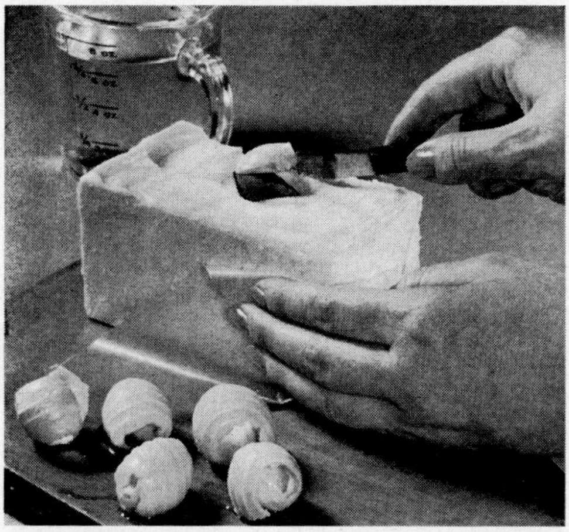

Butter Curls: Dip butter curler in hot water; pull lightly over a pound of butter, making curls about ⅛ inch thick. Repeat hot-water dip each time. Have butter firmer than from butter keeper, yet not hard. (Ditto for balls.)

Butter Balls: Scald paddles in boiling water, *chill* in ice water. Cut firm butter in ½-inch pats. Hold bottom paddle still, move top paddle in circular motion. If butter clings to paddles, again scald and chill the paddles.

Butter Pats: Easy way is to buy butter that's already sliced in serving-size pats. To cut butter in pats, fold strip of butter-wrapping paper over knife. Press down with bold stroke. If you like, trim each pat with parsley.

Butter Roses: Cut stick of butter in 1-inch pieces; let stand till slightly soft. Place forefinger on top of cube; insert tines of chilled fork at each corner, pressing first inward, then upward. Top with parsley. Chill till served.

Index

A

B

C

R

S-T

V-W

Y